# The Sociology of Death

## A selection of previous *Sociological Review* Monographs

Life and Work History Analyses[†]
ed. Shirley Dex

The Sociology of Monsters[†]
ed. John Law

Sport, Leisure and Social Relations[†]
eds John Horne, David Jary and Alan Tomlinson

Gender and Bureaucracy*
eds Mike Savage and Anne Witz

[†] Available from The Sociological Review Office, Keele University, Keele, Staffs ST5 5BG.
* Available from Marston Book Services, PO Box 269, Abingdon, Oxon OX14 4YN.

# The Sociology of Death: theory, culture, practice

Edited by David Clark

Blackwell Publishers/The Sociological Review

306·9
T18678

First published in 1993
Reprinted in 1996

Blackwell Publishers
108 Cowley Road, Oxford OX4 1JF, UK

and
238 Main Street,
Cambridge, MA 02142, USA

*British Library Cataloguing in Publication Data*

A CIP catalogue record for this book is available from the British Library

*Library of Congress Cataloging-in-Publication Data*

The Sociology of death: theory, culture, practice / edited by David Clark.
p. cm.
Includes bibliographical references and index.
ISBN 0-631-19057-0 : 18.95
1. Death–Social aspects–Great Britain. 2. Thanatology.
I. Clark, David, 1953–
HQ1073.5.G7S63 1993 306.9–dc20 93–30934

Printed in Great Britain by Antony Rowe Ltd, Chippenham, Wiltshire.
This book is printed on acid-free paper.

# Contents

# Contents

# Acknowledgements

Several colleagues have contributed in a variety of ways to this volume and I owe them thanks. Ronnie Frankenberg was the first person to encourage me with the idea for the book and I am grateful to him and to his fellow editors at *The Sociological Review*, John Law and Leigh Star, for their enthusiasm and support. Caroline Baggaley, at the journal's office, kept the project moving along smoothly and Pauline Hutchinson, at the Trent Palliative Care Centre, maintained a detailed administrative record of the peer review process. All of the chapters were read and commented on by anonymous assessors and I must thank these for their detailed and helpful observations. Editorial work can involve a mixture of cajoling as well as darker threats; I am more than grateful to all of the contributors for bearing these with humour and efficiency. I trust the finished volume makes it all worthwhile. A number of the papers included here have been presented by their authors at the Leicester Symposia on Social Aspects of Death, Dying and Bereavement; these meetings, which began in 1991, continue to provide an important focus for sociologists working in the field to meet and share ideas. I trust the papers presented here reveal the current state of British sociological interest in death to be in a healthy and expansive state.

# Foreword

There are several paradoxes that mark the management and meaning of dying and death in industrialised nations. These paradoxes are reflected in this timely and stimulating book. Journalists, clinicians and scholars tend to describe death and dying as tabooed subjects; yet there is an increasing literature about these topics (empirical, theoretical or speculative, as in these pages) and one can hardly pick up a newspaper without being plunged into a debate about issues involving some aspect of dying – let alone genocide, warfare or just plain one-to-one killing. Likewise, there is a paradox built into contemporary management of illness *via* a conspicuous array of medical technology. As this technology has increased in sophistication, it has contributed to the suppression of infectious and parasitic diseases, the prevalence of longterm illnesses, and the lengthening of average lifetimes. Yet the increasing reliance on medicine and its technology has been accompanied by anti-medical and pro-humanistic movements, both of which include sociologists. One can see the paradox exemplified in the humanistic thrust of the hospice movement, which sometimes becomes modified when incorporated into the hospitals (at least in the USA). This particular paradox finds sociologists split among themselves. At their most radical, some medical sociologists are virulently anti-medical, though perhaps most have devoted their research and writing to advocating more humanitarian impulses into health care, including that for the dying and their kin.

Among sociologists there are not only specialists and sub-specialists in health or medical care, and 'death and dying,' but also specialists in geriatrics with a tangential interest in the last phases of life. This disciplinary specialisation is sharply criticised by two or three of the authors below, who argue that attention to death as a central feature of life can and should revolutionise our study and understanding of contemporary societies. I do not myself agree with this particular and – I think – very Western ideology, but since it will probably become more widespread, we surely should take notice of it and the consequences of its influence.

Two exciting features of this book are the range of topics addressed and the fact that the authors are not simply specialists in studies of health and illness. Their interests cover a much broader range than is usually found in bibliographies and texts on death. Most of these papers get us out of the hospital and clinic and into less traditional concerns: memorials, inheritance, life courses, demographic and historical trends in Great Britain, an overall characterisation of death in Great Britain, death in 'high modernity,' and the consequences of AIDS. These papers begin to link sociological studies of death with those of historical and political science.

An important aspect of gathering data on death and dying is that of interpretation. Several authors comment that British writing on these topics have been less theoretically oriented than some of the well-known American studies. This book represents a welcome advance in that desired direction. It offers a clear benchmark for looking back some years hence – as we will want to do – to the state of conceptualising these phenomena as they occur in the British Isles.

*Anselm Strauss*
*San Francisco, CA*
May 1993

# Introduction

# Introduction

## David Clark

In his recent and controversial biography of Michel Foucault, James Miller (1993) points out how the French social theorist saw death as the setting wherein the dull monotony of life is transcended to take on a true individuality: as if the approach of death somehow strips away the false trappings of sociality, to reveal the vital heart of an otherwise invisible truth. This apparent contradiction, between death as a final closure and a new unfolding, lies at the heart of this collection of writings, in which a number of claims are made for the importance of death to the sociological project as a whole. Death holds many challenges for sociology. It gives expression to the relationship between the individual and society and to public, private and gendered experiences. Supremely, it presents us with an irreducible facticity: that human bodies are finite. That just as they are born, so too they must die. To be sure, a good deal of sociology has at the least bracketed this point, or indeed ignored it completely. But there is still much to be gained from Berger and Luckmann's (1967) assertion that, in the last analysis, human societies are merely men and women banded together in the face of death.

In much sociological writing however, there has been a tendency to address such issues purely at the level of ideas, values and meanings. The debates about whether death continues to represent a 'taboo' in late modern societies is a case in point (Walter, 1991). More recently, and drawing on a theoretical tradition that goes back at least to the work of Merleau-Ponty, some sociologists have shifted their attention to questions of embodiment. Morgan and Scott (1993) have explained why sociology has for so long been inclined to ignore the body as a subject of enquiry. Part of the reason is undoubtedly to do with the spectre of socio-biology and an unease with reductionist explanations. More generally however – and this is certainly a theme which is raised in the chapters which follow – sociology is itself caught up in a modernising, rationalising narrative. Within this, distinctions are made between the realm of things which are ordered, controlled and abstract set against that where they are disordered, uncontrolled and concrete. Above all, this rationality celebrates the triumph of culture over nature and diminishes bodily matters as an area for serious enquiry. As Morgan and Scott's own collection demonstrates, this is now changing and there is a growing interest in questions of embodiment across a number of substantive fields within sociology.

The present collection contains contributions ranked along this continuum, from 'ideas' to 'bodies' and at times demonstrates the need to move back and forth along it, for example to show how bodily experiences of dying and death make sense within particular historical and cultural constellations of meaning. The book has been grouped, perhaps slightly artificially, into three parts, each reflecting a dominant theme: theory, culture and practice.

Part I begins with an exploration of some central themes concerning the relationship between sociology and death as a field of study. Philip Mellor initiates the debate. His chapter appears initially to be focused on Giddens' notion of sequestration and the place of death in high modernity: on the way in which death is hidden rather than forbidden in contemporary life. Following the collapse of grand narratives, particularly those associated with formal religion, individuals in modern societies must shape their own identities and systems of meaning within a private sphere of social relations. In this context death presents particular problems, threatening alienation and existential isolation. This brings us to Mellor's more fundamental purpose. Given the indivisibility of social representations of death and of high modernity itself, death should not be marginalised to the status of a sub-specialty within the discipline. Rather, death should be of central significance to the discipline as a whole.

The chapters which follow provide a variety of contexts in which to interrogate Mellor's assertion. Writing on the theme of social death, Mulkay continues with a wide focus. Taking a cue from the ways in which the social distribution of death and the social organisation of dying have changed dramatically in industrial societies over the last century, Mulkay draws attention to a problematic underside to the conventional picture of cumulative improvements. Seeing social death as a process wherein individuals cease to become active social agents in the lives of others, 1 argues that, particularly for women, this is an increasingly common and prolonged state in current society.

Finch and Wallis examine some related issues within their unusual analysis of death, inheritance and the lifecourse. This chapter draws attention to an area frequently neglected within sociology (though not in anthropology), namely the material consequences of death. Drawing on a lifecourse perspective, Finch and Wallis show how the management of material inheritance constitutes one of a number of ways in which the anticipation of death, and its aftermath, are socially managed. Jane Littlewood's chapter deals with a more familiar counterpoint to this, picking up the continuing debate on the rites of passage as responses to recurrent social and personal crises created by death. Like Mellor, Littlewood sees the privatisation of contemporary life as a crucial context in which responses to death are enacted. In her analysis this is also linked to the phenomenon of medicalisation, which has subjugated the dying process to expert control and contributed to the relocation of death, from home/community to hospital/institution.

In Part II of the book, the authors provide a more fine-grained insight into the current state of death-related research in British sociology. There are several manifestations here of the phenomenon against which Mellor cautions – an emergent sub-specialty, focussed on the sociology of death. This may yet prove an unstoppable tendency. Sociologists, like other professionals, find support and comfort in familiar surroundings and the dangers of creating a sub-specialty may be offset by the benefits of a shared research agenda and a cumulative approach to sociological problems held in common. In this section of the book we see detailed considerations of a range of cultural and historical themes, often drawing on careful fieldwork using qualitative methods.

There are also hints, in some (though not all) of these chapters, of an applied orientation. This is undoubtedly an important area for sociologists to make their contribution. In the wake of the British hospice movement, there has been a growing interest on both sides of the Atlantic in the development of palliative care as an approach to the needs of those with life-threatening illnesses. Already there have been some significant sociological contributions to this new area of health and social care (Clark, 1993; James and Field, 1992). These developments seem likely to continue. If those who engage in them can continue to draw on the dominant themes and concepts available within current sociology, then a rich contribution can be made to the discipline in its substantive and applied forms.

Small's opening chapter to Part II is a case in point. Here he takes a major public health issue (the HIV/AIDS epidemic) and applies a distinctively sociological perspective, building on recent interest in the analysis of auto/biography to uncover the metaphors and mythologies surrounding those who live with and die from AIDS. Like Finch and Wallis, he is also interested in the application of 'vertical' and 'horizontal' readings of the individual lifecourse.

Jon Davies takes another set of public images and metaphors relating to death: war memorials. Drawing on extensive fieldwork in the British isles, his chapter not only examines the enduring characteristics of war memorials as expressions of collective aggression, guilt and loss, but also reveals their particular place in national and local social identity. Making use of detailed interviews and the analysis of documentary materials, Adams also explores a discrete aspect of death's local management. Her work on the neighbourhood 'layer-out' (the woman responsible for tending and preparing the body of the dead person) like Littlewood's chapter, looks to the modernising influences of medicine and professionalisation as the main explanation for the declining role of the layer-out in the period between the two World Wars. This paper is again rooted in substantial related sociological literatures, particularly those concerned with the formal/informal care distinction. Later in Part II, Jupp's chapter takes up a linked historical theme and presents a detailed analysis of the decline of burial as the preferred method of disposal of the dead, showing how the increasing preference for cremation is connected to social and geographical mobility as well as changes in the role of local authorities, in patterns of family life and in modes of religious expression.

The chapters by Hockey and Field and Johnson in Part II demonstrate the role of sociology in the explication of the work of caring services. Hockey's interest is in how clergy help bereaved individuals to engage in the process of grieving, while constraining behaviours within the limits of agreed, sanctioned norms in a Western context. In an interesting conjunction of *ideas* about grief and the *embodiment* of grieving, she shows how in the West a 'forces' metaphor sees the emotions as something contained within the body which must be released in a controlled and regulated way. By adhering to this dominant model, clergy encounter problems in managing the emotions of others and fail to grasp the possibilities of more dramatistic expressions of grief.

The British hospice movement frequently claims to offer an alternative view of the dying process and the psycho-social significance of death to that prevailing in modern, bureaucratic societies. Field and Johnson conclude Part II with an examination of the role of volunteers in hospices. Paradoxically, hospices face a number of pressures which threaten to undermine their original goals and which potentially routinise an innovative model of care. These pressures also bear on the volunteers who offer their services to hospices. Once again, this paper, drawing on earlier work within a Weberian tradition, applies a particularly sociological analysis to changes within a contemporary social movement in a way which has direct relevance to those working within it.

Part III of the book focusses on a number of themes relating to methodology and the wider practice of sociology. The first two chapters, products of recent doctoral research, concentrate on the generation, collection and analysis of qualitative data in settings which require great sensitivity on the part of the researcher. Howarth undertook a participant observation study of funeral directing. Reflecting the spirit of ethnographic enquiry, her account concentrates on classic problems of bias and confidentiality as well as the passage into, through and out of the fieldwork setting. Costain Schou carried out depth interviews with a group of people with cancer, some of whom were dying. Working within a broadly interactionist framework, her focus here is on the relationship between 'micro' and 'macro' influences in the construction of accounts of the dying process.

The volume comes full circle in the final chapter, by Walter, which returns us to wider debates about the current status and significance of death as a substantive field within sociology. In particular he explores how the concerns of the present book relate to the wider preoccupations of British sociology. Some may disagree with his analysis that sociology in Britain has so far shown only a meagre interest in death and related matters; but most would agree that his distinction between a *sociology of death* and a *mortal sociology* bears closer examination.

I trust that the present volume will convince sceptics that interest in the sociological aspects of death and dying is now becoming widespread among sociologists in Britain. Moreover, I hope the writers here have shown that theirs is by no means an abstracted empirical interest. The papers presented indeed demonstrate clearly that work in the 'sociology of death' has much to give to, and take from, the central preoccupations of the sociological enterprise.

## References

Berger, P. and Luckmann, T., (1967), *The Social Construction of Reality*, Harmondsworth: Penguin.

Clark, D. (ed.), (1993), *The Future for Palliative Care: Issues of Policy and Practice*, Milton Keynes: Open University Press.

James, N. and Field, D., (1992), The routinization of hospice: bureaucracy and charisma, *Social Science and Medicine*, 34, 1363–75.

Miller, J., (1993), *The Passion of Michel Foucault*, London: Harper Collins.

Morgan, D.H.J. and Scott, S., (1993), Bodies in a social landscape, in D.H.J. Morgan and S. Scott (eds), *Body Matters: Essays on the sociology of the body*, London: The Falmer Press.

Walter, T., (1991), Modern death – taboo or not taboo? *Sociology*, 25 (2), 293–310.

# Part 1

# Death in high modernity: the contemporary presence and absence of death

*Philip A. Mellor*

It is no longer the case that death is a taboo subject either in society generally or in sociology in particular. Although many writers (eg. Gorer, 1965; Aries, 1981) have argued that death is a taboo in western modernity, it is increasingly accepted that the recent explosion of academic and popular interest in the subject of death rules out such an argument (Mellor and Shilling, 1993; Walter, 1991). There is now a vast body of literature on death which has been developing over the last decade, and this trend looks set to continue. This cannot indicate a reluctance to talk about death. In relation to specifically sociological literature on the subject we can observe similar developments. Walter (1991) argues that 'British sociologists have kept death at arms' length' but this is increasingly untrue, as this present collection of papers exemplifies. In a sense, then, death is very much *present* in contemporary Western societies.

Nevertheless, although death is not a forbidden subject, it remains a hidden one in the sense that it is generally sequestrated from public space (Blauner, 1966; Mellor and Shilling, 1993). There is a danger that the development of collections of papers such as this one might result only in the creation of a 'sociology of death' specialism within sociology generally, mirroring this hiddeness of death. I suggest that this danger ought to direct our attention to the more widespread sequestration of death from the public domain, the *absence* of considerations of death from social life. Consequently, a sociological consideration of death must reflect upon, and attempt to explain, the apparent contradiction between the *absence* and *presence* of death in contemporary society.

Building upon ideas offered by Giddens (1991) and developed by myself and Chris Shilling elsewhere (1993), I will argue that a theoretical structure aimed at facilitating an adequate analysis of death in contemporary modernity needs to take account of the following three points: first, that the sequestration of death is linked inextricably to central features of what Giddens calls 'late' or 'high' modernity; second, that this sequestration is manifest as the privatisation and subjectivisation of the experience of death, which in turns results in the increased presence of considerations of death *for individuals*; and third, that an adequate integration of death into sociological theory can be achieved only by a partial reorientation of sociology, since sociology itself has been inextricably bound up with the project of modernity. While sociology remains so closely tied to such a project, modernity's systematic sequestration of considerations of mortality will continue to be reflected in sociological theory and practice. Consequently, the task we must set ourselves in the sociology of death should be nothing less than that of contributing to the developing reassessments of, and debates surrounding, the orientations and strategies of sociology, rather than merely striving to carve out for ourselves yet another new specialism.[1]

## Death and ontological security

The term 'ontological security' is central to the recent sociological theory of Anthony Giddens.[2] It refers to persons having a sense of order and continuity in relation to the events in which they participate, and the experiences they have, in their day-to-day lives (Giddens, 1990, 1991). Ontological security therefore depends upon persons being able to find meaning in their lives.[3] Drawing upon Garfinkel (1963) and Heritage (1984), though there are also observable continuities with certain aspects of the work of Gehlen (1956, 1957), Giddens argues that feelings of ontological security find their emotional and cognitive anchors in a 'practical consciousness' of the meaningfulness of our day-to-day actions (1991:36). This meaningfulness, however, is always shadowed by the threat of disorder or chaos. This chaos signals the irreality of everyday conventions, since a person's sense of what is real is intimately associated with their sense of what is meaningful. Drawing upon Kierkegaard's (1944) concept of 'dread', Giddens argues human beings face an ever-present danger of being overwhelmed by anxieties concerning the ultimate reality and meaningfulness of day-to-day life. Society strives to keep this dread at bay by 'bracketing' out of everyday life those questions which might be raised about the social frameworks which contain human existence (1991:37–8). This bracketing process is not always successful, however, since although it is continual it is contingent upon societies being able to control factors which arise which offer particularly potent threats to ontological security, a level of control which varies from society to society. Death is a potent challenge to this bracketing process in all societies.

The existential confrontation with death, one's own or the death of others, has the potential to open individuals up to dread, because it can cause them to call into question the meaningfulness and reality of the social frameworks in which they participate, shattering their ontological security. Death is therefore *always* a problem for *all* societies, since every social system must in some ways accept death, because human beings inevitably die, but at the same time social systems must to a certain extent deny death to allow people to go on in day-to-day life with some sense of commitment (Dumont and Foss, 1972). Nevertheless, as Giddens notes, 'death remains the great extrinsic factor of human existence', something which is ultimately resistant to social containment and control, making any social acceptance of it problematic (1991:162). It is for this reason that Giddens associates death above all else with those 'fateful moments' where individuals have to confront problems which societies have kept away from public consciousness. Here we can draw a clear parallel with Peter Berger's concept of 'marginal situations', which is an expression of broadly the same phenomenon. Again, death is the most significant factor individuals can encounter in marginal situations because it has the potential radically to undermine their sense of the meaningfulness and reality of social life, calling into question even the most fundamental assumptions upon which social life is constructed (Berger, 1967:23).

The similarity between Giddens's work and that of Berger on the significance of death for the social construction, and maintenance, of reality and meaning is a strong one. As Turner (1991) has noted, Berger's *The Sacred Canopy* is exceptional for the number of its references to death, in comparison with other major books in the sociology of religion over the last few decades. Nevertheless, it is also important for the fact that it is a highly significant, though largely ignored, attempt to place the consideration of death at the heart of the sociological enterprise.

Although the book is subtitled 'Elements of a Sociological Theory of Religion', his theory of religion is actually based on a theory of the social significance of death. Expanding upon his sociology of knowledge perspective, developed with Thomas Luckman (1967), Berger argues that all human societies are enterprises in world-building, the 'world' being the meaningful structure persons inhabit, and which gives a sense of what is meaningful and real (1967:3). This world-building enterprise is an ongoing process whereby a relationship with the world is established, giving persons a sense of identity, purpose and place. The power of society is therefore not manifest primarily in 'machineries of social control', but in its representation of what is real, its ability to 'constitute and to impose itself as reality' (1967:12).

The plausibility of this enterprise of world-building is, however, inherently precarious, particularly in crisis (or 'marginal') situations when factors such as death can call into question the socially constructed picture of reality. At these points, the social shield against *anomie* (the terror of meaninglessness) can collapse, causing what Giddens calls the breakdown of ontological security. Since even an individual's biography is the imposition of a socially constructed framework upon personal experiences in order to make them meaningful, the anomic potentiality of death reaches into the innermost depths of people's self-identities. All human beings must inevitably face death at some point, which means that it is always a potential threat to the individual and to the social order as a whole, explaining Berger's point that 'Every human society is, in the last resort, men [and women] banded together in the face of death' (1967:51). The social significance of religion, with which Berger is ostensibly concerned, rests largely on its legitimation of marginal situations through the relation of them to sacred orders, a socially-produced attempt to keep phenomena such as death within the bounds of a socially-produced reality (1967:45). For Berger, death is a fundamental and unavoidable feature of what it is to be a human being, and one with which societies have therefore inevitably to deal. If particular societies fail to deal with death adequately, then not only will individuals have to face extreme terrors of personal meaninglessness, but the social order as a whole becomes vulnerable to a collapse into chaos with a more widespread attendent loss of meaning and order.

## Death, ontological security and high modernity

In a generally positive assessment of Berger's contribution to the sociology of religion, Beckford has criticised the 'Manichaean phenomenology' which he believes underpins Berger's vision of the socially constructed *nomos* shielding persons against the terrors of meaninglessness lurking in the marginal situations of life. This echoes the many criticisms of assumptions both Berger and Luckmann make about human beings' intrinsic desire for meaning (Beckford, 1989:93). Berger and Luckmann work from an anthropological presupposition that human beings crave meaning (Berger, 1967:22, Hamnett, 1974), and argue that human beings are incapable of sustaining a meaningful existence apart from the nomic constructions of society (Berger and Luckmann, 1967:119). The 'transcending potency' of the symbolic universes of meaning which societies create is especially apparent, they suggest, in the ability of a social order 'to enable the individual to go on living in society after the death of significant others and to anticipate their own death with, at the very least, terror sufficiently mitigated so as not to paralyse the continued performance of the routines of everyday life.' (1967:119).

A difficulty apparent with such an analysis is that if we question the fundamental assumption that human beings crave meaning, then the whole theoretical framework looks highly questionable. The analysis is meant to apply to all societies, and this is reinforced by their introduction of examples from a wide spectrum of historical periods and diverse cultures. Although they are particularly interested in modernity, especially in the individual works developed from their collaborations (Berger, 1967; Luckmann, 1967), they are concerned primarily with the secularisation of modern societies and the implications this process has for the continued legitimations of socially constructed realities. In other words, they explore the potential deficiencies of modern mechanisms for the social construction of reality, but see no *essential* difference in these mechanisms from those of pre-modern societies.

I suggest that, despite the obvious similarities between Berger and Luckmann's theoretical framework and that of Giddens, a major difference is discernible here. Beckford argues that Berger and Luckmann's idea that human beings need to construct meaning indicates a psychological functionalism in their approach, but that 'their joint and separate writings contain no suggestion that modern societies are systems with imperative needs for order.' (Beckford, 1989:87). This second point is untrue: it is clear that for Berger and Luckmann *all* societies, including modern ones, are *essentially* ordering systems, as their discussions of death make abundantly clear. Nevertheless, it is true that their analysis of social systems is based on what is essentially a *psychological* requirement of human beings. A more general problem with Berger and Luckmann's theories is also of relevance to us here: ultimately social life seems to exist merely to keep social life ordered, leaving us without anything that could count as the counterfactual (Abercrombie, 1986:27). As Abercrombie notes, human beings can tolerate a good deal of uncertainty, and can even benefit from a measure of uncertainty and risk (1986:28).

Giddens is saying something rather different to Berger and Luckmann. He makes no assumptions about essential, transcultural, transhistorical psychological needs. On the contrary, he is interested primarily in the *distinctiveness* of modern societies, arguing that modernity is characterised by a wholly unprecedented series of mechanisms which remove problems of meaning from public space, relocating them in the privatised realm of individual life and experience, thereby creating historically unique threats of personal meaninglessness. Furthermore, he is able to analyse both pre-modern and modern societies with reference to a framework of trust/risk relations, but notes that the elements of trust and risk in each context are largely different, that the risks in modernity are humanly created, and that risk is often experienced as enabling and even empowering (Giddens, 1990: 102ff.). Consequently, Giddens's discussions of death, despite the many elements shared with Berger and Luckmann, offer us something distinctive and are, I suggest, more valuable for assisting us in our attempts to understand contemporary attitudes towards death.

Giddens's discussions of ontological security are located within his analysis of what he terms 'high modernity'. He believes that we are still living in a culture which can be termed 'modern', despite the arguments of the postmodernists. Postmodernism is characterised by the assumption that western societies have experienced a 'crisis in modernity', involving the loss of the 'metanarratives', such as the idea of historical progress, which have shaped these cultures since the Enlightenment (Foster, 1989). Giddens acknowledges the collapse of many of these metanarratives, but argues that this indicates not the abandonment of the post-Enlightenment modern project, but a further stage in its development. Modernity was characterised initially by a sceptical deconstruction of the metanarratives of religious tradition and their replacement by the metanarratives of modernity. In high modernity, a more advanced stage in the modern project, the 'discontinuist' impulse of modernity has undermined even its own overarching storylines, just as it deconstructed those associated with religion. This produces a sense of disorientation, apparent in the theorists of postmodernity, since we are aware of the inadequacy of our attempts to develop systematic knowledge about the universe of events we are caught up in, but which seem in large part to be out of our control (Giddens, 1990:2–3).

Trust and risk are therefore part of the internal referentiality of modernity: we place our trust in the modern belief that 'risks can in principle be assessed in terms of generalisable knowledge about potential dangers' (Giddens, 1990:111). It is for this reason, rather than for any inherent psychological requirement, that personal meaninglessness becomes a 'fundamental psychic problem' in high modernity, since the moral questions and existential problems posed in day-to-day life are denied answers where answers cannot be found within the internal referentiality of modernity (Giddens, 1991:9). The finitude of human life is paramount amongst these problems, and is the one left most conspicuously unanswered, so that in a cultural milieu which offers unprecedently extreme dangers to the maintenance of ontological security, death is especially hard to deal with.

## Reflexivity and the privatisation of meaning

The fundamentally discontinuist impulse of modernity is expressed in high modernity in the pervasiveness of 'reflexivity', the systematic and critical examination, monitoring and revision of all beliefs and practices in the light of changing circumstances (Giddens, 1990, 1991). Helmuth Schelsky created the term *Dauerreflexion*, meaning 'permanent reflection', to characterise the continuous examination of meaning and values which he observed in the modern consciousness (Schelsky 1965). Giddens's usage of the term 'reflexivity' is consistent with Schelsky's earlier conceptualisation of the systematically-questioning character of modernity. *Dauerreflexion*, or reflexivity, is *chronic*: it is a never-ending process of systematic and potentially radical reappraisals and reassessments of all aspects of modern life, calling everything into question, and undermining any certainty of knowledge so that it can be said that a major feature of high modernity is the pervasiveness of 'radical doubt' (Giddens, 1991:21). Giddens argues that 'We are abroad in a world which is thoroughly constituted through reflexively applied knowledge, but where at the same time we can never be sure that any given element of that knowledge will not be revised.' (Giddens, 1990:39). Gehlen has also written of the constant scrutiny of, and reflection on, motives for action which are no longer located in transpersonal traditions, but in the isolated individual consciousness (Gehlen, 1956, 1957), signalling the same tendency towards insecurity which is at the heart of modernity.

Despite Gehlen's generally pessimistic interpretation of the implications of modern reflexivity for the continuance of the social order as a whole, and for the psychological stability of the individual, a more positive interpretation is possible. A person's experience of this pervasive reflexivity, and its attendent risks, *can* be profoundly liberating and empowering, since there are considerable areas of opportunity available to her/him which would not have been so in the past. Lasch, for example, discusses the ways in which self-development programmes in the United States have encouraged older people to cut their ties with the past and embark upon new marriages, new careers and new hobbies (Lasch, 1991:214). Lasch offers a characteristically bleak interpretation of these activities, which he relates to the 'narcissistic' personality type (Mellor and Shilling, 1993), but it must be acknowledged that the people experiencing such changes in their lives may often find them profoundly empowering, and are often no doubt prepared to accept the so-called 'loss of community' which Lasch, and others such as Sennett (1974), envisage as the price for such empowerment of the individual.

Nevertheless, it is hard to see how this reflexivity can ultimately help individuals deal with the phenomenon of death, since this is a universal parameter within which reflexivity occurs, rather than an object to which reflexivity can be convincingly applied. Although it could be argued that modern societies are culturally diverse, and exhibit a degree of flexibility which allows people to draw upon a variety of cultural resources in order to deal with death, it could also be argued that this diversity compounds the difficulties individuals experience when death is encountered: reflexivity may be increasingly *applied* to death in a multitude of ways, but this multiplicity of *particular* approaches to death accentuates the reality-threatening potential of death in general, i.e. as an unavoidable biological constraint upon various attempts at its cultural containment. The more diverse are the approaches to death in modern societies, the more difficult it becomes to contain it within a communally-accepted framework, and thus limit the existential anxiety it potentially offers to the individual. The apparent cultural diversity and flexibility in modern approaches to death can therefore be explained as being consistent with the sequestration of death from public space into the realm of the personal.[4]

This difficulty of reconciling the dominant reflexivity of high modernity with the brute fact of human finitude is particularly apparent if we relate them both to issues centred on questions of self-identity. These issues are of central significance in contemporary society because modernity has purchased increased control over life at the expense of communally constructed values (Weber, 1948), values being sequestrated from public space into the fragile sphere of the private (Gehlen, 1956, 1957; Bauman, 1989; Giddens, 1991). The concern for issues of self-identity apparent in high modernity is the result of individuals, left alone to construct meaning in their lives, searching for meaning through the creation of a viable and stable sense of self (Sennett, 1974; Rose, 1989). Nevertheless, self-identity is also subject to the pervasive reflexivity of high modernity, so that it is created and maintained through the continual reflexive reordering of self-narratives (Giddens, 1991). Berger argues that 'the individual's own biography is objectively real only insofar as it may be comprehended within the structures of the social world' (Berger, 1967:13), but he prioritises the idea that society assigns an identity to the individual. As Abercrombie notes, those critics who accuse Berger of neglecting social structure are wrong, since the conversation between the individual and social structure is entirely one-sided (Abercrombie, 1986:30). In high modernity, individuals must create their own identities, drawing upon the reflexive mechanisms and socio-cultural resources available to them, but ultimately having to take individual responsibility for the construction of meaning as well as the construction of identity. In this context, death is particularly disturbing because it signals a threatened 'irreality' of the self-projects which modernity encourages individuals to embark upon, an ultimate *absence* of meaning, the *presence* of death bringing home to them the existential isolation of the individual in high modernity.

This idea of the privatisation of meaning, and the difficulties it creates for modern individuals attempting to deal with death, is borne out by a consideration of what are generally acknowledged to be the considerable changes in how people in Europe and North America have approached the phenomenon of death (Aries, 1974, 1981; Vouvelle, 1980; Turner, 1991). Death has gradually been removed from public space, where it was contained in communal, religious beliefs and practices (Aries, 1981), into the seclusion of the hospital (Illich, 1976; Huntington and Metcalf, 1979; Elias, 1985), where it has become a technical matter for medical professionals (Glaser and Strauss, 1968; Giddens, 1991). Funeral rites have similarly ceased to be a concern for the community as a whole, becoming a private matter for the family and friends of the dead person, again organised by a professional group of funeral specialists (Huntington and Metcalf, 1979).

The reflexive deconstruction of communal frameworks for the containment of death has been so extensive that even when persons find themselves at funerals they are often unsure how to act or speak, because prescribed rites of mourning are often no longer available to them (Turner, 1991). As Elias expresses it, 'The task of finding the right word or the right gesture therefore falls back on the individual' (Elias, 1985:26). This point demonstrates how the sequestration of death from public space makes its presence in the personal sphere potentially commanding and threatening. Individuals are likely to experience the tension between the public absence and private presence particularly strongly when they find themselves alone with the task of not merely constructing meaning, but of even knowing how to act, when they are faced with the deaths of those they care about. Gehlen has coined the term *Handlungsverlust*, the decline of the capacity to act, which he associates with the retreat into subjectivism attendant upon the deconstruction of tradition. Together with this deconstruction there is an increase in behavioural insecurity, psychological confusion, and a loss of the capacity to construct socially meaningful human reality (Gehlen, 1957; Zijderweld, 1986). The difficulties modern persons face when confronted with death offer particularly strong supports for this aspect of Gehlen's conceptualisation of modernity.

Nevertheless, the aloneness individuals experience when having to cope with the death of others, is perhaps even more intense when they themselves begin to die. As a result of the reality-threatening power of death, and the increased vulnerability to this threat because of the reflexively-induced disorientations of high modernity, modern persons are increasingly reluctant to come into close contact with those who are dying (Elias, 1985). Since the maintenance of their self-identities is potentially undermined by the presence of death in others, this means that there is a tendency for all persons now to die in situations of unparalleled isolation. Death finds no easy, or generally accepted, place in the conceptions of reality generated by high modernity, and which individuals appropriate in their reflexive constructions of self-identity. Consequently, when death becomes startlingly real in the people around them, their desires for self-preservation encourage them to shut themselves off from those people who are dying; both spatially, sequestrating them in hospitals away from the public gaze, and emotionally, shunning physical contact and denying people the emotional interaction and support just when they are likely to need these things most. Thus, Elias's conception of the loneliness of the dying, the way modern social conditions foster feelings of solitude in those who are dying (Elias, 1985:85), can be extended to include a more general existential isolation encouraged by the reflexivity of modernity. The absence of death from public space makes its presence in private space an intense and potentially threatening one.

Because meaning has been so privatised, any attempts to construct meaning around death are now inherently fragile. Even in the case of the hospice movement, whose development has clearly been part of an attempt to counter certain aspects of these trends, many of the features noted above are still evident. The hospice, like the hospital, remains an institutional expression of the modern desire to sequestrate death away from the public gaze, and individuals in them are still subject to the technical expertise of the medical profession in much the same way, despite the religious patronage of many hospices. Similarly, the location of the dying in a hospice rather than a hospital is unlikely to alter the discomfort of family and friends in the face of the reality of death which the dying temporarily embody. Death may be present in the hospice in a way that it is not in the hospital, but its presence remains a predominantly personally-located one. It is notable that the strategies for dying associated with the hospice movement, such as Kubler-Ross's (1970) various 'stages' in the psychological preparation for death, are directed towards *individuals*, encouraging them to construct some sort of individual awareness of the meaningfulness of their lives and deaths. They therefore offer nothing to counteract the widespread privatisation of meaning in high modernity which is the major source of many persons' contemporary difficulties in dealing with death.

## The sociology of death in high modernity

In linking the modern experience of death to the issues of ontological security, the reflexivity of high modernity, and the subsequent privatisation of meaning, I have sought to indicate that an adequate theoretical analysis of death cannot be conducted at the margins of mainstream sociology, but must locate itself in some of the central sociological debates of the present time. Nevertheless, the absence of much of an interest in death from sociologists in the past is indicative of the fact that there are significant theoretical problems which need to be addressed if the current interest in the sociology of death and the dying is to have the significance to the sociological discipline it ought to have. In particular, the close relationship between sociology and modernity must be examined since, I suggest, the sequestration of death in modernity mirrors the absence of serious attention to death within the discipline of sociology. The increasing awareness of the need to reconstruct sociology in the aftermath of the collapse of the modernist metanarratives, which gave form to political programmes and nation-states as well as to academic disciplines such as sociology, is itself a product of the pervasive reflexivity of high modernity, although it is often articulated as a response to 'postmodernity' (eg Bauman, 1992a). This reconstruction of sociology offers a promising opportunity for the sociology of death to become of central significance to the discipline as a whole.

Sociology is bound up with the project of modernity in two major ways: firstly, it still bears the highly particularised imprint of nineteenth-century social thought concerning modernity; and secondly, the analysis of what modernity continues to bring about remains at the heart of the sociological programme (Giddens, 1987:26). In relation to the first point, it is clear that many sociologists have understood the emergence of their own discipline as a part of the rise of rationalism resulting from the 'disenchantment' of the world attendant upon secularisation

(Weber, 1930, 1981; Wilson, 1982; Giddens, 1987:28). With the upsurge of interest in culture and the collapse of modernist metanarratives, much of the sociology which still bears this nineteenth-century imprint now looks to be of only qualified theoretical value. Archer (1990), Featherstone (1990) and Haferkamp (1987) are among the many sociologists who have sought to develop new theoretical frameworks apart from the rationalisation, modernisation and industrialisation models, recognising their inadequacy in accounting for contemporary social processes and systems.

In relation to the second way in which sociology is bound up with modernity, the continuing centrality of modernity to sociological theory and practice, the extensive publications in sociology debating the nature of modernity and postmodernity exemplify its continuing importance (eg Turner, 1990). Giddens sees these debates, and his own analyses of high modernity, as being part of the 'ambitious task of charting the cultural universe resulting from the ever-more complete disintegration of the traditional world', in other words, of the increasingly radical discontinuist impulse of modernity itself (Giddens, 1987:22–29). Nevertheless, it is also apparent that for this task to be fulfilled adequately sociology must divest itself of the influence of nineteenth-century social thought which has marked it until recently.

Bauman has offered a series of particularly valuable reflections on the major theoretical issues with which sociology must deal in the light of the changed social and cultural circumstances of the contemporary world. Bauman uses the term 'postmodernity' to refer to these changed circumstances, rather than 'high modernity', but this is rather misleading: unlike many of those theorists who locate themselves in a postmodernist perspective, Bauman sees postmodernity as a radical fulfilment of certain features of modernity (at the expense of others), rather than as the abandonment of modernity as such. For example, he suggests that 'The postmodern state of mind is the radical (though certainly unexpected and in all probability undesired) victory of modern (that is inherently critical, restless, unsatisfied, insatiable) culture over the modern society it aimed to improve through throwing it wide open to its own potential (Bauman, 1992a:viii), echoing both Schelsky's and Gehlen's outlines of the insatiable questioning at the heart of modern consciousness and, more specifically, Giddens's discussions of the ways in which the reflexivity of

23

modernity has resulted in the deconstructions of even the modernist metanarratives. Thus, as Giddens suggests, Bauman's 'postmodernity' is modernity coming to terms with itself, 'with the characteristic features of modern social life and thought which were there more or less from the beginning' (Giddens, 1992:21). This is not really *post*-modernity at all, but can more appropriately be described as high modernity. Consequently, I suggest we can modify some of the terms Bauman uses in order to see the value of his theoretical insights with greater clarity.

Bauman offers two routes for the reconstruction of sociology. Firstly, he suggests that it must be transformed into a *postmodern sociology*, where sociology breaks its links with the ontological and epistemological premises of modernity, abandoning any attempt to decode the production and reproduction of cultural meaning through reference to the causal or determining power of social configurations and their dynamics (Bauman, 1992a:26). Secondly, he suggests that rather than revising the traditional strategy of sociology, of relating cultural figurations to transformations in systematic organisation and power arrangements, sociology should adopt a new focus of inquiry, with new sets of categories appropriate to the changed social conditions, but without resigning its formative questions. In this case, sociology would become a *sociology of postmodernity* (Bauman, 1992a: 26–27). In the light of the above discussion, I suggest that the most viable course for sociology at the present time is to adopt the second of these routes, which we could re-term a *sociology of high modernity*. It would be inappropriate for sociology to break its links entirely with the ontological and epistemological premises of modernity, since modernity still shapes the social and cultural systems within which we live. We might add, however, that greater attention to ontological issues should be an important feature of this recasting of sociological categories, a point implicit in Turner's recent arguments for greater attention to the philosophical anthropology of Gehlen (1988) and Plessner (Honneth and Joas, 1988) in the reconstruction of the sociology of religion (Turner, 1991).

The sociology of death and dying ought to find an important place within the sociology of high modernity because the particular nature of death in contemporary societies, both in terms of the individual experience of it and the systemic social features which locate it in the realm of the private, mean that if we can understand the modern approach to death we can understand a great deal about modern society in general. The presence of death poses existential questions for the modern individual. Existential questions concern the basic parameters of human life, containing various ontological and epistemological elements, of which those concerned with the finitude of human life are perhaps the most important (Giddens, 1991:55), particularly as they have immense significance for other existential concerns such as the continuity of self-identity, as noted above. The sequestration, or enforced absence from public space, of death in high modernity intensifies the existential problems created by the fact of human mortality, because death signals the end of reflexive planning, the point at which reflexively constituted knowledge can no longer be applied, thereby opening up individuals to the 'onslaught of nightmare' (Berger and Luckmann, 1967:119), where an understanding of what is meaningful and real disappears. Death has been sequestrated because it is a challenge to modernity itself.

Discussing the sequestration of *morality* by Nazis involved in the extermination of the Jews in the Second World War, Bauman links this sequestration with certain central features of modernity itself. He argues that 'The struggle over moral issues never takes place, as the moral aspects of actions are not immediately obvious or are deliberately prevented from discovery or discussion. In other words, the moral character of action is either invisible or purposefully concealed' (Bauman, 1989:24). The social mechanisms which facilitated this situation were essentially modern: 'The technical-administrative success of the Holocaust was due in part to the skilful utilization of 'moral sleeping pills' made available by modern bureaucracy and modern technology' (Bauman, 1989:26). In a similar way, modernity enables, or encourages, modern persons to forget about *mortality* too. An important feature of modernity is *control*, the subordination of nature to human purposes which, in high modernity, has encouraged the creation of an internally referential system of knowledge and power tied to the colonisation of the future (Giddens, 1991:144). Moral questions and existential issues surrounding death cannot be integrated satisfactorily into day-to-day life in high modernity because they run counter to these dynamics of control. Both morality and mortality are *extrinsic* to the internally referential system of modernity, and are sequestrated from everyday life (Giddens, 1991: 145, 161). This explains the intensity of the existential difficulties facing individuals who have to deal with death, and the general anxiety, confusion and fear they experience in the fact of their mortality.

Death poses further difficulties for the modern person. While it is theoretically conceivable that an individual may go through life oblivious to moral questions, even though this might be conceived of as some sort of mental disorder, mortality is something no human being can ultimately avoid. At various points in their lives all persons will have to deal with, or at least face, the deaths of others and of self. As Turner notes, 'our existential questions are rooted in the biographical history of bodies – their being in and departure from the world' (Turner, 1991:246). Death signals the bodily limitations on the reflexivity of modernity. Although the body has been incorporated into the internally referential system of modernity, becoming a bearer of symbolic value (Shilling, 1991) and the object of various bodily regimes aimed at ensuring its compliance with a reflexively constituted sense of self (Featherstone, 1982, Giddens, 1991), this incorporation remains problematic. Decaying bodies provide unavoidable constraints upon reflexive self-projects – a life spent in the gym will not ultimately stop a person becoming weak and feeble – but dying and dead bodies are even more challenging. Bauman argues that individuals attempt to belie the ultimate limitation of the body encountered in death by concentrating on its *currently* encountered, *specific* limitations (Bauman, 1992b:18). The obsession with health-care apparent in contemporary culture is characterised by this pattern, so that individuals adopt various strategies to avoid dying from lung cancer, or heart disease or liver failure, 'forgetting' that all of these strategies will ultimately be useless since death itself cannot be avoided (Bauman, 1992b:10). Individuals 'forget' this because modernity encourages them to exclude it from their consciousness. Modernity systematically sequestrates all those phenomena which run counter to its own principles of reflexively constituted knowledge, order and control.

## Conclusion

The task for the sociology of death in high modernity must be to illuminate the systemic social and cultural factors which frame our contemporary attitudes to, and experience of, human mortality. If we accept that death has largely been sequestrated from public space, then a sociology of death needs to explore the linkage of this sequestration to the reflexivity of high modernity. This reflexivity fosters the privatisation of meaning, making ontological security increasingly fragile, and is therefore deeply imbedded in modern mechanisms of self-identity. Self-identity is, in turn, constructed within the biographical and biological constraints of the body, which limit the extent to which reflexively applied knowledge and reflexively constructed identity can be sustained. The major limitation here is death, the death of the body and the end of the self-project, which challenges not only an individual's consciousness of what is meaningful and real, but also modernity itself. Death is therefore a problem of meaning, but it is also a problem for sociology, which has not explored sufficiently the linkage between the social construction of meaning in modernity and the way in which sociology, as a modern academic discipline, works within parameters established by modernity.

The sociology of death must both continue certain features of the sociological tradition and simultaneously participate in the branching out of social theory into new directions. It must persist in studying and reflecting upon what modernity continues to bring about, keeping modernity as the central theoretical focus of its discipline, but it must also distance itself from certain features of modernity in order to analyse modernity more effectively. It must align itself with the sociology of identity and the sociology of the body, exploring those aspects of existence which modernity has problematised or sequestrated from public visibility.

Death is one of the very small number of universal parameters within which both individual and social life is constructed, yet historically sociology has been concerned almost entirely with life, at the expense of too little serious attention to death. The sociology of death must not merely reverse this pattern, and ignore life, but must integrate life *and* death into its theoretical programme. If it does not, then the sequestration of death in high modernity will continue to be reflected in the absence of considerations of mortality from the centre of sociological theory and practice, despite the intense and potentially disturbing presence of death in the private lives of modern persons. The sociology of death would become merely an exotic academic specialism, an institutionalised sub-group within sociology which, in its marginality to the fundamental sociological debates of the time, would uncritically mirror other social trends, such as the institutionalised sequestration of the dying into the privatised space of the hospice. In doing so, it would be able to offer only a

*Philip A. Mellor*

limited account of the phenomenon of death which is the focus of its intellectual enterprise. Archer notes that 'social theory must pay its respects to the morality of actors as a generic part of its model of man' (Archer, 1990:113), and we should say the same of mortality too: sociology must develop a view of human beings which is able to account for the fact that people inevitably die, otherwise it will not be able to explain the tension between the public absence and private presence of death in high modernity.

## Notes

1 I should like to acknowledge my debt to Chris Shilling for his contributions to our ongoing discussions of the themes dealt with in this paper, and which we will be developing jointly for a forthcoming book, *Embodiment, Religion and Postmodernity*, to be published by Sage (1995).

2 I shall draw heavily upon the work of Giddens in this paper. Giddens's social theory has been criticised for what is regarded by some as its excessive breadth, and by others for the narrowness of some of its concerns (Bryant and Jary, 1991). I deal with certain strengths and weaknesses of Giddens's approach elsewhere (Mellor, 1993). I have made Giddens's theoretical work central to this present discussion because his recent social theory, along with that of Zygmunt Bauman which I also consider here, has explicitly linked the sequestration of death to structural features of modern societies. Although Giddens's discussion of this subject has been limited, I regard it as a particularly useful basis upon which to develop further the discussion of death in modernity.

3 It has been suggested to me that an 'ontology of the prior subject' is implicit in this theoretical position. This is not so. Giddens draws heavily upon the so-called 'linguistic turn' in social theory; not only with reference to Foucault, but also to Wittgenstein and Mead. Identity comes about through the acquisition of language and the attendent contextuality of social positioning (Giddens, 1984:43). The importance of ontological security has therefore nothing to do with atemporal, non-social assumptions about subjectivity, but the maintenance of a personal identity which is acquired and maintained through interaction with others in communal frames of meaning.

4 It is not my intention to minimise the significance of the fact that a multiplicity of approaches to death are possible within modern societies. Nevertheless, if we consider these approaches within a broad theoretical overview of major trends in the location and significance of death in high modern societies, I suggest it is clear that much of this apparent diversity is entirely consistent with the sequestration, and privatisation, of death which concerns me here. This is not to say that *every* empirically-observable approach to death can be explained with reference to the theoretical framework offered in this paper. The spread of orientations and methods characteristic of modernity, and 'high' modernity, is not a uniform process, and many traditional religious and cultural practices persist which are counterfactual to the arguments presented here. This does not detract, however, from the force of these arguments as an account of the dominant trends in the location and significance of death in high modernity.

# Bibliography

Abercrombie, N., (1986), 'Knowledge, Order and Human Autonomy', in J.D. Hunter and S.C. Ainlay (eds) *Making sense of Modern times: Peter L. Berger and the Vision of Interpretive Sociology*, London: Routledge and Kegan Paul.

Archer, M., (1990), 'Theory, Culture and Post-Industrial Society', in M. Featherstone (ed.) *Global Culture, Nationalism, Globalization and Modernity*, London: Sage.

Aries, P., (1974), *Western Attitudes Towards Death: From the Middle Ages to the Present*, Baltimore: John Hopkins University Press.

Aries, P., (1981), *The Hour of Our Death*, London: Penguin.

Bauman, Z., (1989), *Modernity and the Holocaust*, Cambridge: Polity.

Bauman, Z., (1992a), *Intimations of Postmodernity*, London: Routledge.

Bauman, Z., (1992b), 'Survival as a social construct', *Theory, Culture and Society*, 99:1–36.

Beckford, J., (1989), *Religion and Advanced Industrial Society*, London: Unwin Hyman.

Berger, P. and Luckmann, T., (1967), *The Social Construction of Reality: A Treatise in the Sociology of Knowledge*, London: Penguin.

Berger, P., (1967), *The Sacred Canopy: Elements of A Sociological Theory of Religion*, New York: Doubleday.

Berger, P., (1969), *A Rumour of Angels: Modern Society and the Rediscovery of the Supernatural*, New York: Doubleday.

Blauner, R., (1966), 'Death and Social Structure', *Psychiatry*, 29:378–394.

Bryant, C.G.A. and Jary, D., (1991), *Giddens' Theory of Structuration: A Critical Appreciation*, London: Routledge.

Elias, N., (1985), *The Loneliness of the Dying*, Oxford: Blackwell.

Featherstone, M., (1982), 'The body in consumer culture', *Theory, Culture and Society*, 1:18:33.

Featherstone, M., (1990), *Global Culture*, London: Sage.

Foster, H., (1989), *Postmodern Culture*, London: Pluto Press.

Garfinkel, H., (1963), 'A conception of, and experiments with, "trust" as a condition of stable concerted actions', in O.J. Harvey (ed.) *Motivation and Social Interaction*, New York: Ronald Press.

Gehlen, A., (1956), *Urmensch und Spatkultur*, Munich: Szczesny Verlag.

Gehlen, A., (1957), *Die Seele in Technischen Zeitalter*, Hamburg: Rowholt.

Gehlen, A., (1988), *Man, His Nature and Place in the World*, New York: Columbia University Press.

Giddens, A., (1985), *The Constitution of Society: Outline of a Theory of Structuration*, Cambridge: Polity.

Giddens, A., (1987), *Social Theory and Modern Sociology*, Cambridge: Polity.

Giddens, A., (1990), *The Consequences of Modernity*, Cambridge: Polity.

Giddens, A., (1991), *Modernity and Self-Identity*, Cambridge: Polity.

Giddens, A., (1991), 'Uprooted signposts at century's end', *The Higher*, January 17th.

Glaser, B. and Strauss, A., (1968), *Time for Dying*, Chicago: Aldine.

Gorer, G., (1965), *Death, Grief and Mourning in Contemporary Britain*, London: Cresset.

Haferkamp, H., (1987), 'Beyond the "Iron Cage" of Modernity', *Theory, Culture and Society*, 4 (I).

Hamnett, I., (1974), 'Sociology of Religion and Sociology of Error', *Religion*: 73.

Heritage, J., (1984)., *Garfinkel and Ethnomethodology*, Cambridge: Polity.

Honneth, A. and Joas, H., (1988), *Social Action and Human Nature*, Cambridge.

Huntington, R. and Metcalf, P., (1979), *Celebrations of Death*, Cambridge: C.U.P.

Illich, I., (1976), *Limits to Medicine*, London: Marion Boyars.

Kierkegaard, S., (1944), *The Concept of Dread*, London: MacMillan.

Kubler-Ross, E., (1970), *On Death and Dying*, London: Tavistock.

Lasch, C., (1991), *The Culture of Narcissism*, New York: Norton and Company.

Luckmann, T., (1967), *The Invisible Religion: The Problem of Religion in Modern Society*, New York: MacMillan.

Mellor, P.A., (1993), 'Reflexive Traditions: Anthony Giddens, High Modernity and the Contours of Contemporary Religiosity', *Religious Studies*, Vol. 29.

Mellor, P.A. and Shilling, C., (1993), 'Modernity, Self-Identity and the Sequestration of death', *Sociology*, Vol. 27.

Rose, N., (1989), *Governing the Soul: The Shaping of the Private Self*, London: Routledge.

Schelsky, H., (1965), 'Ist die Dauerrflexior institutionalisierbar?' In H. Schelsky, (ed.) *Auf der Suche nach Wirklichkeit*, Dusseldorf-Koln: Eugen Diederichs Verlag.

Sennett, R., (1974), *The Fall of Public Man*, Cambridge: C.U.P.

Shilling, C., (1991), 'Educating the Body: physical capital and the production of social inequalities', *Sociology*, 25: 653–672.

Turner, B.S., (1990), *Theories of Modernity and Postmodernity*, London: Sage.

Turner, B.S., (1991), *Religion and Social Theory*, London: Sage.

Vouvelle, M., (1980), 'Rediscovery of Death since 1960', in R. Fox (ed.) *The Social Meaning of Death*, Annals of the American Academy of Political and Social Science, 447.

Walter, T., (1991), 'Modern Death: taboo or not taboo?, *Sociology*, 25:293–310.

Weber, M., (1930), *The Protestant Ethic and the Spirit of Capitalism*. London: Allen and Unwin.

Weber, M., (1948), 'Science as a vocation', in H. Gerth and C.W. Mills (eds), from *Max Weber*, London: Routledge.

Weber, M., (1981), *The Sociology of Religion*, Boston: Beacon Press.

Wilson, B.R., (1982), *Religion in Sociological Perspective*, London: O.U.P.

Zijderweld, A., (1985), 'The Challenges of Modernity', in J.D. Hunter and S.C. Ainlay (eds), *Making Sense of Modern Times*, London: Routledge and Kegan Paul.

# Social death in Britain*

## Michael Mulkay

The causes of human death, the social distribution of death and the social organisation of dying have all changed dramatically during the last century in the industrialized societies. Since the nineteenth century, the percentage of deaths arising from short-term infectious diseases has fallen sharply, while the significance of long-term degenerative diseases has greatly increased (OPCS, 1985). Whereas, in the last century, the mortality rate was particularly high among children and continued at what we would regard as a high level throughout adult life, the incidence of death is now heavily concentrated among the elderly. Thus average life expectancy is now much longer. For the majority of people, death approaches slowly over years of gradual decline and its final advent is supervised by qualified personnel in systematically organised settings where technical facilities for prolonging life are to hand. Similarly, disposal of the dead, like the process of dying, has become rationally organised. Unlike the 1800s, when burial was universal and in many areas posed a serious threat to the health of the living, two thirds of human corpses in Britain today are hygienically destroyed by burning. To a considerable degree, death and dying have been taken under human control (Walter, 1990).

This brief outline of the changing profile of biological death in our society is well documented and its main features are unlikely to be challenged. There is, however, another hidden profile of *social* death which is more difficult to observe and is less frequently discussed. Biological death and social death resemble the

* This is a revised a shortened version of a paper written with John Ernst and published under the title 'The Changing Profile of Social Death' in the *European Journal of Sociology*, XXII (1991), 172—196. This version is published with the permission of the *European Journal of Sociology* copyright 1991.

famous drawing of the 'pretty young woman' which, if you look at it in a particular way, transforms itself into a representation of an 'old crone'. In this chapter, I will try to reveal the hidden profile of social death that is buried within the customary picture of cumulative improvement in the pattern of human mortality.

Like the 'old crone' initially unnoticed in the *gestalt* drawing, the profile of social death to be sketched below is less appealing than the picture of progressive demographic change with which we began. But it is perhaps even more important. For changes in our biological existence are significant for us only insofar as they affect our consciousness, our experiences and our conduct. Of course our social death, that is, the termination of our social existence, is linked to our biological cessation and to broader structures of human mortality. But biological death and social death are not identical. Because the two are connected, the profound demographic developments summarised above have brought about extensive alterations in the profile of social death. However, because the two are partly independent and because social death is a contingent cultural response to demographic change, the pattern of social death has come to be redrawn in certain unexpected ways.

In later sections, I will examine the evolving profile of social death with special reference to the basic categories of age and gender. I will be mainly concerned in this discussion with the situation in Britain. But, wherever suitable British material is lacking, I will refer to the extensive American research literature on death.

## The concept of 'social death'

In the major ethnographies concerned with 'social death', the term has been used to draw attention to the way in which the social existence of dying patients is often reduced, and sometimes more or less eliminated, in the hospital setting owing to other parties' physical, emotional and communicative withdrawal. The central observation in these studies has been that patients can cease to exist socially before they have been defined as clinically and/or biologically dead (Glaser and Strauss, 1965; Sudnow, 1967). These ethnographies have helped us to understand how death and dying have come to be managed within the modern hospital. But they have drawn attention away from the wider social context and from the significant fact that, in other settings, social existence may be prolonged well beyond the point of bio-logical termination. If we are to give an accurate account of the overall pattern of social death, we must accept that it is entirely possible for people to sustain a lasting, personal relationship which affects the course of their daily lives with an individual whom they know to be dead (Rees, 1971). The biologically dead can be experienced and addressed symbolically by the living, and they can influence the conduct of the living. In these respects, the dead may continue to participate in the observable social world as that world is understood by their survivors.

As I have argued elsewhere in detail (Mulkay and Ernst, 1991), social death sequences should be conceived as interactional processes which may operate over long periods of time and which may extend either side of 'the grave'. Any particular sequence comes to an end when an individual's actual or impend-ing biological or clinical death is taken as grounds for treating that individual as a non-person. By 'non-person' I mean that the actor has ceased to exist as an active agent in the ongoing social world of some other party. When social death has occurred, other people no longer seek to communicate with that person nor take that person directly into account in carrying out their own actions. Thus social death may precede clinical death; for exam-ple, when a 'hopelessly comatose' patient is treated as 'merely a body' (Glaser and Strauss, 1965). Alternatively, social existence may continue long after death; for example, when distraught par-ents regularly visit the grave of a dead child and talk and write to that child about their previous life together and about the reunion to come (Clegg, 1988).

The defining feature of social death is the cessation of the indi-vidual person as an active agent in others' lives. Individuals can be involved in numerous death sequences and may be, at the same time, dead for some parties yet socially alive for others. Social life is the obverse of social death and depends on the social continuation of the particular person, whether or not that person is biologically living. In certain circumstances, an individ-ual's biological death may initiate a social death sequence for some other person or may create a situation for the other party which is closely analogous to social death. In this sense, social death can be interactionally transmitted.

Let me now show how this conception of 'social death' can be used to throw new light on social responses to the changing character and distribution of biological death in modern Britain.

*Michael Mulkay*

## Social death and the elderly

Social death is the final event in a sequence of declining social involvement that is set in motion either by participants' preparation for, or by their reaction to, the advent of biological death. In order to understand this sequence, it is necessary to consider at what point in people's life cycle this process normally begins. It is, of course, true, as Sudnow emphasises, that we are all in a way dying from birth (1967). It is also clear that, from an early age, we anticipate, in some general sense, our own and others' eventual demise (Kuykendall, 1989). However, because the attribute of mortality is universal, it does not, in itself, lead to variations in social conduct; that is, we do not behave in any special way when we interact with someone who is going to die at some point in the future which is at present quite unknown. In contrast, when the fact of another's mortality becomes more concrete, more imminent, we begin to attend to that person's forthcoming death and our conduct alters accordingly. Similarly, when we come to see the occasion of our own death as part of a tangible, soon to be experienced future, we begin to behave differently with that bounded future in mind. It is these new forms of conduct which, when death is foreseen, mark the beginning of the death sequence.

To ask about the start of the death sequence in our society, therefore, is to ask at what juncture does people's participation in social life begin to change and, in particular, to diminish significantly, quite apart from personal variations in state of health, owing to the socially recognized approach of death? In modern Britain, this major transition typically occurs, particularly for men, at the time of retirement from work (Anderson, 1985). The death sequence begins structurally at this point because retirement typically produces a major reduction in the range of people's social activity and because, as people are well aware, their removal from full involvement in social life is directly linked to the increasing probability of their biological death. Thus in England and Wales, in 1987, 74 per cent of male deaths occurred among those who had lived beyond the age of retirement (CSO, 1989).

As a result of the significant increase in life expectancy during this century, the number of people reaching this age in Britain has grown from 2.2 million in 1901 to 9.7 million in 1981

(Falkingham, 1989). In 1980, 88 per cent of men in this age group were actually retired from work (Turner, 1984). One consequence of this situation has been the formation of an elderly population whose members are socially and economically disadvantaged (Turner, 1984). Not only are the elderly largely excluded from the workforce, they are also denied full participation in the family life of their own descendants and in the wider community. As an indication of the social isolation of the elderly, we can consider the extent to which they are visited by friends and relatives. In Greater London, for example, in the 1970s, only a quarter of elderly people received a visit more than once a week; and one in six were never visited at all. Even in less urban areas such as Yorkshire, only four out of ten elderly people were visited more than once a week (Hunt, 1979).

The general situation, then, is that as people become older and the likelihood of their entering a medically defined dying sequence increases, they are formally retired from paid employment and the social contacts of their mature years are severed. Retirement from work means reduction of income, often to very low levels, which in turn further restricts their social activities. From the time of retirement, elderly people in Britain are channelled collectively away from the main areas of social activity and their social ties with the wider society are progressively weakened in anticipation of their biological end (Williams, 1990).

The death sequence in which elderly people are enmeshed within society at large parallels and provides the background for the death sequences observed by the hospital ethnographers. This is particularly evident in Sudnow's study. Sudnow reports that in County Hospital, in the US, patients are treated by staff as 'dying' only if they are deemed to be 'likely to die on this admission' (1967:69). He notes, however, that there is another sense in which staff deal with *all* their elderly patients in a special way which follows from the latter's proximity, as elderly persons, to biological death. For the hospital physicians and other staff, the absence of a future for old people is taken utterly for granted in routine interaction. Thus dealings with the elderly need not be specially modified at County when they enter the medical death sequence 'insofar as the things one normally discusses with them are not premised on, or take their meaning from, any understanding of a long term future' (1967:70–1). In other words, the death sequences that come to envelop elderly people within the hospital setting are accentuated versions of a broader social death sequence within which such people are already located.

In England today, over 60 per cent of elderly people die in hospitals (OPCS, 1989) where the bureaucratic 'neglect of the patient as a person' (Field, 1989:147) converges with the physical, emotional and communicative withdrawal of the living from those on the death sequence. A smaller, but significant, proportion of the elderly end their days in residential and nursing homes. In 1987, 8 per cent of all deaths among the elderly in England and Wales occurred in such homes; in the case of women, the proportion was 11 per cent (OPCS, 1989). These 'homes' provide an institutionalized form for the final separation of people on the death sequence from 'ordinary' social actors. They are the culmination of the process whereby the elderly are progressively excluded from the ongoing social world.

Residential homes have become an increasingly important location for the enactment of the death sequence amongst the elderly. During the last decade or so, recourse to residential care has become common practice for people over 85 years of age and amongst those who are defined as having 'high dependency' needs. Whereas in some preliterate societies the unwanted old are physically buried alive (Goody, 1961), in our society they are immured in residential homes where, out of sight and largely out of mind, they can be left whilst the process of biological decline takes its inevitable course.

When elderly people enter a residential or nursing home, all those involved are aware that the entrants are most unlikely to come out alive (Hockey, 1985). For those left behind, the symbolic significance of this transition is so evident that in many cases they engage in what Fulton and Fulton (1971) call 'anticipatory grief'. In such circumstances, persons are mourned as if they were biologically dead, even though they may continue to live on in the home for years. Such pre-emptive mourning helps those outside the home to deal with the crisis of separation. It enables them to begin to adjust in advance so that, by the time death comes, they are already 'grieved out' (Glaser and Strauss, 1968). As a result of this process, however, they become more distanced from the person in the home, who is pushed further along the social death sequence as his or her past relationships are disrupted and lose their meaning. Outsiders will often, of course, try to maintain contact with elderly residents. But the symbolic divide between the full social actors on the outside and

© Archives Européennes de Sociologie, 1991

the physically and socially segregated insiders makes such relationships little more than pretence. For, from the outside, the residents are, owing to their inability to perform meaningful social action, effectively dead in social terms.

This does not mean that, internally, residential homes for the elderly are completely devoid of social life. What may often happen in such settings is that the limited range of activities available to residents becomes socially structured in relation to a basic distinction between those who are deemed to be close to death and those for whom death is not thought to be imminent. In situations of this kind, the more active residents strive to re-establish the meaning of their own existence by separating themselves physically and symbolically from other residents. This is well documented in Hockey's (1985) study of a residential home in North Eastern England.

In this home, the 'fit' residents were distinguished by staff and by other residents from the 'frail'. These two categories of residents were kept apart spatially and were treated in quite different ways. In particular, in their dealings with the 'fit', staff stressed their liveliness and talked in ways which denied the immediate relevance of death. In contrast, in their treatment of the 'frail', staff presumed the imminence of biological death and used language forms which referred to death directly as well as by implication. These categories were maintained despite the fact that the 'fit' often died unexpectedly and the 'frail' sometimes lived on well beyond their allotted span.

For the staff, the distinction between the 'frail' and the 'fit' enabled them to focus their attention on the former and, thereby, to sustain a sense that the home was not merely a 'house of death'. Although, from the outside, such homes are seen as locales for the socially dead, on the inside, residents may be defined in ways which emphasise the continuation of social life. This is particularly important for the newer and 'fitter' residents who are even more committed than staff to the spatial and social segregation of the 'frail'. The consequence for the 'fit' is that they can, in this way, retain some vestigial sense of personal worth and social significance. The consequence for the 'frail' of this collusion between the 'fit' and the staff is that they cease to exist as social actors. The ultimate outcome for the 'frail' is that they are systematically prevented from participating in this last, culturally impoverished setting in much the same way that the elderly in general are excluded from the wider society. 'As a result, the final transition of a "frail" resident to sick bay and to the mortuary often goes by unremarked. A much earlier separation ensures that their name and identity is unknown and of little significance' (Hockey, 1985:42; see also Hockey, 1990).

How far Hockey's conclusions apply in detail to other residential homes is not entirely clear; although the findings from various studies suggest that the regime observed by Hockey is unexceptional (Hughes and Wilkin, 1987). Insofar as her study is representative, it shows that, within our residential homes for the elderly, the death sequence of society at large is repeated in microcosm. It is ironic that, even inside these institutions, participants' striving for social existence serves to create yet another manifestation of social death.

### Women and social death

Women have benefited rather more than men from the great expansion in the length of human life that has occurred during this century (Kearl, 1989:132). Furthermore, not only do women now experience a greatly extended lifespan, but they also spend, on average, much less of their lives than in the past bearing and giving birth to children (Turner, 1984). In modern Britain, the vast majority of these children will survive to adulthood and will, indeed, outlive their parents (Anderson, 1985). Throughout the 1800s, in contrast, a large proportion of children were destined to die during infancy. Since then, infant mortality has been reduced to a remarkably low level (Mitchell, 1982; Halsey, 1988). The consequence for British women has been that, unlike their Victorian counterparts, they are very unlikely to spend a significant part of their child-bearing years dealing with the deaths of their own children.

In addition, the general increase in life expectancy means that the deaths of parents and of other close relatives are now likely to occur much later in a woman's life cycle than in the past (Jalland and Hooper, 1986). As a result, during the main years of their maturity, women are now much less involved with death as a normal part of family life. This is, of course, also the case for men. But the social impact of these demographic changes has been much greater for women owing to their central role in domestic activities, including those ritual activities associated with death (Clark, 1982).

In the last century, both children and adults almost always died at home in the family setting (Walvin, 1986). At that time, men passed almost the whole burden of mourning to their womenfolk. In what we may loosely call the 'Victorian middle class', the most lengthy and elaborate of all mourning sequences was that of a wife for a husband. Mourning dress of an exaggerated severity was worn for the first two years by the widow as a sign of 'inner desolation'. Black, light-absorbing crape was used to express her grief and her withdrawal from the world. For the first year of bereavement, the widow could undertake no social activity outside the home. After this she could, if she wished, gradually resume her place in society. It was not unknown, however, for the bereaved woman to remain, like Queen Victoria herself, in more or less permanent seclusion (Gorer, 1965:79; Morley, 1971:68).

When close relatives and particularly when her husband died, the middle-class Victorian woman was required to enter a social death sequence on their behalf; that is, the range of her conduct was drastically curtailed, she was excluded from many of her normal social activities, and indeed she continued to exist only in the most distant fashion for many of the people in her customary social world. The conventional response of the Victorian woman to death in her immediate family was a kind of surrogate death of her own. Given the high adult and infant mortality rates of the time, the great majority of middle class women would have spent many years, in total, enclosed within the ritual death sequences through which expression was given to the collective bereavement of their families.

Among poorer people, for obvious economic reasons, this extended ritual confinement and symbolic adornment of women was impossible (Walvin, 1986). For many Victorian women, the labours required to maintain a daily subsistence for the living had to take precedence over ritual labours for the dead. Nevertheless, the middle-class pattern of activity in relation to death 'percolated to the lower classes' (Morley, 1971:17) and furnished a model of proper conduct to which many less wealthy people aspired (Clark, 1982:132). As in the case of the middle class, the responsibility for mourning lay heavily upon the women of the working class.

The central involvement of women in mourning and the partial social death of bereaved women required by the rules of Victorian etiquette was not only a symbolic expression of loss. It also served as a mechanism whereby the social existence of deceased family members was extended. For one of the primary tasks of bereaved women was to keep alive the memory of the family dead by means of regular prayers, by continuing to celebrate their birthdays and other anniversaries, by visiting their graves, and so on (Morley, 1971; Walvin, 1986). These activities were given significance for the great majority of women by belief in an afterlife and by hope of reunion in a world beyond the grave. Women were required to spend so much of their lives in the borderland between life and death because they were responsible, within the family setting, for maintaining strong social bonds between the living and the constantly increasing number of the dead.

Most of this now, of course, has gone. Belief in the afterlife has greatly declined and with it the rituals of mourning and the other forms of associated conduct (Gorer, 1965; Morley, 1971; Clark, 1982; Turner, 1983). In these respects, modern women may appear to live both longer and freer lives that are less oppressed by the deaths of others. Yet social death is still a more significant feature of women's lives than of the lives of men; although its form today is very different. Because women outlive men, on average, by a considerable margin, most married women alive today are destined to become widows (Kearl, 1989). Thus men are much less likely than women to be left alone as biological death draws near. This suggests that the most extreme form of social death for the majority of women in present day society, as in Victorian times, is likely to occur after the death of their husband.

We observed in the previous section that retirement from paid employment is a major transition in men's lives and that this enforced social disengagement marks for men the beginning of the death sequence. This change in men's status is of considerable importance for their wives, who, in many instances will also retire from the official workforce as the family cycle runs its course. Thus both women and men experience more or less together the marked restriction of social activities that is characteristic of all social death sequences. However, the change is less dramatic and less consequential in the short run for married women owing to the fact that, with few exceptions, their unpaid labour in the home continues undiminished after their husband's or their own retirement. Because caring for their menfolk provides a central focus for the daily activities of most elderly

© Archives Européennes de Sociologie, 1991

women, the character of the death sequence changes most significantly for them when their partner dies. With the advent of widowhood comes a radical alteration of women's social existence and, in many cases, a great acceleration in their move toward social death. It may well be that, for many women, this is where the social death sequence really begins.

Modern widows, of course, are not necessarily old. Nonetheless, the concentration of biological death among the elderly means that widows today will be significantly older collectively than in Victorian times. Yet, owing to their greater longevity, they will often have many more years to live. These long years of widowhood are not subject to the strict control which drastically limited women's social activities in the last century, yet which, at the same time, gave them social significance. They are, rather, likely to be years of increasing personal emptiness and declining social involvement. It may be that, for a proportion of the women now approaching this major change in social status, the consequent reduction in social participation will be less complete and less personally damaging than in the past. 'For more recent cohorts of women . . . individuals may have more anticipatory socializations for widowhood because of earlier divorces and may be less devastated by their spouses' deaths as their identities are more likely to derive from their work' (Kearl, 1989:485). However, this is extrapolation into the future rather than description of a present reality. In Britain today, the majority of elderly widows are well along the social death sequence, with many thousands isolated in their own homes or experiencing the social deprivation generated within the bureaucratic institutions for the aged.

In the course of the last century, then, the profile of social death for women has changed considerably, at least partly in response to alterations in the distribution of biological death by age and sex. In the nineteenth century, women's ritual involvement in social death was a recurring feature of their adult lives. It narrowly restricted the scope of their social activities over extended periods, particularly among the middle class. Yet this continual exclusion from full participation in the social life of their time was not entirely negative. For it entailed important responsibilities in the domestic setting and in the wider network of family relations. In addition, women's conduct in the ritual sequence of social death was seen to have personal and social relevance as a means of contact between the living and the dead.

In the present century, as biological death has become less widely distributed across the generations and more predictably located among the elderly, sustained ritual mourning has virtually disappeared. This has enabled women, on the whole, to put off their entry into the death sequence until relatively late in life. Nevertheless, women's economic and social dependence on men still condemns them, in large numbers, to spend many years in the modern version of the sequence of social death. Women's social exclusion, unlike that of their nineteenth century counterparts, is not spread throughout their mature years but is concentrated into the final decades of elderly decline. Indeed, a large proportion of the extra years gained during this century by increases in life expectancy are spent by women, in growing isolation, in the sequence of social death. In our world, however, this sequence brings with it no active responsibilities and has no wider significance. It has become simply that period in which old women wait for their personal extinction.

## Social death and the young

Social death sequences are likely to precede biological death when participants believe that death can be foreseen. Thus in our own society, where the normal process of dying proceeds slowly among a well-defined segment of the population, it is possible for extended social death sequences to stretch deeply back into people's existence as living organisms. But not all deaths fit this pattern. For instance, accidental deaths occur suddenly and unexpectedly. By their very nature, such deaths cannot be predicted and cannot, therefore, be prepared for in advance. Other deaths are so rare and so out of line with normal expectations that participants experience great difficulty in constructing a suitable social sequence as the process of biological decline unfolds. In our society, problems of this kind are particularly likely to be associated with the deaths of children.

Throughout the nineteenth century, infant mortality was high and, in consequence, children as well as adults needed to be prepared to face death's early arrival. The children's literature of the time carried out this task by constantly rehearsing the death of the young in fictional form and by instructing its readers how to conduct themselves in relation to death in the real world (Walvin, 1986). Equally important was the fact that children's deaths normally took place at home. As a result, children learned how to cope with the death of others, and by implication with their own, in essentially the same way that they acquired the more mundane domestic skills; that is, by observing and taking part in the household's daily activities. Because the great majority of childhood deaths were due to infectious diseases, the process of biological deterioration was usually swift. Nevertheless, the child's move toward social death was normally controlled in accordance with ritual practices that were a familiar part of domestic life and which were based on the assumption that family relationships would continue beyond the grave.

It would be wrong to infer that the frequency with which children died or the assurance of life after death meant that death was accepted without fear by the young or without deep sense of loss by many surviving adults (Jalland and Hooper, 1986). However, such deaths were expected and prepared for in nineteenth century Britain and they took place in an organised manner as part of the recurring pattern of communal life (Walvin, 1986). The marked reduction in the rate of infant mortality since then has transformed people's expectations for their children and this, in turn, has left both adults and children unprepared for death when it does occur. The fear and distress arising from the death of the young that were collectively regulated and socially channelled in Victorian times are now experienced in a society which has yet to develop a social death sequence that is appropriate to the new demographic situation.

In Britain today, excluding stillbirths and neonatal deaths, accidents are the most common cause of death among children (Foster and Smith, 1987). Such deaths are unexpected, not only in the sense that each particular death occurs without warning, but also in the sense that modern parents do not see childhood as a time when death is likely. Thus parents often react initially with disbelief as well as with shock, anger and dismay (Foster and Smith, 1987). The emotional distress of the bereaved is so great, partly because the child's firmly anticipated future in this world is removed instantaneously, but also because expectations of life after death leading to eventual reunion are either entirely absent or are held in most cases with less conviction than in the past. In the great majority of accidental deaths in childhood, the bereaved are deprived of a graduated social death sequence involving the lost child, either before or after the child's death, in the course of which they might adjust to their grief and to the destruction of the personal world in which the child had played such an important part (Foster and Smith, 1987).

Present-day parents have no well-established patterns of social conduct and associated belief to help them through the traumatic events, centred around and processed by the medical bureaucracy, which follow the accidental death of a daughter or son. Acquaintances, friends, even other members of the family network are likely to respond by pointedly avoiding the topic and also by reducing the frequency of their contact with the bereaved (Gorer, 1965; Foster and Smith, 1987). As a result of the death of their child, the social activities of the parents will tend to become restricted in a way that is analogous to, though less formalized than, the restrictions imposed on the grieving Victorian mother. In other words, on the sudden death of a child, parents today are likely to undergo a form of social death sequence by association.

In the modern world, however, this sequence has no wider symbolic or social significance. Parents are no longer ritually separated from the living in order to keep alive the memory of, or to maintain contact with, the newly dead. They are, rather, set apart to forget, and to prepare to replace, the dead (Foster and Smith, 1987). Their social exclusion is, like that experienced by the very old, but another expression of the customary flight from death in our society by those who are not directly affected (Kearl, 1989). The consequence is that the parents, unprepared and lacking social support, typically respond to their bereavement and to the unexpected social isolation that follows with bewilderment accompanied by a devastating sense of personal loss.

In the case of accidental deaths, one source of parents' pain is that they have had no time in which to readjust their relationship with the child whilst the child was still alive (Foster and Smith, 1987). In the case of deaths from cancer, however, which is the second most frequent cause of death among the young in contemporary Britain, time for readjustment is available. Childhood death from cancer is a comparatively slow process. In this respect, it resembles the typical death sequence of the elderly. Indeed, as the disease progresses, children dying from cancer come increasingly to look and act like the aged (Bluebond-Langner, 1978:213).

Yet the social context in which dying occurs is crucially different for children in that children in our society, unlike the elderly

© Archives Européennes de Sociologie, 1991

and unlike the children of past generations, are not expected to die. As a result, although the child dying from cancer, the child's parents and other close relatives have time in which to develop a shared response to the death to come, their reaction typically takes the form of a persistent denial of the imminence of death well beyond the point where the medical prognosis has become unequivocal. In such circumstances, the clinical death sequence is accompanied, not by a change of conduct in recognition of the approach of death, but by a collective pretence of normal social life.

Collective pretence of this kind is not confined in the modern world to the deaths of children. In the case of older persons, however, such pretence is likely to give way, in due course, to a more open recognition that death is finally at hand (Glaser and Strauss, 1965; Field, 1989). This eventual openness is especially permissible in relation to the elderly who are properly expected to die. But, in our world, children are above all people with a future, to be nurtured, protected, instructed, and when necessary cured, with that future in mind (Bluebond-Langner, 1978; Field, 1989). Thus adults' normal dealings with children, in direct contrast to their dealings with the elderly (Sudnow, 1967), address the children's future in innumerable, largely unnoticed ways. Accordingly, when children are transformed by incurable disease into persons with no future, most adults experience great difficulty in knowing what to say or do.

In her moving study of children dying in an American hospital from leukaemia, Bluebond-Langner (1978) shows that the normal response to this dilemma is to restrict the flow of relevant information to the child and to refuse to discuss openly the likelihood of the child's death. Children quickly become aware of adults' reticence on these topics and respond by pretending not to know what lies in store for them. The collective pretence initiated by staff and parents is designed to sustain an illusion of normality. It is intended to reassure the children that, despite their poor health at present and despite the periodic deaths of other sick children, they will in fact recover.

Bluebond-Langner documents the many subtle ways in which this illusion is maintained in adults' dealings with dying children. She emphasises, however, that it is inherently precarious and in continual danger of collapse because all participants, including the children, eventually come to recognise where the process of biological decline is leading. Furthermore, the collective pretence of normality, although it is justified as being in the children's best interests, clearly adds to children's difficulties by creating a situation in which they are likely to approach death in an atmosphere of avoidance, prevarication and distrust.

The deaths of young persons in our society cause special problems, even in situations where the process of dying is slow and where the eventual outcome is recognised in advance by all concerned. The underlying reason for this is that the socially organised death sequences focusing upon the young, which were appropriate in a society characterised by a high mortality rate among children and which provided support and compensation for those involved, have disappeared almost completely as the frequency of such deaths has fallen to remarkably low levels. In our society, as the concentration of death among the elderly has become firmly established and has come to be taken for granted, so the death of the young has come to be almost unthinkable as part of the ordinary course of events.

Yet in a small percentage of young lives, biological death still comes desperately early. Our customary response when such a death approaches is akin to constructing a social death sequence in reverse; that is, instead of initiating an anticipatory process of social decline, we try hard to create a sense of continuing social involvement for the stricken child. We try to pretend, for the child but also for ourselves, that the unthinkable is not happening and to draw the child with us into a world of make-believe where children never die. In this way, we seek to delay the child's social death until pretence and denial are no longer possible.

## Concluding remarks

I have tried to show that the concept 'social death' can be used to elucidate major historical developments in society at large. In order to explore the complex historical changes that have occurred in people's conduct associated with death and dying, I have employed two kinds of systematic comparison. Firstly, I have compared demographic profiles of biological death with profiles of social death. Secondly, I have compared the profiles of biological and social death in modern Britain with those of Victorian times.

The changes that have taken place in the profile of social death during the last century have been brought about by people's collective responses to the changing social distribution of biological death, to the changing social setting of death, and to the changing clinical nature of death. In the previous century, social death sequences were designed to cope with high mortality rates among children, with comparatively modest life expectancy among those who survived childhood, and with the rapid and unpredictable onset of death from infectious disease. The process of dying in Victorian society lay beyond the control of the medical profession and took place overwhelmingly within the domestic setting. In this society, virtually all members were familiar with death from their earliest years and regularly participated in social death sequences of varying degrees of intensity. But women in particular, owing to their subordinate position within the Victorian household, were mainly responsible for carrying out the rituals of mourning whereby family members' often brief lives were continued beyond the grave.

In modern society, biological death has, to a considerable degree, been tamed. It has become largely predictable and occurs mostly within organised bureaucratic structures. One of the unanticipated consequences of this situation is that increasing control over biological death has been balanced by a redistribution of social death. In contrast to the last century, when women's ritual activities operated to continue lives unpredictably cut short, present day social death sequences often work to reduce and terminate people's social existence in anticipation of their biological cessation. Thus in terms of social existence, as distinct from biological functioning, the difference between Victorian times and our own is by no means so great as simple variations in mortality rates seem to suggest. For in our society, not only are there few forms of belief or conduct to keep us living in the lives of others after biological death, but in addition, a substantial part of those extra years of biological functioning that have been acquired during this century are likely to be spent, particularly by women, in a condition closely approaching social death.

The situation regarding the deaths of children is also less straightforward than the dramatic improvement in mortality rates seems to imply. For this very improvement has changed the context in which children die and has destroyed the systems of belief and communal conduct by means of which childhood death was managed in the past. In our society, where parents reasonably expect all their children to survive to adulthood, the social death sequence for the young has atrophied and has been replaced by a process of collective pretence which appears to exacerbate the emotional and interpersonal difficulties of all concerned.

## Bibliography

Anderson, M., (1985), 'The Emergence of the Modern Life Cycle in Britain', *Social History*, 10: 69–87.

Bluebond-Langner, M., (1978), *The Private Worlds of Dying Children*, Princeton: Princeton University Press.

Clark, D., (1982), *Between Pulpit and Pew: Folk Religion in a North Yorkshire Fishing Village*, Cambridge: Cambridge University Press.

Clegg, F., (1988), *Decisions at a Time of Grief*, University of Hull, unpublished.

CSO (Central Statistical Office), (1989), *Annual Abstract of Statistics*, London: HMSO.

Falkingham, J., (1989), 'Dependency and Ageing in Britain: A Re-examination of the Evidence', *Journal of Social Policy*, 18(2): 211–33.

Field, D., (1989), *Nursing the Dying*, London: Tavistock/Routledge.

Foster, S. and Smith, O., (1987), *Brief Lives*, London: Arlington Books.

Fulton, R. and Fulton, J., (1971), 'A Psychological Aspect of Terminal Care: Anticipatory Grief', *Omega*, 2: 91–100.

Glaser, B.G. and Strauss, A.L., (1965), *Awareness of Dying*, Chicago: Aldine.

Glaser, B.G. and Strauss, A.L., (1968), *Time for Dying*, Chicago: Aldine.

Goody, J., (1962), *Death, Property and the Ancestors*, London: Tavistock.

Gorer, G., (1965), *Death, Grief and Mourning in Contemporary Britain*, London: The Cresset Press.

Halsey, A.H., (ed.), (1988), *British Social Trends since 1900*, Basingstoke: Macmillan.

Hockey, J., (1985), 'Cultural and Social Interpretations of "Dying" and "Death" in a Residential Home for Elderly People in the North East of England', *Curare*, 8(1): 35–43.

Hockey, J., (1990), *Experiences of Death: An Anthropological Account*, Edinburgh: Edinburgh University Press.

Hughes, B. and Wilkin, D., (1987), 'Physical Care and Quality of Life in Residential Homes', *Ageing and Society*, 7: 399–425.

Hunt, A., (1978), *The Elderly at Home: A Study of People Aged 65 and Over Living in the Community in 1976*, London: HMSO.

Jalland, P. and Hooper, J., (eds), (1986), *Women from Birth to Death: The Female Life Cycle 1830–1914*, Brighton: The Harvester Press.

Kearl, M.C., (1989), *Endings: A Sociology of Death and Dying*, Oxford and New York: Oxford University Press.

Kuykendall, J., (1989), 'Death of a Child: The Worst Kept Secret Around', in L. Sherr (ed.), *Death, Dying and Bereavement*, Oxford: Blackwell.

Mitchell, B.R., (1981), *European Historical Statistics 1750–1975*, Cambridge: Cambridge University Press.

Morley, J., (1971), *Death, Heaven and the Victorians*, London: University of Pittsburgh Press.

© Archives Européennes de Sociologie, 1991

Mulkay, M. and Ernst, J., (1991), 'The Changing Profile of Social Death', *European Journal of Sociology*, 32: 172–196.

OPCS (Office of Population Censuses and Surveys), (1985, 1989), London: HMSO.

Rees, W.D., (1971), 'The Hallucinations of Widowhood', *British Medical Journal*, 4: 37–41.

Sudnow, D., (1967), *Passing On: The Social Organization of Dying*, Englewood Cliffs, N.J.: Prentice-Hall.

Turner, B.S., (1983), *Religion and Social Theory: A Materialist Perspective*, London: Heinemann.

Turner, B.S., (1984), *Medical Knowledge and Social Power*, London and Beverly Hills: Sage.

Walvin, J., (1986), 'Dying and Mourning: The English Case', in *Consequences of Mortality Trends and Differentials*, New York: United Nations.

Walter, T., (1990), *Funerals: And How to Improve Them*, London: Hodder and Stoughton.

Williams, R. (1990), *A Protestant Legacy: Attitudes to Death and Illness among Older Aberdonians*, Oxford: Clarendon Press.

# Death, inheritance and the life course

## Janet Finch and Lorraine Wallis

Our central purpose in this chapter is to address the question of how to conceptualise the social significance of death. We take a particular approach to this large and important question by addressing it from the perspective of inheritance. In order to do so, we make use of some data from our own empirical research on inheritance in the contemporary English context, but the paper is essentially a conceptual one. It is not our purpose to present an overview of findings from our research, rather in this chapter we are using some empirical data to help us refine conceptual questions.[1]

The perspective of inheritance provides a useful approach for conceptualising the social significance of death because it roots the discussion firmly in material questions. These issues are becoming significant for many more people in the UK, since the rise in home ownership in the past four decades has meant that more people have significant assets to bequeath when they die than would have been the case in the past.[2] This raises certain questions about the social significance of death, which come at the topic from a perspective rather different from that often found in sociological literature on death and dying. Much of the classic sociological work on death tends to focus on the process of dying and the rituals and symbols associated with it (Glaser and Strauss, 1965; Sudnow, 1967; Ariès, 1981). These are important, of course, but they do not tell the whole story. A death also involves the disposal of the deceased's assets. The significance of these material issues, particularly at the micro level, has tended to be overlooked by sociologists.[3] By contrast anthropology has always treated inheritance as being of central importance in understanding social life, and this theme also has been taken up by historians, especially some who have specialised in European societies before industrialisation (Goody, Thirsk and Thompson, 1976; Anderson, 1980).

In this chapter, we aim to begin to redress the balance of sociological interest by suggesting ways in which we might develop a specifically sociological approach to the social meanings of death, taking as our starting point the transmission of property. In considering what type of conceptual framework might be suitable for our task, we have turned to the notion of life course, as developed over the past fifteen years in a body of literature which has been more significant in the United States than in the UK, but which seems of particular relevance to the conceptualisation of death. At first sight this literature does not bear directly on death and inheritance but we would argue that it has considerable potential for development.

Briefly, concepts of the life course provide a framework for understanding the experiences of individuals as they change over time. As individuals move through different life circumstances, a life course perspective seeks to understand these changes as a sequence. By focussing upon sequence at the individual level, and by building in the perspective of time, this approach provides an important counter-balance to the general tendency of sociology to examine social processes from a cross-sectional perspective, and to treat people as aggregate groups which currently occupy a particular life 'slot' (children, young people, parents, the elderly, and so on). Studies of the life course are certainly interested in these different life circumstances. But the particular focus of interest is how they link together: how far people's experiences are cumulative, how far life choices are constrained by what has gone before, how people manage the transitions as they move through different experiences over time (Elder, 1975, 1977; Hareven, 1978; Riley, 1987). Although in a sense a life course perspective takes the individual as its central unit of analysis, the interlinking of individual life courses within the context of families and households is another important component. A further element in life course analysis is that it has a strong sense of the historical circumstances under which people live their lives, in that individuals are treated as people who pass through time not only in the sense of biological ageing, but also in the sense that an individual's life span happens at a particular point in historical time.

Characteristically, therefore, a life course perspective weaves together an understanding of movement through time for individuals, in the context of family (and other close) relationships, and over historical time. The following quotation from Tamara Hareven, who was highly influential in the development of concepts of the life course, encapsulates this:

A life course perspective views the interrelationships between individual and collective family behaviour as they constantly change over people's lives in the context of historical conditions. The life course approach is concerned with the movement of individuals over their own lives and through historical time, and with the relationship of family members to each other as they travel through personal and historical time. (Hareven, 1982:6)

In thinking about how we might use the perspective of inheritance to help understand the social significance of death, we believe that the framework provided by the life course perspective, and associated concepts, has considerable potential. Given that this approach focusses upon the movement of individuals through time (both separately and together), it implies that we should conceptualise death as the end point of the journey of an individual through the particular slice of historical time during which he or she has lived. Interestingly, death has been very little discussed hitherto within the life course literature, though it is an obvious dimension of this approach. It thus enables us to pose sociologically meaningful questions about the social significance of a death for those who remain and the ways in which this might have an impact – either in its anticipation or when the death occurs – upon the relationships and the future life courses of other family members.

Our approach in the rest of this chapter is to select three key concepts associated with theories of the life course. These are: social transition; normative timetables; stages in the life course. For each in turn we ask how it can help us to conceptualise the social significance of death, drawing on our own empirical data to help raise questions and to refine our analysis. Our research on inheritance has not been designed specifically to explore the social significance of death, but it does contain data relevant to this issue. These are of two types. Firstly we have data from a random sample of 800 wills taken from people whose wills were probated in four sample years (1959, 1969, 1979 and 1989) in the north west and south east regions of England.[4] Secondly we have data from 89 in-depth interviews with 99 individuals (some couples chose to be interviewed together) about their experiences of how inheritance is handled in their own families. This study population is not randomly sampled, but has been constructed to ensure, *inter alia*, that it includes people from a wide range of socio-economic backgrounds.[5] In this part of the study we interviewed different members of the same family, wherever feasible, and this was facilitated by our initial contact with the family.

## Death as a social transition

The concept of 'transitions' has played a central part in the development of life course perspectives, and empirical research based upon them. It refers to the movement of individuals between stages or phases of their lives, and seeks to understand the processes through which such movements take place. Work careers provide one obvious example. A focus upon transitions within the career would highlight how – and most importantly, when – people seek and achieve promotion, take an advanced qualification, move into retirement. Transitions between different family circumstances have been a particular focus of much work on the life course, that is, movement into cohabitation or marriage, into parenthood, out of one marriage into another, and so on. Unlike earlier analysis associated with the concept of life 'cycle', this approach does not presume that individuals always pass through any or all of these stages. But it acknowledges that people do experience a sense that their lives move through identifiable phases, especially in retrospect (Demos and Bocock, 1978; Hareven, 1978; Morgan, 1985:159–82).

A life course perspective is particularly concerned with the timing of transitions from one phase to the next, and the personal and structural contexts which lead them to occur at one point in the individual's life rather than another. It is also concerned with the synchronisation of transitions within the context of families – the extent to which the transition of one individual has implications for others within the close family, and how this may be anticipated and may influence individual decisions about transitions. Tamara Hareven's (1978, 1982) work has been particularly influential in developing the conceptual basis for this aspect of life course analysis. She argues that we need to focus upon the complex interweaving of different individual life courses over time within the family context, and points to the importance of analysing how 'individual time' and 'family time' relate to each other. Thus an analysis of the social significance of any event in an individual's life needs to be matched by an analysis of its impact on the people whose lives are significantly interwoven with that individual, always trying to capture the whole as a moving rather than a static picture.

We would propose therefore that the concept of transition, and particularly its emphasis on the interweaving of family time and individual time, can help us to tease out some other facets of the social significance of death. Though the timing of a death is normally outside the control of the person who dies, both the fact that the death occurs, and its timing, can have profound implications for those who survive.

Using the perspective of inheritance brings out this point very sharply. It shows that death does represent a social transition involving a range of people, most evidently the family of the person who has died. One very obvious transition concerns the transmission of the ownership of property from the person who has died to one or more of those who survive.[6] This means that the power to deploy resources, for one's own or other people's benefit, shifts within the family. How far this has a real effect on relationships is a matter for empirical investigation in individual cases, but the potential is certainly there for a shift in the balance of family power, and for the creation of new alliances. Clearly the significance of this is likely to vary with the size of the assets.

The questions which we are posing here concern how far material relationships can consolidate or fracture personal bonds, as these adjustments take place after a death. In turn this raises issues about how such transitions can be managed by any of the relevant parties. In particular can someone with property to bequeath, in anticipation of his or her own death, use the provisions of a will to shape and manage the transition which will occur when the property is transmitted? We can explore this using evidence both from the wills we have studied and from our interview data.

Since wills are legal documents designed for a very specific purpose, normally one would not expect to find clear evidence of an individual's attempt to use a pattern of bequests to manage the transition in relationships which will occur after his or her death. The testator may be seeking to use the provisions contained in the will in this way, but the will itself may not necessarily show clear evidence of such intent.[7] It is certainly true that most wills do not contain explicit evidence of this type. However, a few do. In these cases testators were evidently trying to manage any potential conflict by including specific comments or instructions to pre-empt any such disputes and to ease the transition triggered by their death. Here is a passage from one of the wills (written in 1981) in which the testator attempted to explain the decisions he had made over the division of his estate:

> If any members of my own family shall question my bequest to them or absence thereof I wish to make it clear that no animosity exists between us nor is any neglect of them intended. I have merely disposed of my estate to those who have directly or indirectly been of special service to me and my wife Joy and her family during our lifetime and/or who will in my view best use my estate for the greatest benefit.

Though it is relatively unusual to find a passage like this in a will, it indicates the potential power wills have in sending messages to surviving relatives about their relationship to the testator and about the future relationships between survivors. The power lies in the ability of the testator to manipulate other people's understanding of the meaning of bequests made. In this case, the testator reveals his understanding about normative expectations which might be associated with bequests, especially the expectation that he 'ought' to leave assets to his relatives. Having decided that he was not going to do so, he then uses the will to try to impose his own set of meanings on his actions.

The fact that it is made explicit makes this type of will particularly interesting and suggests that there may be other cases, without explicit comments, where relatives nonetheless are intended to read off messages about relationships from the provisions of a will. Our interview data, which enable us to tap something of the rationale being used by testators, enable us to see that this can indeed happen. In order to explore this we want to look briefly at the case of Alice Hilton. Again, we are selecting a case because it demonstrates this issue particularly clearly. Though we are not claiming that it is statistically representative, there certainly are other cases in our data set in which people anticipate the messages likely to be read off from their will, and the possible consequences for their surviving relatives.

Alice is a widow in her 80s. She lives alone and was recovering from a hip operation when we interviewed her. Alice has two sons, Roy and John.[8] Roy lives locally and, along with his wife, Julie, is the main provider of care for Alice. John works abroad and makes infrequent visits to his mother when in this country. The lack of concern and practical assistance shown by John had caused some distress to Alice. Roy and his wife commented during their interview that Alice had talked of excluding John from her will. As a result Roy and Julie were convinced that Roy's share of his mother's estate would be larger than John's. This, however, was not the account given to us by Alice who implied that her will divided the major part of her estate equally between her two sons. Here she explains her decision to write her will in this way:

> Well I did want to make sure that it were, that no one was going to have a lot of running about . . . Or that there was going to be any disagreement anywhere . . . because it's not nice is it? And if people are left the same then they can't grumble then can they, or do much about it I'm afraid.

Alice appeared to have written a will which, she felt, would cause the least conflict between her sons. Roy and Julie confirmed that, in their view, there was a real chance that John would contest any will which excluded him. By leaving equal shares to her sons, Alice felt she would be avoiding potential conflict. In this case we see something of the processes through which a person anticipates her own death in the foreseeable future and tries to manage the social transition which will occur after it, in which inheritance is a key component.

We would argue therefore that the concept of transition offers a powerful tool for understanding the social significance of death, and that transitions which follow a death can have a clear material dimension in that the re-ordering of relationships can be shaped by who has inherited what. We have focused here on evidence from our current research that the deceased, in advance of his or her death, may try to manage this transition. Yet we feel it is important to point out the possibility that various other parties, including the deceased's relatives, may be involved in managing the transition prior to and maybe after an individual's death. It points to the possibility of applying a life course analysis to the way death and its material elements, related to inheritance, can become interwoven with adjustments and realignments taking place in personal relationships after someone dies.

## Normative timetables for dying

The second concept, which we shall take from the life course literature and apply to our discussion of the social significance of death, is the concept of normative timetables, defined in an influential paper as Elder as:

'. . . a preferred sequence of related activities or stages in a line of activity'. (Elder, 1975:176)

The concept of normative timetables is closely related to the analysis of transitions across the life course, and refers to the empirically recognisable phenomenon that – in the context of a given society – people do commonly share the concept that there is a 'right time' and a 'right order' in which various transitions should happen. These are cultural norms which may sometimes be expressed as age-related; for example, the belief that a man should have married by the time he is 30, a woman somewhat earlier, or that a woman should have become a mother by the time she is in her late 20s. On other occasions they may be expressed as norms of sequence, the sequence often being related more to family time than individual time; for example, a couple should not have children before at least one of them has a well established career or, an elder daughter should marry before a younger one. Though such cultural norms may be relatively weak in contemporary western societies there is evidence, certainly in relation to marriage, that people often do operate with a surprisingly clear view of the appropriate age and sequence in which events should occur (Leonard, 1980; Mansfield and Collard, 1988).

How can the notion of normative timetables inform our understanding of the social significance of death? In general our inheritance data suggest that people do have a strong concept of the 'right time' to die and the 'right order' in which people should die, that is, that there are indeed normative timetables for dying. This is expressed most obviously in generational terms – that parents should die before their children. In this section we explore some of the ways in which this message comes through in our data, and what the consequences are if the normative timetable for dying is violated, by one person's dying 'out of order'. Again, we shall highlight particularly the material dimension of these normative timetables.

Our data from the wills study can be used to explore this issue by looking at the phenomenon of substitution, that is, the circumstances under which a testator indicates that, should their first choice of beneficiary die before the testator her- or himself, the bequest should pass to a named substitute beneficiary. Writing in provision for a substitute implies that the testator has at least thought about the possibility that the first choice beneficiary may die first. A complicating factor is that, where a will has been drawn up by a professional (usually a solicitor) patterns of substitution may reflect professional norms rather than demonstrating the testator's assumptions about who will predecease whom. Our analysis of the wills data shows that there is indeed a difference in substitution patterns between professionally-made and home-made wills. So we are discussing here the data from home-made wills only, where we are likely to gain a clearer picture of the assumptions used by the *testator* (rather than the professional) when thinking about the circumstances of his/her own death.

In general, compared with wills written with the assistance of professionals, home-made wills have far fewer substitutions. Further, in home-made wills spouses are more likely than children to have substitutes and, similarly, sisters are substituted more often than are nieces and nephews. This indicates that testators envisage they are more likely to be predeceased by people from the same generation (spouses, siblings) than by people from the generation below them (children, nieces, nephews). For beneficiaries who are two generations descendant the likelihood of substitution is even more stark. In home-made wills, grandchildren, great-nieces and great-nephews *never* have a substitute. Thus it appears that normative timetables, concerned with the order in which people should die, do influence the way in which wills are written in that, left to their own devices, very few people choose to include substitutes for descendant generations. Presumably substitution is seen as unnecessary, because children, grandchildren, nieces and nephews are not expected to die before the testator.

On one level, it could be argued that this timetable is predictive rather than normative – since life expectancy rates have risen, people may simply feel that it is extremely unlikely that descendant generations will predecease them. The idea of a timetable's being normative implies something beyond the predictive, namely that children 'ought' not to predecease their parents. While our wills data do not enable us to distinguish between these two interpretations, our interview data enable us to gain an understanding of whether people do see this in clearly normative terms. In brief, our interviews suggest that some people do exhibit a strong sense of normative timetabling of the 'right order' in which to die, while other people do not focus on this, or not so strongly. We shall consider briefly the case in our data set that exhibits such normative timetables most clearly. We are not claiming that it is typical (as we have already indicated), though there are echoes of the same phenomenon in some other cases. Our main point is that this illustrates that the concept of normative timetables can be a useful tool for analysing some people's response to deaths in their own families.

It appears that, if people die in the 'wrong' order, this can lead to a sense of confusion, almost of violation. The case which shows this clearly concerns Peter White. Peter is in his 70s. He lives alone and has never married but shared the house with his mother and younger sister prior to both their deaths. Here he talks about the wills they had written, the understandings they all held of the order in which they would die and the plans they had made for inheritance as a result:

> [My mother, my sister and myself bought] this house eleven years ago, we said we'd make wills then and the three of us made wills with the same solicitor who was a friend of ours
> . . . and ur . . . as I say he put it all that it passed from one to the other . . . but even then you can't cater for everything because I've just altered my will because we all presumed that my mother would die first, I would go next, married sister next and younger sister last. And it hasn't happened that way.

Peter then goes on to show how he and his mother had planned the disposal of their assets on the assumption that the younger sister would be the last to die:

> . . . you know, but I've never had anybody leave me any money except my sister and she did . . .
> *Interviewer*: Um, yes, yes . . .
> (There was a pause. Mr White seemed very upset recalling matters relating to his sister. A tear trickled down from his eye.)
> *Peter*: Now it was our idea, her [his younger sister] to have money, being the youngest.

*Interviewer*: Ah yes, right, so she had it, yes.

*Peter*: More interested in her having money behind her than us.

Clearly all the plans which Peter had made for disposal of his assets were based on the notion that his younger sister would survive him. His interview demonstrates the significance of normative timetabling on an individual level. The fact that close members of his family had died in the 'wrong' order caused him considerable distress and confusion. Interestingly, despite his experience, Peter White's second will was still influenced by notions of a normative timetable. In his second will he named his nephews and his second (younger) sister as beneficiaries but was not going to include a predecease clause until this was suggested to him by his solicitor.

Our interviews therefore tend to reinforce the findings of our wills data. Both indicate that people do operate with a strong sense of an order or sequence in which deaths will occur, and we have some evidence that this is normative and not simply predictive. However there certainly is individual variation, with some of our interviewees demonstrating a stronger sense of the normative dimension of timetabling than did others. In those cases, this can strongly influence the way in which people operate, in relation to inheritance, and lend important dimensions to the way in which any death is experienced and handled.

## Death as a stage in the life course

The final concept on which we shall draw in this discussion is that of life 'stages', which focuses upon individual time rather than family time. We shall examine the idea that death can be seen as a stage in the life course of an individual, and consider what this perspective can illuminate about the social significance of death.

If lives can be characterised by phases or stages (at least in retrospect), then death is very obviously the final stage for the individual, even if the consequences of a death continue forward into time in the lives of those who remain, as we have shown. It is curious therefore that the literature on the life course is, for the most part, silent on this final and most predictable stage. A partial exception is Frankenberg's (1987) article which, while not explicitly located in life course analysis, nonetheless does focus upon developing ways of conceptualising death as an integral part of understanding lives over time. He argues that those who study the life course must find concepts to illuminate the ever-present possibility of death, and its ultimate certainty 'however much sociologists . . . may shy away from it' (p. 137). His own preference is for the concept of pilgrimage, to encapsulate a sense of the individual as active agent, moving through time towards death, but within a context which is socially structured.

There are various ways in which the concept of the final stage in the life course can be used to tease out the social significance of death. We have chosen to concentrate on one issue, which is highlighted by our data. We will argue that the central significance of death as a 'stage' in an individual life course is the fact that people anticipate it – indeed it is the only life event that can be anticipated with total certainty. In this context it is also important to note that demographic changes in life expectancy (especially in the twentieth century) have meant that people can expect to live well into their 70s.[9] As a result people may delay thinking about the consequences of death, including the disposal of their assets, until much later in life than might have been the case in the past.

From a sociological perspective, there are a range of fascinating conceptual and empirical questions about *how* people anticipate death, *when* they do so, and the effect which this has upon the way in which they shape their life choices and their social relationships. In this chapter, we are concentrating on one particular way in which death is anticipated, through plans made for the disposal of one's assets. By focusing on the issue of inheritance, we are able to explore the ways in which the significance of death varies with the particular point in the life course which an individual has reached. We can also see that it is grounded in the life course of those who would be left behind.

In essence, we wish to suggest that younger people anticipate the possibility of their death and its consequence in a rather different way than is the case for older people, and that this is revealed in the ways different age groups approach the writing of a will. To begin with some specific examples from our interview data, we focus first on Nick Murray, a single man in his early 20s. Here he considers to whom he would leave his possessions if he were to write a will:

*Nick*: Ur, probably to my father again.
*Interviewer*: Yeah.
*Nick*: 'cause, 'cause I've spent you know so much time with my father, him first, first and foremost I think –

His young step-sister, present during the interview, interrupts:

Sister: No, but if you wrote it to Dad, um, Dad's older than you and he may die before you, you should write it to me, ur, ur only, about ur, nearly twenty years younger than you.

It is clear even to Nick's seven year old step-sister that the desire to name a parent as a beneficiary conflicts with the concept of normative timetabling which, as we have seen, more usually informs the way people write their wills. Yet Nick Murray was not alone in considering the inclusion of a member of the ascendant generation in his will. Five of our interviewees had written a guardianship clause into their wills and all but one had named their parents as guardians, indicating that these particular (relatively youthful) testators are using wills to address their needs and responsibilities at the particular point in their life course which they had reached currently. They were not, in a sense, expecting their wills to last them through to death if this did not occur until old age. Other interviewees, in different ways, also made apparent the transient nature of wills written by younger people. Here Wendy Kahn, aged 42, talks about the will she had written some years previously and indicates the extent to which it represented a set of concerns and circumstances specific to that stage in her life:

So we thought, you know, sort of what would happen to them [her children], and with me being the only one, it was that sort of thing that made us make a will, rather than the possessions side of thing . . . yeah, our will is quite simple, very, very, simple unless and until as it stands now, because you know, you don't have anything do you really . . . nothing really to give anybody, only what you have if it is sold you know, sort of the house and things.

Now Wendy feels:

. . . as time sort of goes on, and you think about things slightly differently, and your children have grown older, erm, there might be specific things that I might want to leave to one, erm, you know which, I haven't given it a great deal of thought . . . but, erm, you know, in the future I might think about it a little bit more deeply.

Our wills data also lend support to the claim that wills made by younger people are transient in nature and not intended to cover a death which might ultimately occur in old age. Amongst the 800 wills in our sample, 74 per cent of our testators under 60, compared with 48 per cent of those aged 60 plus, wrote a simple will which did not make specific gifts of, for example, cash or personal property but simply bequeathed their estate as a totality. Older will-writers are more likely to include such gifts, which indicate that thought has been given to acknowledging the value of a range of personal relationships, at the end of one's life. So both our wills and our interview data suggest that people who write wills at an early age are anticipating the possibility of their death and its consequences in a rather different way than is the case for older people.

When we explore these patterns in the light of our interview data, another facet of this phenomenon emerges. It would appear that something more complex is happening to trigger the writing of a will – and the form which a will takes – than simply the ageing process, though clearly this is important. Other changes in life circumstances can also be triggers, especially if such changes would have further consequences if a death occurred. In short people seem to review their wills as they *and* their beneficiaries grow older. Norman and Doris Clegg, now both in the early 70s, made their first will more than ten years ago when both of their two daughters were married without children. Here Doris talks about their plans to add a codicil to their will to cater for the events of their daughters' predeceasing them.

> *Doris*: And we have made wills. We've made wills in favour of our daughters but since we made the will, they've both had children and next month we have made an appointment to see our solicitor to make sure that if anything happened to our daughters, our grandchildren would benefit.
> *Interviewer*: Right.
> *Doris*: Not that we don't trust our sons in law, cos we do know of many cases where the surviving husband has married again and all the money has gone to the family of his second

wife, which means that your own grandchildren could be cut out. So this is just a precaution. I trust the boys implicitly but I think in this life you've got to do things.

The Clegg case does suggest ways in which we can understand how ageing relates to the anticipation of one's own death, and why younger people's wills often take a different form from those of older people. It is not simply that through ageing people come to believe more in their own mortality, but also that they can see in more concrete terms what might be the consequences of their death for other people. However, wills written by people who are younger and healthy seem to have different personal meaning for the testator, acting in effect as a fail-safe device for circumstances they do not really expect to occur. We get hints of this, in different ways, in interviews other than those we have already quoted. For example, a number of younger people told us that they had first considered seriously writing a will when taking a plane journey to go on holiday. They felt that they ought to make sure their children would be provided for in the event of a fatal accident. In these circumstances a will is clearly being seen as no more and no less than a safety net for a possible, yet unlikely, eventuality.

By contrast the process of thinking about asset disposal in later in life seems to involve a much clearer sense of death as a concrete event, which is anticipated in an active sense, and which forms an end-point of a life. In these circumstances people seem more likely actually to anticipate how they would like their assets to be distributed, and how such a distribution might acknowledge the strengths of their different relationships. For them, death becomes the final stage of life in a very meaningful sense. By taking actions which anticipate it in specific ways, inheritance rounds off the relationships formed throughout the life course.

## Conclusion

We began the analysis contained in this chapter with the intention of exploring new ways of conceptualising the social significance of death, taking one particular angle on death, namely the perspective of inheritance. Thus our intention has been to focus on the material dimensions of death, and their social meanings, which often are overlooked in sociological work on death and dying. In selecting a conceptual framework, we have drawn on concepts of the life course and have developed these to apply to the specific dimensions of death which we have highlighted.

Our main conclusion is that life course concepts have indeed proved a potentially valuable tool with which to generate new insights into the social significance of death, and that this approach would repay further development. We are very conscious that we have opened up this line of analysis only in a limited way. For example in discussing death as the last 'stage' in the life course, we have developed one particular line of analysis, namely the way people anticipate the final stage. But there may well be other ways of developing the concept of death as the final stage in the life course. Similarly, we have made little use of the dimension of historical time, which is so important in life course analysis. Yet clearly there is potential for asking sociologically interesting questions about the effect of reaching this stage of life at one point in historical time rather than another. However we believe that we have done enough to indicate the potential of this approach for the sociology of death and dying.

Our own use of life course concepts in this chapter has suggested four themes which are important to a sociological understanding of death. These themes are linked by a common focus on time. First, we have argued that life course analysis directs us to look at the interweaving of individual time and family time, and that employing this perspective helps us to understand the kinds of adjustments in relationships which occur following a death. Second, we have argued that it directs us to look at one person's death in relation to another's, and to see the social significance of the sequence in which deaths occur. Third, we see life course analysis directing us to examine the ways in which people look forward to and anticipate their own death, especially as it approaches more closely. Fourth, it would seem that people anticipate death in ways which are fundamentally social, attempting to manage the consequences of their own death for those who remain, and to round off their lives in a way which provides a satisfactory conclusion to their close relationships. In relation to each of these, we have provided some data which indicate that they are phenomena worthy of study, but we have not attempted (nor could we, on the basis of our existing study) to give a definitive account of the experience of the majority of people. Our focus has been conceptual rather than empirical, as we indicated at the beginning of the chapter.

Thus in this chapter, we have done no more than open up the potential of life course analysis in the sociological study of death. We have tackled it specifically from the perspective of inheritance, but we certainly believe that the potential of life course analysis could be exploited in studying other dimensions of death. Nonetheless we would argue that taking the perspective of inheritance has also helped to redress some imbalances in the sociology of death and dying, in that we have shown that material considerations can be fundamental to the ways in which death is experienced and handled. In a British context where inheritance is becoming a more significant factor in many more families, sociologists do need to ensure that material issues are central to any rounded analysis of the social significance of death.

## Notes

1 The project on Inheritance, Property and Family Relationships is funded by the ESRC (Grant number 000232035). Its central purpose is to explore how questions of inheritance are handled in contemporary families in the UK. The research team comprises Janet Finch, Jennifer Mason and Judith Masson as directors, plus Lynn Hayes and Lorraine Wallis as research associates. This paper is co-authored by Janet Finch and Lorraine Wallis, who would like to acknowledge the assistance of other members of the team in data collection and preparation, and in developing the ideas which are explored here.

2 Between 1961 and 1991 the number of owner-occupied dwellings doubled. Now more than two-thirds are owner-occupied. (*Social Trends*, 1993:114).

3 At a societal level sociologists have looked at the socio-economic impact of inheritance for example, on the distribution of wealth (Harbury and Hitchens, 1979; Scott, 1982) and the class structure (Saunders, 1990). Further, sociologists and historians have illustrated the way in which gender inequalities implicit in laws and customs relating to inheritance have served to perpetuate patriarchal relationships (Goody, 1976; Delphy and Leonard, 1984; Davidoff and Hall, 1987). However the impact of inheritance on interpersonal relationships has been little explored.

4 Once wills have been probated, they become public documents. Our sample was taken from the Probate Registers for our four sample years. Though they are documents on public access, we have treated them with the same degree of confidentiality as we would for any other personal data, including concealing the identity of individuals.

5 Names of potential interviewees were taken from the electoral register. They were contacted first by letter and then by phone to ask if they would be willing to take part in a study which focussed on how families passed things on from one generation to the next. All interviewees were assured of the confidentiality of their information. We have honoured this by the use of pseudonyms and by altering any details which may reveal the identity of the interviewee.

6 Though transfers of property can and do occur before death (and indeed are

one way in which people anticipate their own death), the more usual case in the UK context is that it occurs after death.

7 We are aware that the feminine of 'testator' is 'testatrix'. However since this term is less widely understood, the term testator throughout the chapter refers to both male and female writers of wills.

8 We have discussed aspects of this case in more detail in Finch and Wallis (1992).

9 Life expectancy, calculated at birth, is now 73 years for men and 78 years for women. (*Social Trends*, 1993:97)

# References

Anderson, M., (1980), *Approaches to the History of the Western Family 1500–1914*, Basingstoke: Macmillan.

Ariès, P., (1981), *The Hour of Our Death*, London: Allen Lane.

Davidoff, L. and Hall, C., (1987), *Family Fortunes: Men and Women of the English Middle Class, 1780–1850*, London: Hutchinson.

Delphy, C. and Leonard, D., (1984), Class analysis, gender analysis and the family. In R. Crompton and M. Mann (eds), *Gender and Stratification*, Cambridge: Polity.

Demos, J. and Bocock, S.S., (eds), (1978), *Turning Points: Historical and Sociological Essays on the Family*, Chicago: University of Chicago Press.

Elder, G.H., (1975), Age differentiation and the life course, *Annual Review of Sociology*, 1:165–90.

Elder, G.H., (1977), Family history and the life course, *Journal of Family History*, 2:270–304.

Finch, J. and Wallis, L., (1992), 'Inheritance, care bargains and elderly people's relationships with their children'. Paper presented to the BSG conference, to be published in D. Challis and B. Davies (eds), *Health and Social Care: International Perspectives*, Aldershot: Gower.

Frankenberg, R., (1987), Life: cycle, trajectory or pilgrimage? A social production approach to Marxism, metaphor and mortality in A. Bryman, B. Bytheway, P. Allatt, and T. Keil, (eds), *Rethinking the Life Cycle*, London: Macmillan.

Glaser, B.G. and Strauss, A.L., (1965), *Awareness of Dying*, London: Weidenfeld and Nicholson.

Goody, J., (1976), Inheritance, Property and Women: some comparative considerations. In J. Goody, J. Thirsk and E.P. Thompson (eds), op.cit.

Goody, J., Thirsk, J., and Thompson, E.P., (1976), *Family and Inheritance: Rural Society in Western Europe 1200–1800*, Cambridge: Cambridge University Press.

Harbury, C.D., and Hitchens, D.M.W.N., (1979), *Inheritance and Wealth Inequality in Britain*, London: Allen & Unwin.

Hareven, T.K., (ed), (1978), *Transitions: Family and the Life Course in Historical Perspective*, New York: Academic Press.

Hareven, T.K., (1982), *Family Time and Industrial Time*, Cambridge: Cambridge University Press.

Leonard, D., (1980), *Sex and Generation*, London: Tavistock.

Mansfield, P. and Collard, J., (1988), *The Beginning of the Rest of Your Life: A Portrait of Newly-Wed Marriage*, London: Macmillan.

Morgan, D.H.J., (1985), *The Family, Politics and Social Theory*, London: Routledge.

Riley, M.W., (1987), On the significance of age in sociology, *American Sociological Review*, 52:1–14.

Saunders, P., (1990), *A Nation of Home Owners*, London: Unwin-Hyman.

*Social Trends*, (1993), Central Statistical Office, London: HMSO.

Scott, J., (1982), *The Upper Classes: Property and Privilege In Britain*, London: Macmillan.

Sudnow, D., (1967), *Passing On: The Social Organisation of Dying*, Englewood Cliffs, NJ: Prentice-Hall.

# The denial of death and rites of passage in contemporary societies

## *Jane Littlewood*

This chapter explores two questions which are central to the development of the sociology of death, dying and bereavement. The first question relates to the denial and associated medicalisation of our understanding of death-related issues. It will be argued that this process is relatively recent and has resulted in the removal of death and dying from the community and to its relocation in the hospital or similar institution. The second question of relevance relates to the role which rituals in general and rites of passage in particular play in contemporary society. It will be argued that death-related rituals are still widely performed but, outside of certain specific and relatively rare circumstances, such rituals have themselves been removed from the community and have been relocated in the private world of individuals who have been bereaved. As Ariès (1983) has indicated, the contemporary situation is one in which:

> The relative of the cremated person rejects the physical reality of the site, its association with the body, which inspires distaste, and the public character of the cemetery. But he accepts absolutely the personal and private nature of regret. For the cult of the tomb he has substituted the cult of memory in the home (Ariès, 1983:577).

## The medicalisation of our understanding of death, dying and bereavement

A great deal of discussion has taken place concerning the denial of death in contemporary cultures. Ariès (1983) has suggested that the general attitude of western societies towards death is characterised by fear and shame. People who are dying provoke unease and embarrassment, therefore it is seen to be appropriate that they are removed from the community to die in the isolation which he sees as characterising the modern institutional death. Gorer (1965) has suggested that this isolation also seems to affect people who have been bereaved. As living reminders of the unavoidable reality of death they may be avoided rather than supported, 'mourning in reverse'.

Illich (1977) is another critic of the contemporary way of dying. He suggests that contemporary attitudes towards the medicalisation of death are primitive. For example:

> the witch hunt that was traditional at the death of a tribal
> chief is being modernised. For every premature or clinically
> unnecessary death, somebody or something can be found who
> irresponsibly delayed or prevented a medical intervention
> (Illich, 1977:85).

He argues that this situation has arisen out of a misguided notion of progress originating from the late Victorian period which led to the belief that scientific medicine would ultimately be able to overcome death itself. Cannandine's (1981) analysis of war deaths might be taken as supportive of this view since he indicates that death, particularly death on the battlefield, was seen as both romantic and unlikely during the late Victorian/early Edwardian period.

> . . . social Darwinism and the stridently athletic ethos of the
> late Victorian and Edwardian public school, produced an
> atmosphere in which soldiering and games were equated, in
> which death was seen as unlikely, but where, it if happened it
> could not fail to be glorious (Cannandine, 1981:195).

Gorer (1955) argued that death had replaced sex as contemporary society's major taboo topic. He was concerned with what he called the 'pornography' of death and the presentation of dying in an unrealistic framework. Gorer believed that, as the actual experiences of deaths in the community became rarer and fewer people saw corpses or experienced bereavement, a relatively realistic view of death had been replaced by a voyeuristic, adolescent preoccupation with it. For Gorer, a return to the mourning customs of the past, ie the Victorian Celebration of Death with all of the communal ritual involved, provided an answer to the problems he identified.

However, the appropriate 'place' of death was, by this time, firmly located outside of the community and within the hospital. The medical profession was seen, and possibly saw itself, as being responsible for keeping it there. Bereavement was similarly medicalised. In a highly influential paper written in 1944, Lindemann referred to the 'Symptomatology and Management of Acute Grief' and by 1961 Engel was considering grief in terms of the manifestations of the experience being similar to that of a disease. However, if cultural denial of death and bereavement, coupled with the medical profession's management of it, may be said to have characterised attitudes in the 1950s, such attitudes were almost immediately, although by no means entirely successfully, challenged. During the 1960s an explosion of literature concerning the social organisation of dying and the psychological consequences of such an organisation occurred. Specifically:

1 Sudnow (1967) looked at the social organisation of dying and emphasised the ways in which dying was routinised and thereby moulded to fit the day-to-day functioning of the hospital.
2 Glaser and Strauss (1965a, 1965b, 1968, 1971) published a series of works concerned with death and dying as a social process.
3 Kübler-Ross's (1969) influential work, which addressed itself to the psychological processes associated with the ways in which people cope with terminal illness, was published.

The 1960s also saw the establishment of the modern hospice movement in Britain together with the growth of the death awareness movement in North America.

Despite the work of Sudnow and Glaser and Strauss being highly critical of the social context and social organisation of dying, ie things which could potentially be changed, it was Kübler-Ross's work, which was essentially acontextual, which received and continues to receive the most attention. Kübler-Ross indicated that the people she interviewed went through five, generally progressive emotional stages: denial, anger, bargaining, depression and finally acceptance. This work was one of several stage/phase types of analyses which were invoked concerning the experiences of both dying and bereavement in the late 1960s and early 1970s. For example Averill (1968) identified shock, despair and recovery as the relevant stages of grief and Kübler-Ross's (1969) analysis has also been applied to bereavement. In addition, Parkes (1972) identified numbness, pining, depression and recovery as the relevant stages which followed the loss of a loved person.

The most significant criticisms of Kübler-Ross's work come from Kastenbaum (1975), Germain (1980) and Charmaz (1980). Specifically, Kastenbaum and Germain both address the problems of stage theories in general and show us how any theory which encourages the notion of one developmental path also implicitly encourages the labelling of any deviation from it as abnormal. There is also the danger, as Eisenbruch (1984a, b) and Kellehear (1990) both indicate, that cultural differences in coping may be interpreted in terms of personal inadequacy. There is the risk that professionals may misread description as prescription (Littlewood, 1992). Also, Fitchett (1980) has pointed out that not only is there little agreement amongst health care professionals concerning which stage/phase a given person is actually in but, when experience is controlled for, what inexperienced staff tend to categorise as acceptance more experienced staff tend to categorise as denial.

Charmaz (1980) takes these criticisms further and suggests that Kübler-Ross's theory does not necessarily reflect coping with the process of dying but rather more reflects adaption to the social context in which death occurs. Consequently, it might be suggested that dying at home or in a hospice might result in very different patterns of adaption. In addition, Marshall (1980) has suggested that despite a lack of description of the sample characteristics, there are indicators that the interviewees were relatively young adults. If this is the case then the work would share this tendency with some of the early work conducted in connection with widowhood, eg Marris (1958) and Parkes (1972). However, given that the majority of people who die or who are widowed are over the age of sixty-five, these samples are likely to be unrepresentative.

Nevertheless, perhaps the most informative analysis, in terms of identifying the attraction of stage/phase types of analyses comes from Kaufmann (1976). In a chapter sardonically entitled 'On Death and Lying' Kaufmann identifies an interesting contradiction between Kübler-Ross's perspective and her actual findings. He notes that in the introduction to her work she suggests that the denial of death is psychologically inevitable and yet she goes on to record interviews with literally hundreds of dying people who were not apparently 'inevitably' and uniformly denying death. Kaufmann notes that Kübler-Ross does not comment in any great depth upon this aspect of her research. Perhaps she was expressing a cultural preference rather than a psychological inevitability? If this is the case then it seems reasonable to suggest that people who are close to death and people who have been bereaved may not be in a position to exercise an essentially unrealistic position regarding the issue of their own and other people's mortality. It may also be suggested that the presence of people who are dying or have been bereaved might be perceived to be highly threatening at both an individual and a social level. This in turn puts members of the medical profession in a particularly difficult position, ie they are expected, and may expect themselves, to embody a culture which denies the very experiences many of them have to face on a day-to-day basis.

The attraction of stage/phase types of analyses may well lie in their ability to represent the experiences of people who are dying and people who are bereaved in a culturally acceptable manner (ie as an experience which follows an ordered linear progression). However, the experiences associated with grief are probably better characterised in terms of wave after wave of violently contradictory emotional impulses, cf Smith (1982), Marris (1986), Littlewood (1992)). Paradoxically, the stage/phase presentation may only ever make sense to people who have not experienced bereavement, eg, in all probability most young to middle-aged health care professionals in contemporary societies. Perhaps it is to this audience that such a presentation is addressed.

Whilst it must be said that the work of Kübler-Ross has been of great value in terms of promoting our attempts to understand the anguish suffered by people who are dying, it seems reasonable to suggest that given the socio-cultural context of the work, the criticisms of it, particularly those which imply that it may be used as a defensive attempt to deny the emotional reality of the subject, are likely to benefit from a certain degree of accuracy, eg Kaufmann (1975) and Kalish (1985). However, it must also be said that the sociological literature does little to illuminate these and associated problems.

As Kellehear (1990) has indicated, the sociology of death, dying and bereavement is still in its infancy. The majority of work in this area is descriptive rather than theoretical and the bulk of it is primarily concerned with caretaker behaviour rather than the experiences of people who are dying or who have been bereaved.

In connection with death and dying, possible exceptions to this general tendency lie within the work of Glaser and Strauss (1971) and Kellehear (1990). Glaser and Strauss adapted and updated Van Gennep's (1960) observations regarding rites of passage to introduce the concept of death as a status passage. This concept is a broad one which readily contains notions about conflict and change without consensus either being implied or assumed.

Alternatively, Kellehear's work is concerned with our understanding of the 'good death' and adds much of value to Ariès's (1983) proposition that such deaths are unlikely in western societies by identifying the social context in which a good death may be said to occur. However, in connection with bereavement, there is a relatively large, and potentially useful body of literature concerning rites of passage in particular and ritual in general which has the potential to further our understanding of the experience of bereavement in contemporary societies.

## Rites of passage

Van Gennep's work has often been cited in connection with the helpfulness of funeral rites, eg Clark (1982), Kellehear (1991) and Littlewood (1992). Van Gennep was concerned with a wide range of rituals of which funerals were only one sub-set. His thesis was that all rituals involving passage from one state to another (eg single\married, child\adult, alive\dead) share a single tripartite structure of rites. The first rites involve the separation of the individual or group from their previously held social status or position. The second series of rites involve transition, in which the individual or group may be seen as between social states and is often physically or symbolically excluded from the society. The final series of rites are those of incorporation, which involve the individual or group being incorporated into a new social state or position. Van Gennep was of the belief that this general structure was adhered to in most societies. As Huntington and Metcalf point out:

> There is a deceptive simplicity to Van Gennep's notion, which at first sight seems to amount to little more than an assertion that rituals have beginnings, middles and ends. However, Van Gennep was the first to notice just how similar are the beginnings, middles and ends of an extraordinarily wide range of

rituals. Van Gennep emphasised that these similarities are not random analogies but part of a single general phenomenon (Huntington and Metcalf, 1979:8).

From his survey of death rituals throughout the world, Van Gennep came to the conclusion that it was the theme of transition rather than that of separation which dominated funeral rites. He further concluded that the deceased's next-of-kin (however that might be culturally defined) were subject to the rites along with the dead person. Van Gennep's conceptualisation of the rites of passage is as follows:

| Rites | The Dead Person | People who are Bereaved |
|---|---|---|
| Separation | From the living members of society | From the living members of society |
| Transition | From the world of the living | From the world of the dead |
| | towards the world of the dead | towards the world of the living |
| Incorporation | Into the world of the dead | Into the world of the living |

Whilst Van Gennep himself did not claim that funeral rites could ease the transition for people who have been bereaved, the work has attracted the interest of many researchers who claim that the potential for them to do so is present, eg Clark (1982), Kellehear (1991), Walter (1991) and Littlewood (1992).

Funeral rites of separation in contemporary societies are relatively straightforward. As Kübler-Ross (1983) has indicated, they simply involve the public acknowledgement of the death of a person significant in our private lives. However, the theme of transition has been investigated independently by Turner (1969). Turner argued that a long transitional period in rites of passage may, under certain circumstances, be extremely beneficial to the passengers of such rites. Following Van Gennep's original analysis he suggests that the transitional period is one where people are 'betwixt and between' social states and therefore have the potential to meet as true equals in a position where considerations of status, power and social worth do not apply. Consequently, long periods of transition have the potential to be times of respite and communality. Obviously, this type of analysis is more relevant to situations in which large numbers of people go through the same rite at the same time.

Some contemporary evidence may be taken to indicate that

facilitating rather than impeding the situation which Turner describes may be beneficial. For example, Miller (1974) has poignantly described the aftermath of Aberfan, a disaster in which many children lost their lives. According to Miller, the situation was one in which communal grieving was handled relatively well by the surviving community. People were described, in keeping with Turner's hypothesis, as coming together as equals, thereby facilitating the expression of grief.

Alternatively, Erikson (1979) documented the aftermath of a similar disaster in Buffalo Creek, USA. In this case an intervention programme in which people were randomly placed in caravan parks, thereby disrupting any potential for mutual social support, was undertaken. This type of relocation had extremely adverse effects. Specifically:

> . . . two years after the flood, Buffalo Creek was almost as desolate as it had been the day following, the grief as intense, the fear as strong . . . they rarely smiled and rarely played . . . they were unsettled and deeply hurt (Erikson, 1979:137).

Walter (1991) has argued that the belief that bereaved people have lost touch with mourning rituals was challenged by an extensive display of spontaneously generated rituals on Merseyside following the Hillsborough tragedy. Walter utilises Turner's (1969) observations and argues that, while loss by an entire community was probably the major factor which provoked the display of ritual behaviour, it was the temporary breakdown of hierarchy which empowered ordinary people to act.

In terms of rites of incorporation, it has been suggested by Gorer (1965), Parkes (1972) and Marris (1986) that such rites may play an important role in terms of the time-limitation of the grieving process. They may also prove valuable as a gesture from other members of the community that people who have been bereaved are welcome back into the everyday reality of their particular social group. However, in societies where the everyday reality of dying and bereavement are effectively denied in the first instance, it is difficult to envisage exactly how such a ritual of incorporation might be generated.

## The role of ritual in contemporary society

Cheal (1988) has recently attempted to clarify the role of ritual in contemporary, complex and largely secular societies. He identified three types of ritual. Specifically:

1 Rituals of reification, (which he associated with the past);
2 Rituals of resource management, (which he associated with the present);
3 Rituals of reproduction, (which he associated with the future).

Cheal was concerned to generate:

a new approach to the existence of ritual in secular, technologically advanced societies (1988:280).

His concept of rituals of reification is of particular interest. According to Cheal, rituals of reification:

are believed to have their origins in traditions inherited from the past, which cannot be changed because the flow of time cannot be reversed. These rituals of reification have most useful effects in maintaining boundaries and internal solidarity of social groups, and they have a conservative social influence. They are therefore particularly highly valued by people whose position and authority depends upon maintaining the integrity of existing social structures (1988:283).

There are many examples in the literature pertaining to death, dying and bereavement of an apparent desire, perhaps fuelled by denial in the present, to reclaim the traditions of the past.

For example, Gorer's (1965) work has been extremely influential in portraying the Victorian era as a 'golden age' for grief. Marris (1986) continues this tradition in the following vein:

Traditionally, full mourning in England would begin with the shuttering of the house and the hanging of black crepe while the dead person was laid out in his or her old home. The funeral procession itself was decked with as much pomp as the family could afford or its sense of good taste suggested. Thereafter, the nearest relatives wore black for several months

and then half-mourning for a while, gradually adding quiet colour to their dress . . . and when the period of mourning is over it [the family] can take up the thread of daily life without guilt because the customs of society make this its duty.
(Marris, 1986:29–30).

There appears to be a general consensus in the area that the rituals of the past must be helpful to people who have been bereaved but it remains undemonstrated exactly how such rituals might be rehabilitated in order to fit contemporary, complex and secular societies.

This consensus, however, has recently been challenged but the challenge tends to be on the basis of the interpretation of the past rather than upon its relevance to the present. For example, Cannandine (1981) takes issue with Gorer's analysis and strongly suggests that the decline of the Victorian Celebration of Death, which Gorer associated with the onset of World War I, actually coincided with a decline in the death rate which followed dramatic improvements in public health. For Cannandine, ritual and the ubiquitiousness of death are strongly related and furthermore, ritual expressions may change. For example, he noted that following World War I when, in terms of overall mortality rates in the community, most people would have been familiar with death, a different type of the ritual expression of grief evolved, ie Armistice Day and the Cenotaph.

Richardson (1988) adopts a similar approach to these issues in her consideration of the treatment of people dying in poverty in the early nineteenth century. Specifically, those who failed to provide for themselves in death were taken naked, wrapped only in paper or a strip of calico stretched over the corpse. Relatives were denied the customary farewell and were allowed no say in where the burial might take place. Given the scale of death rites prevalent at the time, a more brutally calculated statement of the social worth of the poor is difficult to imagine. However, although the past is open to various interpretations, it is still the past, and in the present, as Cheal (1981) points out, cultural variation and the consequent dissolution of many traditional solidarities has led to fewer and fewer rituals of reification being either performed or taken seriously.

Alternatively, rituals of resource management may be particularly relevant to modern conditions and share many similarities with rites of passage:

Rituals of resource management celebrate success in 'doing something about the situation' through rational use of the available resources. The origin of these rituals is in the present which is experienced as a boundary between the limitations of the past and the prospects for a better future (Cheal, 1988:284).

The importance of rituals of resource management would seem to lie in their ability to operate in a similar manner to a rite of passage, ie to mark the end of one phase in a person's life and the beginning of another. Furthermore, there is a good deal of evidence which suggests that people in contemporary societies are apparently of the belief that undergoing another rite of passage, such as a birth, marriage or re-marriage, following their bereavement, will restore them to a more favourable social and personal position. For example:

A woman in her twenties, whose father had died, was very clear that her reason for marrying so soon after her father's death was 'to get back to normal'. However, the transformation she'd hoped for had not occurred. Nevertheless, she was expecting her first baby in a few months time and that she thought 'would do it' (Littlewood, 1992:25).

For other people, being on the brink of a birth, marriage or re-marriage may precipitate a desire to appropriately 'close' a previous experience of bereavement. For example, a man whose daughter had died of leukaemia over a year before he was interviewed wanted to express his belief that, as part of his life, the experiences which followed his daughter's death were over. He particularly wanted the hospital to know this because he was looking forward to the birth of twins in a few months time (Littlewood, 1992).

The desire to have a child following an experience of bereavement can be a particularly strong one for some women. In the case of parents who have lost children, Videka-Sherman (1982) has suggested that having another child is one of the signs of positively adjusting to the loss of the previous child. In all of these cases the investment would seem to be in a better future for the individuals involved.

A variation on this general theme might be what Raphael (1984) calls 'reparation' ie the attempts made by some individuals, following their bereavement, to secure funds for research into the disease which precipitated their loss. In this way, it might be suggested, people invest in the future of others rather than themselves. Further examples might include the activities of parents who had lost adult children in the Zeebrugge disaster. As Hodgkinson (1989) has pointed out:

> Their avowed aim was to see the prosecution of the ferry operator for negligence and the institution of safer ferry standards (Hodgkinson, 1989:354).

There are many pressure and/or self-help groups campaigning for change in the ways in which bereavement is dealt with at the social level, eg the Stillbirth and Neonatal Death Society (S.A.N.D.S.) and the National Association of Widows (N.A.W.). The membership of such groups consists, almost in its entirety, of people who have undergone a particular type of bereavement and who wish to help others, in numerous ways, who subsequently sustain a similar loss. It might be suggested that some of these groups foster the development of the contemporary version of 'communitas' described by Walter (1991), ie people who have undergone a similar type of experience gather together under conditions where considerations of social worth and hierarchy do not apply.

According to Cheal (1988) rituals of reproduction are derived from representations of the end and serve to protect the present by promising a continuing social future. Cheal is of the belief that fear of premature endings, in the absence of new beginnings, fuels rituals of reproduction in contemporary societies. Greeley (1987) has argued that many of the rituals which facilitate interaction with the dead, in either life or the afterlife, are good examples of rituals of reproduction. Greeley further suggests that remarkably little is known about these rituals, which may be largely unaffected by the decline in organised religion. It is interesting to note that both Parkes (1972) and Bowlby (1980) suggest that rituals involving the social acknowledgement of an ongoing relationship between the person who has died and the people who have been bereaved would be helpful. At one level it would seem strange that we do not have such rituals, for if any anthropologist wanted an example of a society within which the dead lay heavily upon the shoulders of the living for some considerable amount of time following a death, and in some cases perhaps forever, they need look no further than western European ones. Any consideration of the experiences of individuals following the death of someone they were closely involved with, would strongly suggest a preoccupation with an ongoing relationship with the dead person.

However, while it might be accurate to suggest that there is little in the way of sociological research which illuminates death-related rituals of reproduction, there is a good deal of evidence, mostly derived from literature concerned with 'pathological grief' to indicate that such practices are relatively widespread in contemporary societies. Furthermore, it seems reasonable to suggest that the location of these practices tends, at least outside of disastered communities, to take place at an individual rather than a communal level.

A classic example of a ritual of reproduction designed to deny the end would be Gorer's (1965) concept of mummification. Mummification is a process in which the world of the bereaved individual appears to be frozen in time following a death. The grieving person often acts as if the dead person will return at some future date. Gorer cites Queen Victoria's response to the death of Prince Albert as an example of this form of grief. Marris (1986) makes a similar point in connection with loss in general and cites an example from literature, that of Miss Haversham, a character in Dickens' *Great Expectations*, who waited forever, in her tattered wedding gown, by the ruins of what should have been her marriage feast. In addition, virtually all of the clinical evidence associated with the use of 'linking objects' (Volkan, 1975, 1981 and 1985) might be interpreted as a ritual of reproduction which relies on the presence of a particular object in order for it to occur.

Raphael (1984) and Littlewood (1992) have both suggested that, among elderly people resident in the community, daily conversations between the living and the dead partner are relatively common-place. For these individuals, who usually hold beliefs concerning an afterlife, their daily conversations guarantee their social future as a couple – in this world and the next. If death and dying have been confined to the hospital or a similar institution, it might be said that rituals of reproduction have been confined to the home. Furthermore, when such rituals are publicly acknowledged, they tend to fall prey to notions of pathology and are often seen to require the intervention of a health care professional.

Jane Littlewood

## Conclusion

Overall, it may be concluded that the social organisation of death, dying and bereavement generally takes place outside of the community. In the instance of death and dying, the occurrence of these events has been institutionalised within the hospital and in the instance of bereavement outside the practice of rituals of resource management, the experience has been privatised and remains largely located within the home.

However, when whole communities are affected by disaster, the evidence would suggest that people can and do use communal rituals, quite often spontaneously generated, in order to express their sense of loss. Nevertheless, it must be said that such examples are relatively rare occurrences in contemporary societies. The reality for many individuals who have been bereaved would seem to lie in the various forms of rituals of resource management and, perhaps at the risk of contravening contemporary cultural norms, rituals of restoration.

Perhaps the best that can be hoped for is that people who are dying become aware of the possibilities inherent in Kellehear's (1990) examination of the 'good death' within contemporary cultures and that people who have been bereaved may begin to consider new ritual expressions of grief appropriate to themselves and to their immediate mourning group. It can be hoped too that people outside of those groups will welcome this change rather than try to deny it or associate it with rituals of the past. For ultimately, our own deaths are inextricably intertwined with our future and the present is a situation in which:

Anything that you have, you can lose, anything you are attached to, you can be separated from, anything you love can be taken away from you. Yet, if you really have nothing to lose, you have nothing (Kalish, 1985:181).

## References

Ariès, P., (1983), *The Hour of our Death*, Aylesbury, Peregrine Books.
Averill, J.R., (1968), Grief: Its Nature and Significance, *Psychological Bulletin* 70, 721–48.
Bowlby, J., (1980), Attachment and Loss Vol. III, *Loss, Sadness and Depression*, London: Hogarth Press.
Cannandine, D., (1981), War and Death: Grief and Mourning in Modern Britain

in Whaley J. (ed.), *Mirrors of Mortality: Studies in the Social History of Death*, London: Bedford Square Press.

Charmaz, K., (1980), *The Social Reality of Death*, Reading Mass. Addison-Wesley.

Cheal, D., (1981), Ontario Loyalism: a socio-religious ideology in decline, *Canadian Ethnic Studies*, 13:40–51.

Cheal, D., (1988), 'The Postmodern Origin of Ritual', *Journal for the Theory of Social Behaviour*, 18: 3 pp. 269–290.

Clark, D., (1982), *Between Pulpit and Pew: Folk Religion in a North Yorkshire Fishing Village*, Cambridge: Cambridge University Press.

Eisenbruch, M., (1984a, b), Cross-Cultural Aspects of Bereavement I and II, *Culture, Medicine and Psychiatry*, 8:283–347.

Engel, G., (1961), Is Grief a Disease? *Psychosomatic Medicine*, 23:18–22.

Erikson, K.T., (1979), *In the Wake of the Flood*, London: Allen and Unwin.

Fitchett, G., (1980), It's time to Bury the Stage Theory of Death and Dying, *Oncology Nurse Exchange*, 2(3).

German, C.P., (1980), Nursing the dying: Implications of the Kübler-Ross staging theory in: R. Fox, *The Social Meaning of Death*, Annals of the American Academy of Political and Social Science, 447: p. 46–58.

Glaser, B.G. and Strauss, A.L., (1965a), *Awareness of Dying*, Chicago: Aldine.

Glaser, B.G. and Strauss, A.L., (1965b), Temporal Aspects of Dying as a Non-Scheduled Status Passage, *American Journal of Sociology*, 71:48–59.

Glaser, B.G. and Strauss, A.L., (1968), *Time for Dying*, Chicago: Aldine.

Glaser, B.G. and Strauss, A.L., (1971), *Status Passage*, London: Routledge and Kegan Paul.

Gorer, G., (1955), 'The Pornography of Death' (revised) in Gorer, G., (1965), *Death, Grief and Mourning in Contemporary Britain*, London: Cresset Press.

Gorer, G., (1965), *Death, Grief and Mourning in Contemporary Britain*, London: Cresset Press.

Greeley, A., (1987), Hallucinations among the Widowed, *Sociology and Social Research*, 71:258–265.

Hodgkinson, P.E., (1989), Technological Disaster – Survival and Bereavement, *Social Science and Medicine*, 29(3): 351–6.

Huntington, R. and Metcalf, P., (1979), *Celebrations of Death: The Anthropology of Mortuary Ritual*, Cambridge: Cambridge University Press.

Illich, I., (1977), *Limits to Medicine: Medical Nemesis and the Expropriation of Health*, Harmondsworth: Penguin.

Kalish, R.A., (1985), *Death, Grief and Caring Relationships*, 2nd Edition, California: Brooks Cole.

Kastenbaum, R.J., (1988), 'Safe Death in the Post Modern World' in A. Gilmore and S. Gilmore, (eds), *A Safer Death: Multidisciplinary Aspects of Terminal Care*, New York: Plenum Press.

Kaufmann, W., (1976), *Existentialism, Religion and Death*, London: New English Library.

Kellehear, A., (1990), *Dying of Cancer: The Final Year of Life*, London: Harwood Academic Publishers.

Kübler-Ross, (1969), *On Death and Dying*, New York: Macmillan.

Kübler-Ross. (1983), *On Children and Death*, New York: Macmillan.

Lindemann, E., (1944), Symptomatology and the Management of Acute Grief, *American Journal of Psychiatry*, 101, September, 141–8.

Littlewood, J., (1992), *Aspects of Grief: Bereavement in Adult Life*, London: Routledge.

Marris, P., (1958), *Widows and their Families*, London: Routledge and Kegan Paul.

Marris, P., (1986), (Rev. Ed)., *Loss and Change*, London: Routledge and Kegan Paul.

Marshall, V.W., (1980), *Last Chapters: A Sociology of Ageing and Dying*, Monterey: Brooks Cole.

Miller, J., (1974), *Aberfan: A disaster and its Aftermath*, London: Constable.

Parkes, C.M., (1972), *Bereavement*, New York: International Universities Press.

Raphael, B., (1984), *The Anatomy of Bereavement: A Handbook for the Caring Professions*, London: Hutchinson.

Richardson, R., (1988), *Death, Destitution and the Destitute*, London: Routledge.

Smith, C.R., (1982), *Social Work with the Dying and the Bereaved*, London: Macmillan.

Sudnow, D., (1967), *Passing On: The Social Organisation of Dying*, Englewood Cliffs N.J.: Prentice-Hall.

Turner, V., (1969), *The Ritual Process*, Chicago: Aldine.

Van-Gennep, A., (1960), *The Rites of Passage*, Chicago: University of Chicago.

Videka-Sherman, L., (1982), Coping with the Death of a Child: A Study over Time, *American Journal of Orthopsychiatry*, 51(4): 699–703.

Volkan, V., (1975), Re-grief Therapy in Schoenberg B. *et al*, (eds), *Bereavement: Its Psychosocial Aspects*, New York: Colombia University Press.

Volkan, V.D., (1981), *Linking Objects and Linking Phenomena*, New York: International Universities Press.

Volkan, V.D., (1985), Psychotherapy of Complicated Mourning in Volkan, V.D., (ed.), *Depressive States and their Treatment*, New Jersey: Jason Aronson.

Walter, T., (1991), The Mourning After Hillsborough, *The Sociological Review*, 39 pp. 599–625.

# Part 2

# Dying in a public place: AIDS deaths

## Neil Small

The public presentation of AIDS has fused AIDS and death in such a way as to make the former a synonym for the latter. I will consider the way that AIDS discourses have developed and specifically will review the contribution that the biographies and autobiographies of individuals who have lived with, and died from, AIDS have had on defining the epidemic. In particular I consider the way celebrity diagnosis, illness and death has been introduced and commented on in the public sphere. In what follows I argue for the importance of personal accounts. In so doing I look to John Paul Sartre's horizontal and vertical reading of biography to help locate this material alongside other ways of looking at the epidemic.

There is a conventional orthodoxy that sees ours as a death-denying culture whose taboo about discussing this subject even exceeds our reluctance to talk about sex. AIDS, and the fear of AIDS, speaks directly to these subjects and then compounds the likely difficulty in establishing a discourse by mixing in the taboo-ridden and vilified homosexual, drug addict, prostitute and prisoner. Yet a particular image of AIDS and AIDS deaths has become well established. AIDS is very visible – or at least a particular construction of AIDS is very visible. Part of that visibility involves a juxtaposition of AIDS and a stylised 'AIDS death'. Dying with AIDS involves dying in a public place at the very least because this public construction of AIDS and AIDS death structures the experience of the person living with, and dying from, AIDS. Explicitly public deaths have been sometimes sought, sometimes ascribed, sometimes ducked but not avoided.

Socially this is an epidemic defined by its paradoxes. Stereotyping the epidemic has made its public face what it is. Personalising the epidemic has provided a space for considerable individual achievement. But it has also been a source of individual grief and crass exploitation.

By the spring of 1992 the World Health Organisation were estimating that, worldwide, the cumulative total of people HIV positive by the end of this century would be between 30 and 40 million. They estimated that 90 per cent of these people would live and die in the developing world.[1] In the UK, figures published in January 1992 show a cumulative total of 5451 cases of AIDS of whom 3391 had died. The cumulative total of reports of HIV infection was 16,282[2]. Estimates of real HIV prevalence total 30,000 (World AIDS 1991). In the USA cumulative totals of AIDS cases, as of summer 1991, were 191,601[3]. In what follows I concentrate on the experience of those people in the UK and USA. I do so aware that this includes only a small proportion of those touched by the epidemic. I do so also in the awareness that there is a danger, evident in the literature on HIV and AIDS, of marginalising the experience of those outside these countries.

## AIDS discourses

Representations of AIDS have been evident in many different places, in science, in autobiography, in the literature of resistance. They have also been present in popular discourses, both in the media and in the street.

> By referring to meanings in different systems, the terms of AIDS discourse also relate to different already inscribed relations of power. Given the multiple levels and domains of power relations implicated in AIDS discourse, no system or situation can ever be compared by simple analogy to the next, or totalized by structural analysis (Patton, 1990a:1).

Patton argues a Kuhnian position that knowledge is only coherent within a given paradigm (see Kuhn, 1962),

> the newness of retroviral research and the association of a newly identified disease with social stigma argues, in Kuhnian terms anyway, that we ought to be in the middle of a paradigm shift (Patton, 1990:5).

A 'progression' of the 'master science' from bacteriology through endocrinology and immunology to virology and retrovirology reflects changes in solving problems but carries with it different views on the nature of the body, the role of the individual and of social metaphor more generally. Bacteriology saw the body as somewhere static before and after the assault of germs; endocrinology was replete with gendered and emotional tropes (Patton, 1990) as the body ran hot and cold, oily and dry. Within an ascendancy of immunology health becomes sustained by careful management. The fluid and the fragile produce a delicate balance. It is a balance that accommodates the individual and environment. Sustaining health became a question of constructing and maintaining a defense. Virology shifted paradigmatic thinking towards a more aggressive resort to 'magic bullets' to knock out a virus.

At a time when the shift from immunology to virology was not complete along came HIV, a pathogenic disease of the immune system, something that stopped you repairing the defensive walls immunology had elevated to the ascendent. It spoke to two agendas immediately. First, it stripped bare that aspect of immunology's social metaphor that implies health is about balance, and is up to the individual to achieve and maintain. To be ill means you have not been responsible, you have failed. Blame and guilt are intrinsically tied to this metaphor. Second, it reinforced a shift to virology and legitimised the headlong pursuit in pharmacological research into 'magic bullet' responses to the epidemic. A single cause/single response research establishment triumphed. It appeared that the paradigmatic shift had occurred.

But another factor was evident in this epidemic. This paradigmatic shift was being constructed without a voice for the person infected. And they were to have a voice.

> People living with HIV illness organised with sympathetic clinicians and researchers to form community research initiatives which investigated simple, often natural, organic compounds to improve morbidity. Working within an ecological/immunological framework, they confronted head-on the highly individualistic and single response-oriented research establishment as well as the cultural metaphors on which it rests (Patton, 1990a:11).

People with HIV and AIDS, and their most immediate supporters, reconstructed drug test protocols, they helped change the treatment regimes of many health facilities and, most crucially, they confronted the language of AIDS – its talk of guilt and innocence, its construction of a dangerous understanding of risk and, particularly, its equation of diagnosis with death.

Social metaphors exist in a layered way – new ones covering, but not removing, old. Social or personal rifts can open up the underlying strata of belief and of expression. Old ideas bubble up. The triumph of science has not really replaced a belief in fate. Individuals can reconstruct community metaphors and challenge social ones. The metaphor of an AIDS death has been so challenged.

Since at least the early nineteenth century, responses to epidemics, of various sorts, had been shaped by moral assumptions about the sexual behaviour of those they affected. These assumptions infiltrated medical theories and responses and, in turn, shaped and reshaped popular attitudes. We see, in relation to cholera, typhoid, TB and cancer, links made between individual failings (particularly sexual ones), social marginality, moral inadequacy and a tendency to acquire one or the other of these diseases (Mort, 1987). Even more clear are the links made *vis-a-vis* venereal disease (Davenport-Hines, 1990).

But the discourse on AIDS has not been just about sex. Sexuality, social marginality and disease intersect in a matrix that is, itself, both an indicator of the social anxiety and a conductor of the social tension that are central to both personal identity and social policy. AIDS has become the symbolic bearer to a host of meanings about contemporary culture – its social composition, racial boundaries, attitudes to social marginality, moral configurations and social mores – as 'different histories intersect in and are condensed by AIDS discourse' (Weeks, 1989:2).

Simon Watney has argued that, just as developments in immunology and virology permitted the identification and isolation of HIV in 1983, so modern cultural theory with its emphasis on signification and narrative has allowed for a better understanding of what is and what is not being done in response to the epidemic. But this opportunity has not yet been realised. The cultural agenda of AIDS has fixed, and reinforced, heavily medicalised perceptions. The person with AIDS has been marginalised and is, discursively, largely absent (Watney, 1989:64–5).

The person is only introduced into the AIDS agenda in two ways. Firstly, as a place in which the virus resides. This means they are marginalised, feared and seen as doomed – dying from, not living with, AIDS. Secondly, and in contrast, the person has been introduced through the efforts of those resisting the dominant cultural agenda of AIDS.

> I belong to a community which has faced, collectively and individually, the social challenge presented by HIV. In that community, people with HIV have not been ostracised: they have not had their autonomy threatened by calls from the uninfected majority for coercive measures to protect them. Members of that community have volunteered in their thousands to provide financial, practical and emotional support to those infected. And as a result I, and many other people with HIV, have been able to achieve our own personal and private victories against this disease (Grimshaw, 1989:217).

AIDS is presented discursively and metaphorically. The way things are represented 'is not merely a reflection of "real life" but an integral part of it' (Watney, 1987:4). If gays are depicted as expendable – government responses to the epidemic seemed to follow a recognition that the virus might enter 'the majority of the population'; or if an automatic progression from HIV to AIDS to wasting and death is made in the media – the Health Education Authority's campaign 'What's the difference between HIV and AIDS? – Time' for example; then such pictures structure the expectations and the lives of individuals and of communities. If AIDS metaphors are used that talk of plague and retribution then these shape individuals worlds, and the worlds of research and social policy (Sontag, 1983, 1988). It is not that we should seek to dispose of metaphor – it is one of the ways we have sought to make sense of the senseless throughout history. Nor should we seek to make rational, to reduce to biomedics, what is in essence a subjective encounter with our bodies and our mortality (see Frankenberg, 1990:351). Rather, we should use metaphor to help explain and open up, not to construct and to constrain, our realities.

## The individual and the social – a problem of mediations

The place of the individual person in the epidemic can be sought *via* life stories. There is a considerable history of life story methods in sociology. Characteristically, there would be a combination of life story material and public and private archive data; newspapers and diaries for example (Thompson, 1978). Each serves to complement the other by adding relevant detail and by establishing validity through triangulation (Denzin, 1970). Alternatively one might seek breadth and validity not by the use of documentary evidence, or a recourse to what expert opinion said was going on in the time covered by the life story, but by amassing a number of different life stories based around the same theme. These might be concerned with the same historical period or be drawn from the same geographical area (Bertaux, 1981:7). The task in using such life history is to illustrate:

> the objectivity of a fragment of social history on the basis of the non-evaded subjectivity of an individual history . . . (we seek) access to the universal and the general (society) starting from the individual and the singular (Ferrarotti, 1981:21).

Jean Paul Sartre (1963) argued for a horizontal and a vertical reading of biography. The former was made up of the individual's immediate social context and then the context of that context – and so on. The latter was made up of a chronology of sites of individual praxis, the family, peer groups, work places. What such a reading leaves us with is the need to understand how the horizontal and the vertical are mediated in an individual life. This Sartre defined as the 'problem of mediations'. There must be some understanding of a hierarchy of such mediations at any specific juncture. There will also be pivotal hinges around which:

> the social fields wherein the self-objectifying praxis of man and the universalising efforts of a social system meet and confront each other in a more direct way (Ferrarotti, 1981:23).

Methodologically identifying the relationship between the individual and the social system necessitates practice that is both heuristic and dialectic. How do the individual and social interact and how does each change the other? It is by pursuing such questions that we can consider social change in three strata. First, the deep contradictions of social and economic organisation. Second, the pressures that are exerted collectively and institutionally. Third, the decisions that individuals make that might have a cumulative pressure for change either in one person's life or, if many are making such decisions at the same time, on social change itself (Thompson, 1981).

In relation to AIDS the institutional and social context is not supportive of many of the understandings individual accounts seek to transmit. Nor is the institutional and social context supportive of the ability of the individual to live and to die with the autonomy they seek.

The dominant rhetoric emerging from the Department of Health and the Health Education Authority is that AIDS is everybody's problem. It is not just a concern for drug users or homosexual men. In fact, in the US and UK at least until the mid 1990s, most people who develop AIDS will belong to one of these groups. There is a danger that some sort of 'liberal even-handedness' will lead to a 'degaying of AIDS' (Patton, 1989). To be gay and to have AIDS does present specific problems and possibilities. The problems include geographic concentrations and age profiles and the absence of social support through families (McCann, 1990). But these can also represent possibilities for self-help, community programmes and care in the community that does not depend on the unpaid labour of women in the home.

Other problems are of stigma. Marginalisation and hostility to gays, and gay organisations, have been evident throughout the history of AIDS. Examples are legion, hostility is certainly evident in the media but also in the accepted rhetoric of research and planning (see Black, 1986:53 on the identification of AIDS with the Four H Club – Homosexuals/Haitians/Heroin Addicts/ Hookers). Hostility also takes a more immediately direct form – petrol bombs and physical violence for example. During 1984 and 1985 there was an 89 per cent increase in violence towards gays in San Francisco. In New York the number of cases of anti-gay violence increased by 100 per cent (Black, 1986:173). The US National Gay Task Force estimated incidents of violent harassment of gays at about 1000 a month (Amis, 1987:191).

Marginalisation takes many forms. Ignoring AIDS, not spending enough and blaming victims are some (Small, 1988 on the first two, Altman, 1986 on the third). Excluding those most centrally involved from the process of planning is another. Perhaps most pervasive is a tendency to sacrifice the interests of those with HIV and AIDS for the sake of those uninfected. Health education campaigns and medical opinions that talk up risk provide examples. So do those who posit an inevitability between infection, illness and death. Such approaches are experienced by those already HIV positive, and trying to live with the felt implications of that, as serious blows[4].

The medical debate on the likely future of those with HIV infection – is it a 'one way trip' or are co-factors necessary to generate a transfer to AIDS – is something fought out *via* epidemiological studies and mathematical projections (Adler, 1987: Webster *et al*, 1989). As such it is a debate that has a profound effect upon lives. Firstly, the debate influences the allocation of research and development budgets. Secondly, if HIV/AIDS is like many cancers, the morale of the person effected will have an impact on the likely development of the virus[5]. The personal, the institutional and the wider social represent different sites of praxis. They are often in conflict but it is a conflict in which each shapes the other. The social and institutional response to HIV and AIDS structures the lives and deaths of individuals and does this in ways that contribute to the interests of the collectivity and not of the individual. But the system is not a closed one. Social fields in which the self objectifying praxis of individuals and groups acts on the social system do exist and examples of the former shaping the latter can be found.

## Making your voice heard: autobiography and AIDS

HIV infection and AIDS has generated a considerable body of autobiographical writing. Much of this comes from the USA. Collectively it represents the beginnings of an oral history of the epidemic. Common concerns are evident in a number of these autobiographies:

### The world has changed

Most of the autobiographical literature has been written by gay men. It reflects a sense that not only has AIDS changed their lives and the lives of those around them but that it has changed a large section of the community. Paul Monette, for example, asks:

> remember when all we worried about was whether the melon was ripe (Monette, 1988:37.)

Writing about 1987 he says:

> Now in the seventh year of the calamity, my friends in LA can hardly recall what it felt like any longer, the time before the sickness (Monette, 1988:2).

## *Being gay has changed*

Richie McMullen (1988) writes that when he was told he had HIV disease he felt, as an initial response, dirty, guilty and ashamed. Despite, he says, having been 'out' for many years the pain was in part a shame at being found out.

> My HIV disease had, at that time, the perfect host in which to do its worst. Where had all my development gone? (McMullen, 1988:24).

Monette argues that, in 1985, hate was the only public health tool available (Monette, 1988:166). Emmanuel Dreuilhe (Dreuilhe, 1987:34) asks:

> How can homosexuals and drug addicts feel patriotically inspired in their private war when they don't even like them-selves, or may actually hate themselves because of a self-image that reflects society's contempt for them? If the opinion of others finally convinced you that you are morally and physi-cally deficient, how can you believe in yourself or in the importance of your own survival?

John Money continues to develop the same point:

> How are you supposed to feel about yourself when you are derided, arrested and called immoral? (Money, 1987:53).

But he also recognises that, dangerous as such social atmospheres are, they can be compounded. He says that there is a need to for-give historical trespass – that nursing a grudge is life-threatening to an ill person. McMullen goes further in saying that moral projections say more about the persons who make them than those they are directed at:

> I am proud to be associated with an international Gay com-munity which has achieved so much in the field of caring responsibility (McMullen, 1988:66).

## *A sense of separateness*

The autobiographical material considers two sorts of separateness – one imposed and one chosen. Money writes that he experienced society's fright of contagion as creating a scenario where he felt more of a kindred spirit with the plague victims of the thirteenth century than with the beneficiaries of twentieth century medicine. He and many others recount stories of absurdly cautious doctors and other health workers. John Mordant (1989), who had contracted HIV through sharing needles, underlines the separateness by recounting how, after his diagnosis, he went to Narcotics Anonymous to seek help with his addiction. But:

> HIV freaked them out. I was their living nightmare sitting among them (Mordant, 1989:105).

But a sense of separateness can also come from an overriding preoccupation with AIDS. Monette again:

> this sense of separateness would grow so acute that I really didn't want to talk to anyone any more who wasn't touched by AIDS, body and soul (Monette, 1988:94).

### Sexual expression

Autobiographical material offers many areas of shared concern, in addition to the few examples presented above. It also presents other areas of social change. These include a collapse of faith in medical technology, a change in the nature of sexual expression and a shift in family relationships. The latter occurs most profoundly when people with AIDS die before their parents.

Returning to changes in sexual expression, an example is provided by Dreuilhe:

> What had been exciting in sexual practice was anonymity: the fact that one didn't know one's partner made him all the more desirable and the impersonality of the places where one met was precisely what made these surroundings seem supercharged with sexuality . . . These days the situation is reversed, and those who still lead an active sexual life are looking instead for comrades, partners in whom they can have confidence and whose medical history is well known to them. (Dreuilhe, 1987:69).

This sort of change is chronicled in many places. For example in the medical discourse where the incidence of rectal gonorrhoea is cited as evidence of changing sexual practice by gay men, as are the dramatic reductions in HIV infection rates (Peters *et al.*, 1991). It is chronicled in the literature on the politics of AIDS. For example the debates about the proposed closure of the bath houses in San Francisco included a consideration of how the promiscuity of gay men attending such places had to be understood using two determining constructs. Firstly, that of the oppressive nature of anti-gay society and, secondly, the pleasure and sense of liberation that such a lifestyle gave many (see FitzGerald, 1987:100).

As well as the shared themes evident in much of the autobiographical material on AIDS, there are also shared metaphors and a sense of a personal narrative in conflict with a dominant social narrative. I will offer an example of each.

The military metaphor, discussed by Susan Sontag in her book on AIDS and metaphor (Sontag, 1988), is frequently present. Paul Monette talks of 'pushing the enemy back' and of being 'back from the front line' (Monette, 1988:42). Emmanuel Dreuilhe's work is infused with the metaphor, 'a positive test isn't a death warrant, it's really a declaration of war' (Dreuilhe 1987:95).

The difference between individual and social narrative is most evident in the preoccupation of the former with living with AIDS and the latter with dying of AIDS. Monette again:

We chose to see the diagnosis not as a death sentence but as a life challenge (Monette, 1988:80).

As well as presenting numbers infected and projections of rates of increase, the public discourse on AIDS has involved personalised presentations of living with, or dying from, AIDS. Terry Madeley began television's 'AIDS Week' on 27 February 1987 by becoming the first man on British TV to say he had AIDS. His appearance on 'Day to Day' was followed on 6 March by an appearance on BBC1's 'Open Air AIDS Special', on 26 June he was on 'Wogan'. Following his death he was the subject of 'Remember Terry' shown on BBC in November 1987. In this last programme Dr Richard Smith, from the British Medical Journal, argued that Terry's appearance on TV had contributed to a new sort of public discussion on AIDS in which there was 'not so much rubbish in the papers' and not so much terror in the public's encounters with the epidemic. Eminent AIDS researcher and clinician Dr Michael Adler is reported as having said that Terry's appearance on TV had put the 'cause' forward 10 years. Terry's physician Dr Caroline Bradbear thought that 'AIDS was the making of Terry, he had become what he had always wanted to be. He had achieved celebrity'.

Keith Alcorn's critique of television's 'AIDS Week' (Alcorn 1989) raises many important points about TV and the epidemic, and about the relationship between the media and the emblematic Terry. Alcorn argues that personalised accounts are always justified by current affairs programme makers by claiming an intention to foster identification. But identification can operate in two modes. Watney distinguishes between the transitive sense of identifying self in relation to the difference of the other, and the reflexive sense of identifying self in relation to resemblance to the other (Watney, 1987).

Alcorn argues that the programmes featuring Terry centred on two implied questions. First, 'Do you want to end up like him?' and second, 'What shall we do about people like him?' Both these questions continue to imply difference between the viewer and the subject. They also build on and reinforce an established image of a person living with AIDS.

It may be that Terry became emblematic but the integrity of his position, and the resonance of his lifestyle and attitudes, risk being devalued by attributing such a label. Terry's assertion of life; his despair; his impact on those around him; his mother's resoluteness and her eventual hurt and anger; his theatricality – both in his concern to play his part on a wider stage than the one he had achieved as an actor and in the orchestrated extravagance of his funeral; his fear of loosing his good looks and his even greater fear of indignity and dementia are all things repeated time and again in the autobiographies of people living with AIDS.

There have been many other personalised accounts in the media. In 1987 Chris Dale (a pseudonym) wrote an occasional column for the *Guardian* that began on May 6 under the headline, 'The diary of a condemned man'. One of its strengths was the range of considerations he addressed. For example there is a pointed critique of available medical care and of the links between treatment and funding in the NHS (see The *Guardian* 3 June and 30 September 1987.) In the USA the televised diary of Paul Wynne, a person living with AIDS, claimed to present 'the face of AIDS' to the US public. France had the work of novelist Herve

Guibert, notably in his 1990 book *'To the Friend Who didn't save my Life'* and in a controversial TV film *'La Pudeur et L'Impudeur'*.

French intellectual Paul Aron achieved headlines by talking about 'my AIDS' in the French press. Andy Warhol's *'Diaries'* (1989) include fascinating, typically idiosyncratic and oblique, references to the arrival of AIDS as an issue of concern for New York's glitterati – including the AIDS deaths of Rock Hudson and Liberace.

A sense of AIDS and the person is also evident in the increasing number of obituaries we read. (The person on TV's 'Remember Terry' who said 'someone as young as me should not be going to so many funerals' provides as good an encapsulation of one of the cultural meaning of AIDS as any.) Actor Ian Charlston's death at the beginning of 1990 was plagued by the intrusions of the tabloid press (it seems Dr Richard Smith's belief that 'not so much rubbish was in the press' after the 1987 'AIDS Week' was a little premature). Author Bruce Chatwin's death was plagued by the intrusions of the self-righteous presumption of the 'outers' – people who decide they know best about what should be public knowledge.

Television has approached HIV and AIDS in some popular series. Channel 4's *'L.A. Law'*, early in 1991, included an episode considered the legality of 'Outing'. *'Midnight Caller'*, in its 1989–90 series included two episodes about a woman with AIDS, who happened to be the series hero's former girlfriend. In the UK *'East Enders'* has an ongoing story line featuring an HIV positive male character. Its treatment of this has occasionally appeared sensitive but more often, for example in its initial fatalism, has been clichéd and misleading.

Film has also contributed to the presentation of personal stories about living with AIDS. Arthur Bressan's *'Buddies'* (1985) was a fictional account that juxtaposed its moving story with a computer print-out of the names of those who had died in the epidemic over the opening and closing credits. Rene's *'Longtime Companions'* came out in 1990 and achieved some critical acclaim and a fairly wide distribution. Robert Epstein and Jeffrey Friedman's film *'Common Threads: Stories from the Quilt'* (first shown in Britain in 1990) achieves a dignified resumé of the San Francisco based 'Names Project' – a project which helps the bereaved to commemorate their loved ones with quilt sections (see Ruskin, 1988).

The Theatre saw Larry Kramer's *'The Normal Heart'* premiered in the USA in 1985 and later transferred to the UK. There have been a number of other plays, including John Roman Baker's *'The Ice Pick'*, the first National Theatre production to consider the epidemic, premiered in 1991 and *'Angels in America'* by Tony Kushner which opened in the UK in 1992.[6]

Through 1991 there continued to be personal accounts on TV and in the press. John MacLachlan's accounts of living with AIDS appeared in the *Observer*[7]. As to TV, the programme on 24 April 1991, 'Inside Story – AIDS in the Family', provides an interesting point of focus on the use of personal accounts. It was very much a presentation of AIDS in the heterosexual family. Within these limitations it addressed important issues. But these limitations are very important – they reinforce the otherness of the homosexual and they build on the bifurcation between the innocent victim and, by inference, the guilty. The public presentation of personalised accounts of living with AIDS have multiplied but not progressed.

## Magic, Mercury and Ashe – celebrity and AIDS

The public face of AIDS was, for many people, constructed out of the illness and death of film star Rock Hudson, who died on October 2nd 1985. By then five and a half thousand other Americans had died, over eleven thousand had contracted the virus and new cases of AIDS were running at about a thousand a month in the USA. Hudson's death generated considerable publicity. More concretely he had left $240,000 to launch the 'American Foundation for AIDS Research', chaired by Elizabeth Taylor. The other film star, Ronald Regan did not make a public speech about AIDS until 1987, by which time 36,058 Americans had been diagnosed and 20,849 had died (Shilts, 1987:596).

Before Hudson's death there had been widespread speculation in the US that a major film star had AIDS. Top of the speculators' list was Burt Reynolds. Shilts reports a 1985 conversation with a San Franciscan columnist on a gay newspaper:

> I don't want to hear that it's not true . . . if we are to survive, we need it to be true (Shilts 1987:544).

There was a belief that the social reverberations that a celebrity AIDS case would create might convince the press and Federal government that the epidemic should be taken seriously.

Celebrity has remained an important factor in the public image of AIDS. It brings gains and losses, which I will consider in relation to three recent celebrity examples. Earvin 'Magic' Johnson, US basketball star, announced in November 1991 that he was HIV positive. Arthur Ashe, former tennis star announced in April 1992 that he had AIDS. Freddie Mercury, pop singer, died from AIDS in November 1991. Both the presentation of and the response to these events help us understand the way AIDS is being constructed in popular discourse and the impact that individual accounts can have.

Johnson announced at a press conference that he had 'attained' the HIV virus and was to retire immediately. At the same time he reassured people that his wife was negative. He planned to 'become a spokesman for the HIV virus for the young people so they will practise safe sex, because sometimes people are a little naive and they think it can't happen to them.' He continued 'This is not like my life is over. I'm going to live a long time . . . I'm going to beat it and I'm going to have fun.' Johnson announced the establishment of the 'Magic Johnson Foundation for AIDS Prevention, Education, Research and Care'.

It would be hard to overestimate Johnson's public profile in the USA. Likewise it would be hard to overestimate the extent of publicity following Johnson's announcement of his HIV status. TV networks broke into normal programmes, newspaper headlines accorded it the same status as the death of a major head of state. The President and Vice President expressed publicly their sadness at Johnson's illness – they have not had a high profile in sympathy and concern for HIV and AIDS before. President Bush invited Johnson to serve on the National AIDS Commission.

As is often the case, interest in seeking either information or reassurance about HIV increases greatly after all concentrated periods of publicity. St Mary's Hospital in London saw a fourfold increase in the number of people seeking a test for HIV during the first British government publicity campaign about HIV and AIDS (Beck *et al*, 1990). In Johnson's case the impact was major. Calls to the US Centre for Disease Control, in Atlanta Georgia, increased from 3000 to 40,000 a day. The San Francisco AIDS Foundation reported an increase from 200 to 2000 calls a day. The bulk of callers inquired about safe sex and the use of condoms. The price of condom stock went up by $3 a share (Benjamin, 1991).

At the centre of Johnson's impact on public consciousness was a wish on his part to end the innocence of heterosexuals – 'If I can get it, and I'm healthy, wealthy and heterosexual then anyone can' seemed to be the message. Of considerable significance also was his appeal to Americans of colour:

> I particularly hadn't paid attention to the figures showing that AIDS is a huge problem in the black community. I didn't know that half of the Americans currently suffering from the disease are either black or Hispanic. Like most other blacks, I was denying that AIDS was spreading through our community like wildfire while we ignored the flames (Johnson, 1991).

But the response to Johnson, and to the reactions to Johnson's announcement, have not been entirely supportive and uncritical. First it is important not to equate interest directly with understanding or with change. For example, publicity generates a considerable response from the 'worried well' who present, even after publicity campaigns, confused understandings of routes of infection (Davey, Green, 1991). Enthusiasm for the message of celebrities is quickly dissipated. In Johnson's case Vice President Dan Quayle was quick to shift the prevention agenda from condom use to abstinence. The press engaged in smear by allusion as to Johnson's sexual preference. In the summer of 1992 Johnson's (ghosted) book, praised by the American Medical Association and the American Foundation for AIDS Research (Johnson, 1992) was banned as being 'not in keeping with what our customers tell us they want to read' by three of America's largest chain stores. Johnson's book describes frankly, using the vernacular of the young, behaviour that puts people at risk. This violates what chain stores call a 'clean magazine' policy that also bars magazines such as *Penthouse* and *Playboy*[8].

The public profile of celebrities with AIDS does not end the bifurcation characteristic of the epidemic in which a distinction between the guilty and innocent is created and maintained. Indeed in many cases it reinforces it. Tennis star Martina Navratilova criticised double standards of public morality; Johnson had spoken of the large number of women sexual partners he had and she argued that such an admission by a heterosexual woman would lead to ostracism[9]. Novelist Sarah Schulman believed Johnson was:

re-igniting a particularly loathsome rhetoric that views women solely as 'modes of transmission' bringing AIDS to men and children[10].

If Schulman is correct then the split between 'guilty' injecting drug users and homosexuals and the 'innocent' is changing. The 'innocent' used to embrace haemophiliacs, others infected via blood products and children. Now it includes the hapless male heterosexual. The 'guilty' is expanded to include the 'infecting woman'. It is a development that echoes other prejudices evident in our society.

Arthur Ashe had a number of heart by-pass operations. The blood transfusions they necessitated led to his contracting the HIV virus, either in 1979 or 1983. He did not discover his status until 1988, by which time he was diagnosed as having AIDS, and announced it (prompted by news of a forthcoming newspaper report) in 1992. Blood transfusions have been linked with 4770 cases of AIDS in the US, 2 per cent of the total. Ashe remained firmly within the 'innocent' construction. What he did, as Johnson does to a lesser extent, was to present a challenge to the juxtaposition of a diagnosis of being HIV positive with sickness and of AIDS with death. Ashe was leading an active public life[11].

In his press conference Ashe spoke of the impact Susan Sontag's book *'AIDS and its Metaphors'* (1988) had on him. Sontag identified the metaphors surrounding AIDS – an invasion, a pollution, an alienating repulsive taint of deadly sin – as things intensifying the deep fears of degrading pain felt by people with AIDS. The cultural messages accompanying AIDS spread panic, encourage hatred and offer a rhetorical opportunity to fulminate against sufferers as blameworthy and deserving of punishment.

Some of the impact of these metaphors, and the ambiguity of celebrity and AIDS, is clear in the life and death of pop singer Freddie Mercury. Mercury died in November 1991 having just made public his AIDS diagnosis. He had not made his diagnosis known before because he wished to protect the privacy of those around him. He had lived as a virtual recluse for the previous year but when he had appeared in public had been described as appearing 'gaunt and painfully thin'[12].

Freddie Mercury was what the press choose to call 'an admitted bisexual' and it was this that shifted him into the cohort that does not excite automatic support from the press and public opinion. Indeed some of the response to his death was savage. Joe Haines in the *Daily Mirror* of 28 November 1991 reaches the depths.

> He was sheer poison, a man bent – the apt word in the circumstances – on abnormal sexual pleasures, corrupt, corrupting and a drug taker . . . for his kind, AIDS is a form of suicide . . . his private life is a revolting tale of depravity, lust and downright wickedness.

Mercury's death prompted widespread sympathy and public attention as well as the knee jerk homophobia of the Daily Mirror. But that publicity appeared to depict Mercury as an exotic creature, different from the ordinary world. Such distancing prevents the public nature of his diagnosis and death having a major impact on the social construction of AIDS and AIDS deaths.

## Dying and epidemics

There is a psychology and sociology of death and dying and a psychology and sociology of epidemics. This epidemic requires them to be brought together as it also requires bringing together individual and social histories. Kelleher (1990) argues that although, from the 1970s, many more people were writing about death and dying, the emphasis was on clinical opinion, theory, and patient care. A sociology of dying was still in its infancy. He identifies an organising construct which he terms 'a good death'.

> Cast your mind back to that old painting or movie set in Victorian times which portrays a scene of a dying person. There lays the limp figure of the dying person. Here are the friends and close family of the dying around the bed. To the side stands the clergyman (Kelleher, 1990:3)[13].

The features such a picture assumes include an awareness of dying; social adjustment and personal preparation – including religious preparation; and the making of last farewells.

Such 'good deaths' are maintained in popular and personal constructs and provide frameworks for locating one's own experiences. They are constructed around some important, but not universal, features of modern death. Many more dying patients now know their prognosis (Veatch, Tai, 1980). Over two thirds of all deaths that occur each year in industrialised countries happen to people over 65 years of age (Lancaster, 1979). The majority of these people will die of cardiovascular system disease and/or cancer (Hetzel, 1980). With increased life expectancy will come the increased possibility of having a lengthy dying process (Charmaz, 1980). Most people who are dying will die in hospital, but will spend an increased amount of their time in other settings, particularly at home (Veatch, 1976). Further:

> Overall, it is clear that a broad trend in favour of awareness and control of dying has made itself felt in Britain and America, as elsewhere, and this seems to be part of a general historical reaction in the West against extremes of heroic medicine and the lifesaving ethic (Williams, 1989:207).

AIDS deaths in the western world fit with some of these overall social and clinical changes but not with all. The average length of time from diagnosis of having AIDS to death has increased, although it is influenced by class, age and gender differences (Squire, 1990). The majority of AIDS deaths occur in a cohort younger than average in terms of overall profile of deaths in Western countries. Indeed, in some areas of the US AIDS deaths are *en route* to becoming the single largest cause of death for young adults (Freudenberg, 1990). Projections suggest that in some parts of Africa, progress in reducing infant and child mortality will be reversed because of the impact of AIDS (Chin, 1990). Although most people with AIDS can live outside of a hospital setting for much of the time, their characteristics as a population mean they are not able to access the more common forms of informal care and support (Dixon, 1990). There are more negative social and professional reactions to people with AIDS than those with other illnesses (Clever, 1988:523). Finally, despite the development of the hospice movement for people with AIDS (Small, 1993) there is still a considerable recourse to 'heroic' medical interventions throughout the duration of a terminal illness (Gill, 1990). The construct of what is a 'good death' will have to be redrawn for people with AIDS.

An epidemic psychology designed around AIDS, or able to encompass it, is taking shape. Frankenberg (1988) and Weeks (1989) identify this, and both offer thoughts on controlling, epidemic psychology. In addition, Rosenberg (1989) has looked at the common social trajectory of major epidemics. Strong (1990) sees fatal epidemics as having the potential:

> to create a medical version of the Hobbesian nightmare: the war of all against all . . . The human origin of epidemic psychology lies not so much in our unruly passions as in the threat of epidemic disease to our everyday assumptions, in the potential fragility of human social structure and interaction, and in the huge diversity and elaboration of human thought, morality and technology. . . . (Strong, 1990:258).

What can bring these disparate concerns together? Sociology now has begun to look at human embodiment and to use that as the basis for considering the complex way the diseased body is used, metaphorically, as a reflection of social disruption (Turner, 1991:266). There is a:

> reciprocal manner in which the sick experience their state, express it, and organise it, and . . . the collective discourse that sets up the scheme of biological misfortune and gives it meaning (Herzlich, Pierret, 1987:xi).

## The individual and the social – across the boundaries

Zygmunt Bauman (1992) argues that the necessity of human beings to live with the constant awareness of death accounts for crucial aspects of the social organisation of all known societies. He identifies, as a defining characteristic of modern society, a deconstruction of mortality by translating the insoluble issue of death into the many specific problems of health and disease, which are soluble in principle. But death as a taboo subject, or as a denied object, can be challenged by the individual:

> The impact of death is at its most powerful (and creative) when death does not appear under its own name; in areas and times which are not explicitly dedicated to it; precisely where we manage to live as if death was not or did not matter, when we do not remember about mortality, and are not vexed by the thoughts of the ultimate futility of life.

Such a life – life forgetful of death, life lived as meaningful and worth living, life alive with purpose instead of being crushed and incapacitated by purposelessness – is a formidable human achievement (Bauman, 1992:7).

There are examples of autobiography and AIDS that display the creativity that can be generated from a proximity to death. Life lived with purpose is present in much that the epidemic has generated. That sense of purpose, that refusal to accept being crushed and incapacitated by what is around is evident in, for example, those situations where individuals have reached across boundaries and sought to change institutional and social responses to the epidemic.

I have argued above that social and institutional factors can be seen shaping individuals' experience of AIDS. I will conclude with two examples that show the relationship between the individual and the social as a more dynamic and reciprocal one. Elizabeth Glaser counts as a US celebrity with the virus. Her HIV status received extra publicity because she is married to a television star, Paul Michael Glaser (best known for his role in 'Starsky and Hutch'). While giving birth to her daughter in 1981 she received a transfusion of contaminated blood and subsequently found she, her new baby daughter and a son subsequently born, were all HIV positive. Paul was negative. Elizabeth's daughter died in 1988, the same year as Elizabeth was instrumental in setting up the 'Paediatric AIDS Foundation' in the US. In 1991 she published a book about her experiences (Glaser, Palmer, 1991) and in July 1992 Elizabeth addressed the Democratic Parties' National Convention and sought to place the issue of AIDS prevention and AIDS care firmly on the agenda for that political party.

The Names Project Memorial Quilt has provided a means for individuals to record the passing of their loved ones. It has been a focus for the establishment of locally organised support for the bereaved and it has acted, particularly via the unfolding of the Quilt in Washington D.C., as a dignified but clear notice to the US government and people of the need for urgent action. In October 1992 the Names Project AIDS Memorial Quilt, last displayed in its entirety in 1989, was laid near the Washington Monument. It consisted of 18,000 panels each one remembering a person who has died of AIDS. Names Projects now exist in 22 countries including the UK[14].

These two are examples of the many cases of individuals' experience reaching across boundaries and leading to institutional change and, perhaps, cultural change. The reverse occurs where social attitudes and institutional practices impact upon individuals; where government neglect, institutional hostility, and media exploitation shape peoples lives and structure their deaths. AIDS is a public phenomenon and a private experience. To have AIDS is to be caught in this nexus. Individual accounts offer pictures of the experience and, sometimes, a way to make one's own sense of what is happening to you, to those around you and to a world living with AIDS.

## Notes

1  World Health Organisation, Press Release, 12 Feb 1992.
2  Department of Health, Press Release, 29 January 1992.
3  World Health Organisation, Global AIDS Statistics, 31 August 1991.
4  A study of the response to media treatment of disaster survivors (Shearer, 1991) found that insensitive reporting added to the distress of victims. Victims wanted television coverage to help those who have suffered some tragedy to recover some control over events.
5  'Medicine Now', BBC Radio 4, 13 Feb 1990.
6  Goldstein (1991) has produced a bibliography of HIV and AIDS related work in film, theatre, music, dance and photography.
7  *The Observer*, 13 January 1991.
8  The *Guardian*, 6 Aug 1992.
9  The *Guardian*, 21 November 1991.
10  The *Guardian*, 19 November 1991.
11  This chapter was completed before the death of Arthur Ashe.
12  The *Guardian*, 24 November 1991.
13  The Italian clothing company 'Benetton' caused great controversy early in 1992 by proposing an advert for their products that featured David Kirby, a 32-year-old American who was dying with AIDS, on his deathbed with his family at his side.
14  The Names Project, International Newsletter No 8 Summer 1992.

## Bibliography

Adler, M., (1987), 'Care for patients with HIV infection and AIDS', *British Medical Journal*, Vol. 195, pp. 27–30.
Alcorn, K., (1989), 'AIDS in the public sphere', in E. Carter and S. Watney, (eds), *Taking Liberties*, London: Serpents Tail.
Altman, D., (1986), *AIDS and the New Puritanism*, London: Pluto Press.
Amis, M., (1987), *The Moronic Inferno*, Harmondsworth: Penguin.
Bauman, Z., (1992), *Mortality and Immortality and Other Life Strategies*, Cambridge: Polity Press.

Beck, E.J., Donegan, C., Cohen, C.S., Moss, V. and Terry, P., (1990), 'An update on HIV testing at a London STD Clinic: Long term impact of the AIDS media campaigns', *Genitourinary Medicine*, 66 (3), pp. 142–7.

Benjamin, P. (1991), 'Do you believe in Magic?' The *Guardian*, 16 Nov, pp. 20–1.

Bertaux, D., (ed.), (1981), *Biography and Society: The Life History Approach in the Social Sciences*, London: Sage.

Black, D., (1986), *The Plague Years*, London: Picador.

Charmaz, K., (1980), *The Social Reality of Death*, Reading, Mass: Addison-Wesley.

Chin, J., (1990), 'The Global Epidemiology and Trends of HIV-AIDS'. Paper presented to the Royal College of Nursing/British Medical Association Conference, *AIDS: The Challenge for the Community*, Cardiff, 18–20 April 1990.

Clever, L.J., (1988), 'AIDS: A special challenge for health care workers', *Death Studies*, Vol. 12, No 5–6, pp. 519–530.

Davenport-Hines, R., (1990), *Sex, Death and Punishment*, London: Collins.

Davey, T. and Green, J., (1991), 'The worried well: ten years of a new face for an old problem', *AIDS Care*, Vol. 3, No 3, pp. 289–93.

Denzin, N.K., (1970), *The Research Act*, Chicago: Aldine.

Dixon, P., (1990), 'Changing patterns in AIDS Home Care', Paper presented to the Royal College of Nursing/British Medical Association Conference, *AIDS: the Challenge for the Community*, Cardiff, 18–20 April 1990.

Dreuilhe, E., (1987), *Mortal Embrace. Living with AIDS*, London: Faber and Faber.

Ferrarotti, F., (1981), 'On the Autonomy of the Biographical Method', in D. Bertaux, (ed.), *Biography and Society*, London: Sage.

FitzGerald, F., (1987), *Cities on a Hill*, London: Picador.

Frankenberg, R., (1988), 'Social and cultural aspects of the prevention of the three epidemics (HIV infection, AIDS and the counterproductive societal reaction to them), in A. Fleming *et al* (eds), *The Global Impact of AIDS*, New York: Alan R. Liss Inc. pp. 191–9.

Frankenberg, R., (1990), Review article: 'Disease, literature and the body in the era of AIDS – a preliminary exploration', *Sociology of Health and Illness*, Vol. 12, No 3, pp. 351–360.

Freudenberg, N., (1990), 'AIDS prevention in the United States: lessons from the first decade', *International Journal of Health Services*, Vol. 20, No 4, pp. 589–99.

Gill, S.K., (1990), 'Clinical Aspects of HIV and AIDS,' *AIDS Care*, Vol. 2, No 4, pp. 359–61.

Glaser, E. and Palmer, L., (1991), *In the absence of Angels*, New York: Putnam.

Goldstein, R., (1991), 'The Implicated and the Immune', in D. Nelkin, D.P. Willis, and S.V. Parris, (eds), *A Disease of Society*, Cambridge: Cambridge University Press.

Grimshaw, J., (1989), 'The Individual Challenge', in E. Carter and S. Watney, (eds), *Taking Liberties*, London: Serpents Tail, pp. 213–17.

Herzlich, C. and Pierret, J., (1987), *Illness and Self in Society*, Baltimore: John Hopkins University Press.

Hetzel, B.S., (1980), *Health and Australian Society*, Harmondsworth: Penguin.

Johnson, E., (1991), 'Magic: My AIDS Nightmare', *Sports Illustrated*, 18 Nov.

Johnson, E., (1992), *What you can do to avoid AIDS*, New York: Times Books.

Kellehear, A., (1990), *Dying of Cancer*, Chur, Switz: Harwood Academic.

Kuhn, T.S., (1962), *The Structure of Scientific Revolutions*, Chicago Ill: University of Chicago Press.

Lancaster, H.O., (1979), 'Ageing and mortality statistics in Australia', in J.M. Donald, A.V. Everitt and P.J. Wheeler, (eds), *Ageing in Australia*, Sydney: Australian Association of Gerontology, 28–30.

Monette, P., (1988), *Borrowed Time*, London: Collins Harvill.

Money, J.M., (1987), *To All the Girls I've Loved Before*, Boston: Alyson Publications.

Mordaunt, J., (1989), *Facing up to AIDS*, Dublin: The O'Brien Press.

Mort, F., (1987), *Dangerous Sexualities*, London: Routledge and Kegan Paul.

McCann, K., (1990), 'The role of informal carers and volunteers in providing community care for gay men who are HIV positive,' Research Paper, Institute for Social Studies in Medical Care, London.

McMullen, R., (1988), *Living with HIV in Self and Others*, London: The Gay Mens Press.

Patton, C., (1989), 'Resistance and the Erotic', in P. Aggleton, G. Hart, and P. Davies, (eds), *AIDS: Social Representations, Social Practices*, London: Falmer Press.

Patton, C., (1990), 'What Science Knows: Formations of AIDS Knowledge', in P. Aggleton, P. Davies, and G. Hart, (eds), *AIDS: Individual, Cultural and Policy Dimensions*, London: Falmer Press.

Patton, C., (1990a), *Inventing AIDS*, London: Routledge and Kegan Paul.

Peters, B.S., Beck, E.J., Coleman, D.G., Wadsworth, M.J.H., McGuiness, O., Harris, J.R.W., and Pinching, A.J., (1991), 'Changing disease patterns in patients with AIDS in referral centre in the UK: the changing face of AIDS', *British Medical Journal*. Vol. 302, 26 Jan, pp. 203–7.

Rosenburg, C., (1989), 'What is an epidemic? AIDS in historical perspective,' *Daedalus*, 118, 2, 1–18.

Ruskin, C., (1988), *The Quilt: Stories from the Names Project*, New York: Simon and Schuster.

Sartre, J-P., (1963), *Search for a Method*, New York: Alfred Knopf.

Shearer, A., (1991), *Survivors and the media*, London: John Libbey.

Shilts, R., (1987), *And the Band Played On*, Harmondsworth: Penguin.

Small, N., (1988), AIDS and Social Policy, *Critical Social Policy*, 21, pp. 9–29.

Small, N., (1993), 'HIV/AIDS: Lessons for Policy and Practice', in D. Clark, (ed.), *Death and Dying: future issues in policy and practice*, Buckingham: Open University Press.

Sontag, S., (1983), *Illness as Metaphor*, Harmondsworth: Penguin.

Sontag, S., (1988), *AIDS and its Metaphors*, London: Allen Lane.

Squire, S.B., (1990) 'Advances in clinical management', *AIDS Care*, Vol. 2, No 4, pp. 363–6.

Strong, P., (1990), 'Epidemic psychology: a model', *Sociology of Health and Illness*, Vol. 12, No 3, pp. 249–259.

Thompson, P., (1978), *The Voice of the Past: Oral History*, Oxford: Oxford University Press.

Thompson, P., (1981), 'Life Histories and the Analysis of Social Change', in D. Bertaux, *op. cit.*

Turner, B.S., (1991), Review article: 'Missing bodies – towards a sociology of embodiment,' *Sociology of Health and Illness*, Vol. 13, No 2, June, pp. 265–272.

Veatch, R.M., (1976), *Death, Dying and the Biological Revolutions: our last quest for responsibility*, New Haven: Yale University Press.

Veatch, R.M. and Tai, E., (1980), 'Talking about death: patterns of lay and professional change,' in R. Fox, (ed.), *The Social Meaning of Death*, Annals of the American Academy of Political and Social Science, 447: 29–45.

Warhol, A., (1989), *Diaries*, New York: Simon and Schuster.

Watney, S., (1987), *Policing Desire. Pornography, AIDS and the Media*, London: Methuen.

Watney, S., (1988a), 'The Spectacle of AIDS', *October*, No 42.

Watney, S., (1988), 'AIDS, "Moral Panic" theory and homophobia', in P. Aggleton, and H. Homans, (eds), *Social Aspects of AIDS*, London: Falmer Press, pp. 52–64.

Watney, S., (1989), 'The subject of AIDS,' in P. Aggleton, G. Hart, and P. Davies, (eds), *AIDS: Social Representations, Social Practices*, London: Falmer Press, pp. 64–73.

Webster, A., Cook, D.G., Emery, V.C., Lee, C.A., Grundy, J.E., Kernoff, P.B.A., and Griffiths, P.D., (1989), 'Cytomegalovirus infection and progression towards AIDS in haemophiliacs with human immunodeficiency virus infection,' *The Lancet*, July 8, pp. 63–6.

Weeks, J., (1989), 'AIDS: the intellectual agenda,' in P. Aggleton, G. Hart, and P. Davies, (eds), *AIDS: Social Representations, Social Practices*, London: Falmer Press.

Williams, R., (1989), 'Awareness and control of dying: some paradoxical trends in public opinion,' *Sociology of Health and Illness*. Vol. 11, No 3, Sept, pp. 201–212.

World AIDS, (1991), November, No 1, London: Panos Institute.

# War memorials

## Jon Davies

As raw data, British war memorials present problems. There is no agreed statistical 'population' of war memorials – indeed there is no agreed definition of what a war memorial is. Even if both of those problems were solved, it would take a very sophisticated type of stratified sample to cover the full range of iconographical, epigraphical and topographical symbolism that one finds associated with war memorials: the First World War memorial at Skelton, Cumbria is a lych gate, the second a bus stop (Dawson, 1992). The memorial at Bamborough, Northumberland is a Calvary, and that at Darlington is a hospital (Davies, 1992). There is a memorial fireplace in a surgery at Dudley, North Tyneside (Newcastle Evening Chronicle, 1992). The problem of variety is even greater if one tries to cover all of the Western war memorials, which symbolise an even greater variety of histories, religions, and national, regional, and local cultures. There is no British or European list or census of war memorials. The Imperial War Museum is currently engaged on a census of British war memorials, but there is no similar European venture. The most general remark that one can perhaps make is that war memorials are probably the most widespread of European public statuary, to be found in capital cities, small villages and mountain tops, in great city squares and in windswept cemeteries. They are also the most commonly understood of our public symbols or 'art' forms. The biggest statue in the world is the war memorial at Stalingrad, now Volgagrad (Kohout, 1992:100–101).

This chapter will discuss the question of war memorials, war remembrance and 'the dominant ideology' thesis. It will then concentrate on four themes expressed on, in and by war memorials: war memorials as religious symbols; war memorials as gender-defining icons; war memorials as a common European cultural 'lapidary text'; and war memorials as the central 'totem' of ritual practice, in which notions of sacredness and community are construed in contradistinction and opposition to the secular and the profane. Most of the empirical material will be British, focussing on the First World War. The main exception to this reliance on British material will be the use made of Abraham Lincoln's Gettysburg Address (Lincoln, 1863).

## 1 War Memorials – the symbol of a dominant ideology?

War is one of the sovereign acts of state; and no ruling élite can ignore the issue of 'managing' patriotism. As Stephen Hill points out (Hill, 1990:2) the question of 'the dominant ideology' must at some point be addressed *empirically*, and in the case of war memorials this would seem to be a fairly simple matter: were they built by the hegemonic class in order to manipulate the lower classes? This runs into another problem discussed by Hill (Hill, 1990:13), the relative inaccessibility of hegemonic classes to empirical researchers. It is generally rather difficult to do much more than to impute to them, in a somewhat unempirical way, a particular ideology or ideological intent. Indeed, in 'normal' times, the activities of the dominant ideologues may be so diffuse and inexplicit as to be immune to empirical research.

At times of crisis, however, and in particular at times of war, the dominant ideology will be made both explicit and purposeful; and the activities of the dominant élite will become much more centralised in the institutions of the state. At the time, of course, the dominant group will protect its ideological purpose through censorship and police activity: but as Price demonstrates (Price, 1972) in retrospect at least such activities are amenable to empirical research: Price shows how on the occasion of the Boer War the British Government and upper class made very clear efforts to mobilise working class support for the war – and failed.

This chapter is a discussion of the ideological nature of *war remembrance*, rather than of war mobilisation or of war practice. An ideology is as much a re-ordering, a remembering, of the past as it is a call for action and conformity in the immediate present or an invitation to orientate behaviour in terms of a particular view of the future. The business of constructing appropriate war remembrance rituals and symbols is an occasion for explicated

113

ideological dispute, and therefore capable of being researched. In the case of the Great War we do in fact have at least three excellent empirical studies of the attitudes of the British dominant élite to war remembrance: David Cannadine (Cannadine, 1981) and Alan Wilkinson (Wilkinson, 1978 and 1986).

Cannadine states (Cannadine, 1981:241) that his essay rests 'far too extensively' on the documented attitudes to war (the Great War) and to war remembrance of an élite: and Wilkinson's work of 1978 is clearly about another part of that élite, the established church. Both authors show an élite largely unsure of itself, and indeed rather incapable of doing much other than to try to come to terms with its own grief, sorrow and sense of loss and incompetence. Equally, they show how popular and spontaneous was the insistence on proper and prolonged war remembrance and on the business of creating appropriate war remembrance symbols and practices, whether the élite was or was not able or desirous to turn these symbols and practices to ideological purpose. The demand for highly ritualised, endlessly repeated, properly respected war remembrance came from a cultural source well beyond the reach of any manipulative ideology. Wars as part of the profane world have to be dressed in the ideology of the State. In a deeper sense, though, wars as death reach into the archaeology of our culture, into the elementary forms of our religious life, where they are part of the Sacred. War, in this century above all others, is not something which has happened 'in between History', in between long periods of normalcy, as an event to which ordinary people can be summoned by a blast on the ideological whistle, then to be sent home again. War and war remembrance is a part of our primary socialisation, obdurate rather than malleable.

The thousands of war memorials in villages and small towns were built and maintained by people who could not be so easily manipulated because the memorials were in such large measure the gravestones of their children, public expressions of private grief for young men and boys whose bodies were in the mud and soil of Northern France. In the village of Keld, in North Yorkshire, the war memorial is part of a dry stone wall and helps to keep sheep in a field. It was paid for, in cash and kind, by the people of the village. The poem on it, unique to the village, was written by Miss Parkin, schoolmistress of the Congregational village school, who had it pinned up in the school, where it was seen by members of the war memorial committee. Miss Parkin had taken over the school when the head teacher went off to war. When he came back, she left – her only record now the poem on the memorial. The stone for the memorial came, donated, from the local quarry, dressed by two village masons who had themselves recently returned from the war. The Congregational minister presided at the 1921 dedication service, which has been held every year since then. The four names on the memorial all had, and have, family living in the village: and the poem is to be found repeated on plaques in the local URC, Methodist and Established Churches. The memorial site was chosen because that is where the young men used to gather, quite close to the pub (since closed), with a view of the River Swale, and visible by everyone using the road from Reeth to Kirkby Stephen. The pressure for the memorial – if pressure there had to be – came from the mothers of the non-returning boys because the soldiers who did return had all been given village medals, while their own sons – until the memorial – had nothing to commemorate them. One of the four dead soldiers was in fact later buried in the local church – his parents could afford to have his body brought over: one of the others was much later discovered in a grave in France: his parents could not afford to have him returned, according to his surviving brother, no matter how dearly his mother wanted that. The other two men simply disappeared. The poem says:

> Those whose names are on this wall
> For their country gave their all
> Coming hither passing hence
> Hold their names in reverence

The monument is as plain as the poem – there was little interest in the more 'Catholic' style of funerary architecture in nonconformist Upper Swaledale! The memorial is as vernacular as you can get, a more permanent version of the hundreds of the wayside shrines and makeshift memorials that appeared on street corners and in churchyards in 1914 and 1915 as the lists of the dead grew. There has been a remembrance service at the Keld memorial every year since its dedication in 1921 and the current URC Minister says that of all the obligations in his calendar, Remembrance Day is the one he would least dare to vary (Davies, 1992, field research, ongoing).

In Europe in particular – where we demarcate the century by

reference to war, pre-war, inter-war, post-war – the experience of war is deeply rooted in our everyday life, addressing, among other things, the nature of our religion; the relationship between the sexes; our identity as Europeans; and our sense of community. We are a bellicognisant, though not necessarily a bellicose society. War memorials, in iconography, in epigraphy and in topography, carry much of the symbolic weight attached by Emile Durkheim (and others) to the totemic constructs of primary religions (Durkheim, 1982 [1915]).

War memorials – whether in the shape of great spaces (Trafalgar Square, the Battlefield of Culloden or Gettysburg), national monuments (The Cenotaph, the Arc de Triomphe, the Australian National War Memorial), fireplaces (Dudley, North Tyneside), flower gardens (Newcastle University), sunken warships (Pearl Harbour) or memorial hospitals (Darlington) – are the most ubiquitous forms of public architecture and statuary, and of all such 'art' forms probably the ones most widely understood, primarily because they combine the essence of Europe's history (war) with the essence of the West's most deeply-rooted religion, Christianity and the Passion story of Christ.

## 2 War memorials as religious symbols

War memorials often carry religious texts; they are even more often shaped as crosses, carry crosses on them or are to be found near churches, in graveyards or in cemeteries. Not all memorials carry such clear religious statements, and in Republican France were actually forbidden to do so: but where they do, as is often the case, they carry specifically *Christian* symbols. For the best part of two thousand years, Europe has been the subject of intense Christian missionary activity. The religion was spread not by the enunciation of complex theology or the reading of Bible and commentary, but by the dramatic enactment of the Christian story in ritual, morality plays, Holy Day enactings, Church processions and decorations, icons, hymnals, liturgies (see Dix, 1945, Warner, 1981, Paxton, 1990, Young, 1933, Hardison, 1965, Gurevich, 1990). In this drama the story of the Passion, ie, the suffering of the crucified Christ (a young celibate male) is the central Christian message: it is icon, text, history and atonement. The essential elements of this Passion story are: 1, death as voluntary self-sacrifice: 2, the danger of betrayal, both before and after the sacrifice: 3, salvation, resurrection or redemption via self-sacrifice: 4, salvation and refutation of betrayal *only* by repeated acts of remembrance on the part of those for whom the sacrifice was made. As noted above, war memorials are many and varied: but the word most commonly found on them is the word GAVE, the word denoting voluntary self sacrifice. At St. Hedda's Church, Egton Bridge, near Whitby, the war memorial is visually part of the Stations of the Cross which are fixed on the outside of the Church: the memorial at Bamborough, Northumberland, is in the form of a Calvary, as is that near the parish church of Twickenham (Davies, 1992). At Queen's Gate, Kensington we read 'This Calvary was erected by their friends 1919–20'. This memorial was restored in 1982 in memory of those who died in the Falklands (McIntyre, 1990:205). The Anglican Communion liturgy presents Christ as suffering 'Death upon the Cross for Our Redemption', and as instituting 'A Perpetual Memory of that His Precious Death'. In response, the People 'Present Ourselves, Our Souls and Bodies to be a Reasonable Holy and Lively Sacrifice' (Book of Common Prayer, 1662). These words and images are echoed in many war memorials, as the following juxtaposed columns show. The inscriptions are to be found on the memorials themselves or in McIntyre, 1990 or Boorman, 1988.

*The Priest*:

Didst give Thine only Son Jesus Christ to suffer death upon the cross for our redemption . . . who made there (by His one oblation of Himself once offered) a full perfect and sufficient sacrifice, oblation and satisfaction for the sins of the whole world

THEY DIED THAT WE MIGHT LIVE (Kilmartin, Argyllshire).

THROUGH THE GRAVE AND GATE OF DEATH WE PASS TO OUR JOYFUL R E S U R R E C T I O N (Sandridge, Herts).

. . . And did institute and in His holy Gospel command us to continue, a perpetual memory of that His precious death, until His coming again. This is My body which is given for you . . . This is My blood which is shed for you . . .

BE THOU FAITHFUL UNTO DEATH AND I WILL GIVE YOU A CROWN OF LIFE (Great Milton, Ox.).

THIS CALVARY WAS ERECTED BY THEIR FRIENDS (Kensington).

Do this . . . in remembrance of Me. Take this in remembrance that Christ died for thee . . .

THEY GAVE WE HAVE (Bloxham, Oxon).

WHEN YOU GO HOME TELL THEM OF US AND SAY; FOR THEIR TOMOR-ROW WE GAVE OUR TODAY (Newcastle).

GREATER LOVE HATH NO MAN THAN THIS THAT HE LAY DOWN HIS LIFE FOR HIS FRIENDS (St. John, 15,13).

*The People*:
We Thy humble servants . . . offer and present unto Thee, O Lord, ourselves, our souls and bodies, to be a reasonable, holy and lively sacrifice unto Thee. . . Although we be unworthy through our mani-fold sins, to offer Thee any sacrifice, yet we beseech Thee to accept this our bounden duty and service. . .

THESE GAVE THEIR LIVES THAT WHO YOU LIVE MAY REAP A RICHER HARVEST ERE YOU FALL ASLEEP (Shrewsbury).

THEY SHALL NOT GROW OLD AS WE THAT ARE LEFT GROW OLD; AT THE GOING DOWN OF THE SUN AND IN THE MORN-ING WE SHALL REMEM-BER THEM (Binyon, 1919 p. 98).

*The Priest*;
The body of Our Lord Jesus Christ which was given for thee preserve thy body and soul unto everlasting life. Take, eat this in remembrance that Christ died for thee. And feed on Him in thy heart with thanksgiving

IN LOVING MEMORY AND SURE HOPE OF LIFE ETERNAL THE KING OF THE WORLD SHALL RAISE US UP WHO HAVE DIED FOR HIS LAWS UNTO EVERLASTING LIFE (Hollybush, Worcs.).

LES ENFANTS DE CHATEAU SUR LE LOIR MORTS POUR LA FRANCE (Chateau sur le Loir, Davies, 1992).

War memorials rarely mention the enemy, rarely mention killing – except indirectly, through the portrayal of weapons. They are, then, works of fiction, of what Auden called 'parable art' (Auden, 1935:14), designed to indicate not so much what actually happened, but what moral lessons needed to be drawn from the events to which the memorial is directing our attention. As sacralised monuments, as permanent wayside funerals, as the sites of annual acts of remembrance, they insist on a contemplation of the transcendent meaning of the deaths of so many young men in war. The First War memorial at Heriot's School, Edinburgh, utilises the Horatian epigram '*Dulce et decorum est pro patria mori*', while the Second War text states of the dead boys that 'Their lives they gave for Freedom Truth and Right' (Davies, 1992).

The chronology is perhaps important, the theme very definitely so. The patriotic motive is not removed, but it is now legitimated by reference to a specific set of abstract virtues. The 'conclusion' drawn from so many deaths is neither pacifist or revanchist/jingoist, but rather one in accord with the duties and purposes expressed in Christian 'Just War' doctrine and the example of the self-sacrificing Christ, as expressed on so many war memorials. Pacificism was strong during the interwar period, as was appeasement and its opposite, revanchism. The story in each country varies in accordance with the different experiences of victory, defeat and post war social disruption. War memorials retain the military option for the West, but now as grim duty, not mindless bellicosity. In this sense their authors predicted the lesson or verdict of the Spanish Civil War, the Second War and indeed of general post-war Western attitudes to military activity, ie that the use of military force is seen to be a necessary if unwelcome duty if 'proper' values are to be upheld. In spite of so much death in war, neither the West nor Europe is a pacifist culture (see Watkins and Worcester, 1986, pp. 49–50) and our war memorials (rather than war poets) express this sense of the Duty of the West.

This duty in practice falls upon men: and the version of military duty which war memorials proclaim is a Christian version of a much older heroic male tradition going back beyond Rome and Greece to the earlier cultures of the Middle and Near East. War and the remembrance of war, the story of Dead White European Males, underpins (for better or for worse) the separate socialisation of men and women.

119

*Jon Davies*

## 3 War Memorials as symbols of Male Duty

There are war memorials which honour women who died in war. Outside the National Portrait Gallery in London is a memorial to Edith Cavell. Ironically, this is one of the few British war memorials actually to mention and censure the enemy. Edith Cavell's insistence that 'Patriotism is Not Enough' appears in lower case lettering, and is semi-obscured by grime, while larger letters proclaim the agency of the Germans in her death and the need for loyalty to King and Country (Davies, 1992).

Where women do appear on war memorials, they do so within the allegorical tradition of monumental statuary, as Angels of Victory or Death, handing out laurel crowns or wreaths. In some French war memorials they appear realistically as part of family tableaux assembled in sorrow around the body of a slain son: and in Russian/Red Army memorials they appear as gigantic Mother Russia figures alongside equally gigantic Soviet heroes. The town of Stromness, in the Orkneys, has a single representational female figure as its war memorial. On a first war memorial at Newcastle upon Tyne women appear as wives and mothers kissing their men goodbye (this particular war memorial is used by Alan Borg as the dustcover for his book *War Memorials* (Borg, 1991).

Overwhelmingly, war memorials, in iconography, epigraphy and topography, are about men. As symbols of 'the supreme sacrifice' they subsume under the notion of self-sacrificing, dutiful death all the greater and lesser chivalries which mark out the division of social responsibilities between men and women. This division of tasks and the taking on, by men, of the military duty, long predates our own culture: 'I must die in shame', says Enkidu in *The Epic of Gilgamesh*, 'I shall not die like a man fallen in battle; I feared to fall, but happy is the man who falls in the battle' (Sanders, 1972:93). When Enkidu dies, Gilgamesh sets off on one of those long journeys which war so often entails, rejecting as he does so the joys of domesticity offered him by the young woman Siduri who invites him to 'Let your clothes be fresh, bathe yourself in water, cherish the little child that holds your hand, and make your wife happy in your embrace' (Sanders, 1972:102). Gilgamesh rejects the offer because he loves Enkidu, a theme of love between men, especially men as warriors, repeated in the much later Christian epics such as the *Song of Roland*

120    © The Editorial Board of The Sociological Review 1993

(Burgess, 1990) or the German medieval epic *Willehalm* (Gibbs and Johnson, 1984). In these, and many other similar and earlier epics such as the *Iliad*, the same themes are repeated: the imperative to leave home (ie female company) in order to find honour and virtuous company by doing good and/or defending the community – and to die in so doing. As Maurice Keen notes, 'The life of honour has to be lived through to the end: the final seal of approbation . . . is a sepulchral monument' (Keen, 1984:250).

In one way or another, this male tradition, pre-Christian and Christian, continues into the modern era: 'Some talk of Alexander, and some of Hercules, Of Hector and Lysander, and such great names as these' goes the 1780 song *The British Grenadiers* (Langbridge, 1890:258). The carnage of the First World War put an end to any cheerful version of the epic military tradition. The British 'War Poets' and films such as *All Quiet on the Western Front* insisted that the entire tradition was bogus and evil. War memorials, however, re-focussed the tradition into the self-sacrificing and sombre version of male duty that we see on war memorials, where it still remains as something to be taken as paradigmatic of the obligations of men in general. It is men who are seen as giving their lives so that the community is protected – and women who are seen both as being protected and as obliged to await the return of men, whether as memory or as homecoming hero. Needless to say, the waiting women are assumed to be waiting in a state of virtue, otherwise the sacrifice will be sullied and de-sacralised. Girouard (1981, Chap. 18) deals with the British version of this chivalric tradition. The many war memorials using Crusader or knightly symbols (eg the Cavalry memorial in Hyde Park) bear witness to the strength of the tradition.

## 4 War memorials as a common Euro-christian symbol

Robertson argues that we should be

> more conscious of the intentional, fabricative aspect of
> national-identity formation. . . Dominant ideologies are
> produced and reproduced largely in the course of interaction
> between and politically structured comparisons with other
> societies, within the broad context of the shifting structure of
> the world system. (Robertson, 1990:194–5).

*Jon Davies*

A major, if not the major form of 'interaction' between European societies and between Europe and the rest of the world has been war. By 1930, not only had Europe effectively conquered and colonised itself but also it had achieved domination over 84 per cent of the globe (Encyclopoedia Americana 1980, 14:821). The Common European travelling through his inherited lands may not find one common language but he will surely find one immediately understandable symbol: which European does not know the meaning of the trinity shown in Figure 1?

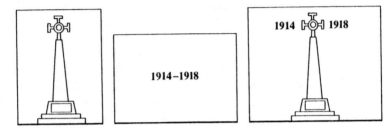

**Figure 1**

War memorials may be 'read' as a guide to the archaeology, history and contemporary cultural configurations of Europe and the West: where comprehension of these memorials ends, so does 'Europe'. War memorials are part of a huge war remembrance effort in, for example, cemetery and battlefield pilgrimages, cemetery construction and architecture, and regimental, battalion and campaign reunions and re-dedications. War memorials should be read as the lapidary texts of a bellicognisant Western culture, a war-echoing culture, in which war is a dominant part of human socialisation. War memorials mark out with our dead (to paraphrase Kipling's *The White Man's Burden*) the external boundaries and internal configurations of Western history. They are a kind of contemporary archaeology, bearing symbols which trace the course of Western history from origins to destiny, from tribal gatherings to great empires. They are, as places, at the same time occasions for rituals of both unity and disunity, capable of reinvigorating old enmities and of providing an opportunity to transcend them. They do this by calling upon the common experience of death in war as interpreted in an inheritance of shared symbolism. The Scottish National War Memorial in Edinburgh Castle has in its central 'Shrine' (the term used in the official guidebook) a sculpted figure of St. Michael, Captain of the Heavenly Host. This figure is fixed to and soars up into the vaulted ceiling, whence he looks down upon the Stone of Remembrance, set upon an undressed rock representing the highest point of the last primeval volcanic eruption. The Shrine is replete with an array of pagan, non-Christian and Christian symbols. On one of the accompanying Regimental Memorials is to be found the passage from Pericles' *Oration* of 430 AD:

> The whole earth is the tomb of heroic men, and their story is not graven in stone over their clay, but abides everywhere without visible symbol, woven into the stuff of other men's lives.

The Scottish National War Memorial was dedicated in 1927. In Moscow in 1991 Boris Yeltsin seemed to echo Pericles when he and the people of Moscow buried the three young men killed in the August *coup* attempt: 'Sleep well, our heroes: sleep well – let the whole earth be your soft pillow' (*The Sunday Telegraph*, August 25, 1991). In November 1863 Pericles' *Oration* was used at the dedication of the memorial cemetery at Gettysburg by the official Orator, Edward Everett, calling the guests' attention to 'our obligations to the martyrs and surviving heroes of the Army of the Potomac'. Lincoln, in a short and rather ill-received speech, ignored the partisanship of the Orator's words, speaking rather of 'These brave men who struggled here' (deliberately not singling out the Union dead), insisted that no words of his could add to their deeds and stated that:

> From these honored dead we take increased devotion to that cause for which they gave the last full measure of devotion, that we here highly resolve that these dead shall not have died in vain, that this nation, under God, shall have a new birth of freedom (Lincoln, November 1863).

Lincoln is trying here to use the memorial occasion, the sacrifice, to transcend the causes of the conflict and to move the unit of collective loyalty from a small to a larger frame and purpose. War memorials and war cemeteries not infrequently perform this function – not always with success (President Bush at Pearl Harbour) or without controversy (President Reagan at Bitberg). British efforts to create a memorial for their Crimean War dead in Russia were more successful, eliciting from Soviet Rear Admiral Alexeyev the sympathetic comment that 'Only a people which respects its history has the right to dream of a better future' (*Guardian*, November 2, 1991).

Any evolving common European culture will, indeed already does, address the matter of the pattern of enmities created by European and Western wars. War memorials, as objects and as places of pilgrimage, can contribute to the re-ordering of those enmities into a broader, shared understanding of the West and its place in the world. While ancient internal enmities may in this way be neutralised, externally this culture will no doubt find new enemies where the definitive 'Euro-christian' boundary ends, most probably in the world of Islam, the classical location of 'non-Europe'. Internally, a Euro-christian view of war and its place in our history may well run the risk of re-invigorating one of Europe's oldest bigotries, anti-semitism, because the business of 'winding up' World War Two and the Cold War may well produce an agreement to forget, if not actually forgive, what happened to Europe's Jews. Here again, the controversies about appropriate memorials of war are instructive guides to contemporary European cultural concerns – see Webber, 1993, Young, 1989 and Wyschgood, 1990.

## 5 War memorials as elementary forms of community life

Edward Tiryakian (Tiryakian, 1988:58 *et seq.*) describes the role played by religion in creating 'the new moral community' in which an authentic sense of nationhood is mobilised and set against the artificial, alien and secular institutions of an exploitative state. Tiryakian is describing revolutionary events in Iran, Poland and Nicaragua. The post World War One war memorials represent an effort by the living to create or reclaim some authentic sense of community with the dead. In the Great War over 60 million men had been mobilised (from a continent of approximately 120 million households), 22 million had been wounded and 10 million killed (Singer and Small, 1970, p. 52 *et seq.*). Attempts were made, more or less successfully, to render these deaths authentic, that is to say to sacralise them, at a national level by the institutions of the state. The Cenotaph was deliberately designed so as to be as inclusive as possible of all the nations and faiths of the Empire: it bears no religious or national symbols, no marks of regiment or rank. The Tomb of the Unknown Warrior is not quite so inclusive, as it is within a Christian – indeed an Anglican – religious building. Both these war memorials are, of course, in London. The work of Cannadine and Wilkinson referred to above indicates that in Britain at least these commemorative activities of the State were in no way experienced as alien – indeed, they reflected popular demand, as did the national Two Minute Silence. The same cannot be said for the recent (1992) statue erected to 'Bomber Harris', which clearly split the community, evoked a secular rather than a religious response and debate, and by doing so undermined the very purpose of a memorial.

In their search for an effective sacralisation of what had happened between 1914 and 1919 – a disaster unparalleled in our history, whether for the victors or for the losers – the living sought to locate their memorials as close as possible to where they felt the community to be. The national symbol system worked at one level but, as the Bomber Harris incident perhaps shows, national state commemorative activities tend to be unable to address the elementary need of primal communities for an appropriate sacralisation of *their particular, irreplaceable loss*. In the Orkneys the largest island ('Mainland') has 14 war memorials. In 1911 Mainland had a total population of 14500. Over half of the memorials are located in graveyards or cemeteries, where they are by far the most dominant stone, situated on a mound or on the central place of the burial ground. On one of the smaller islands, Egilsay, the First World War memorial, a substantial granite obelisk, has but one name on it. Typically, the memorial will refer to 'The men of this parish', without specifying the name of the parish (Davies, Field research, ongoing). The parish is one of the oldest of our collective identities; and in leaving out the name the memorial builders are serving notice that this is a 'private', that is to say a communal matter: they are talking to themselves of the dead they know to be their dead. The parish is also the primary religious collectivity, the cemetery a primary sacred place, regularly visited by those who live in the parish. The memorials on Orkney, Mainland, also locate the parish within the broader society of which it is part: foreign battle sites and the places where the soldiers died are listed, as is the fact, where relevant, that the dead soldier died in the forces of New Zealand, Canada, or Australia, the major places of emigration of the Celtic diaspora. These memorials, therefore, sum up and symbol-

125

ise the story and sacrosanct character of the primary community: they invoke its religion, they say what happened to its men, they re-integrate the non-returning soldiers into the memory of the community, they comprehend the larger world, and they state, without dispute, the primal loyalty of the living to the dead. As Durkheim puts it,

> Without symbols social sentiments could have only a precarious existence. . . . If the movements by which these sentiments are expressed are connected with something that endures, the sentiments themselves become more durable. These other things are constantly bringing them to mind and arousing them: it is as though the cause which excited them in the first place continued to act. Thus these systems of emblems, which are necessary if society is to become conscious of itself, are no less indispensable for assuring the continuation of this consciousness. (Durkheim, 1915; 1982 edn. p. 231).

The tribal societies on whose practices Durkheim commented have no doubt long since disappeared, either subsumed into or wiped out by the dominant cultures of the West. The communities which produced our thousands of war memorials may also disappear, for different reasons perhaps. They will however, leave behind them, in the shape of war memorials, potent symbols of the history and culture of our bellicognisant society.

## Note

There is no 'list' of war memorials, but the British range is well covered in Derek Boorman, *At the Going Down of the Sun*, Colin McIntyre, *Monuments of War*, Rose Coombs, *Before Endeavours Fade* and Alan Borg, *War Memorials*. Bruce Kapferer, *Legends of People, Myth of State*, deals with the Australian National War Memorial and its significance in the formation of an Australian national identity. Antoine Prost, *Les Anciens Combattants et la Societe Francaise* and David Troyansky, 'Monumental Politics . . . French Monuments aux Morts' deal with France. George Mosse, *Fallen Soldiers*, deals with Germany and Michael Ignatieff, 'Soviet War Memorials' deals with Russia. American studies are to be found in General of the Army George C. Marshall, 'Our War Memorials Abroad; A Faith Kept' and in Edward Chase, *Beautiful Arlington, Burial Place of America's Illustrious Dead*. J. Mayo, 'War Memorials as Political Memory' is also worth reading. The Jewish concerns for appropriate war memorials are dealt with by Webber, 'A Memorial for Auschwitz?' and by Young, *The Texture of Memory: Holocaust Memorial and Meaning*.

# References

Auden, S., (1935), 'Psychology and Art Today', quoted in Hynes, S., (1976), *The Auden Generation*, London: The Bodley Head.

Binyon, L., (1919), 'For the Fallen', in Benn, (1986), *Memorials*, London: Ravette.

Boorman, D., (1988), *At the Going Down of the Sun*, York: Ebor Press.

Borg, A., (1991), *War Memorials*, London: Leo Cooper.

Burgess, G., (ed.) and translator, (1990), *The Song of Roland*, Harmondsworth: Penguin.

Cannadine, D., (1981), 'War and Death, Grief and Mourning in Modern Britain', in *Mirrors of Mortality*, (1981), J. Whaley, (ed.), New York: St. Martin's Press.

Chase, E., (1928), 'Beautiful Arlington, Burial Place of America's Illustrious Dead', *National Geographic*, vol. 54.

Coombs, R., (1990), *Before Endeavours Fade*, London: Battle of Britain Prints.

Davies, J., (1992), Fieldwork ongoing, Newcastle University.

Dawson, B., (1992), Ph.D. Thesis, ongoing, Newcastle University.

Dix, G., (1945). *The Shape of the Liturgy*, Westminster: Dacre Press.

Durkheim, E., (1982), [1915], *The Elementary Forms of the Religious Life*, London: George Allen and Unwin.

*Encyclopaedia Americana*, Connecticutt: Groliev.

Gibbs, M. and Johnson, S., (eds), and translators, (1984), *Willehalm*, by Wolfram von Eschenbach, Harmondsworth: Penguin.

Girouard, M., (1981), *The Return to Camelot, Chivalry and the English Gentleman*, New Haven CT: Yale University Press.

Gurevich, A., (1990), *Medieval Popular Culture*, Cambridge: Cambridge University Press.

Harding, *et al.*, (1986), *Contrasting Values in Western Europe*, London: MacMillan.

Hardison, O., (1965), *Christian Rite and Christian Drama in the Middle Ages*, London: The John Hopkins Press.

Hill, S., (1990), 'Britain: the Dominant Ideology Thesis after a Decade', in *Dominant Ideologies*, Abercrombie, (ed.) (1990), London: Unwin Hyman.

Ignatieff, M., (0000), 'Soviet War Memorials', *History Workshop*, No 17.

Kapferer, B., (1988), *Legends of People, Myth of State*, Washington DC: Smithsonian Institute Press.

Keen, M., (1984), *Chivalry*, New Haven CT: Yale University Press.

Kipling, R., (1899), 'The White Man's Burden', in T.S. Eliot (ed.), (1987), *A Choice of Kipling's Verse*, London: Faber and Faber.

Kohout, P. *et al.*, (1992), *Disorientations – Eastern Europe in Transition*, London: Thames and Hudson.

Langbridge, F., (ed.), (1890), *Ballads of the Brave*, London: Methuen & Co.

Lincoln, A., (1863), The Gettysburg Address, in Nicolay, J. and Hay J., (eds), (1890), *Abraham Lincoln*, London: T. Fisher Unwin.

McIntyre, C. (1990), *Monuments of War*, London: Hale.

Marshall, G., (1957), 'Our War Memorials Abroad: A Faith Kept,' *National Geographic*, June 1957.

Mayo, J., (1988), 'War Memorials as Political Memory,' *Geographical Review*, Spring 1988.

Mosse, G., (1990), *Fallen Soldiers*, Oxford: Oxford University Press.

*Newcastle Evening Chronicle*, May 20, 1992.

Paxton, I., (1990), *Christianising Death*, Ithaca NY: Cornell University Press.

Price, R., (1972), *An Imperial War and the British Working Class*, London: Routledge and Kegan Paul.

Prost, A., (1977), *Les Anciens Combattants et la Societe Française*, Paris: Presses de la Fondation Nationale des Sciences Politiques.

Robertson, R., (1990), 'Japan and the U.S.A.: the interpenetration of national identities and the debate about orientalism', in *Dominant Ideologies*, Abercrombie *et al*, (eds) (1990), London: Unwin Hyman.

Sanders, P., (ed.), (1972), *The Epic of Gilgamesh*, Harmondsworth: Penguin.

Singer, J. and Small, M., (1970), *The Wages of War, 1816–1965, A Statistical Handbook*, Michigan: Ann Arbor.

Tiryakian, E., (1988), 'From Durkheim to Managua: revolution as religious revivals', in Alexander, J., *Durkheimian Sociology: cultural studies*, Cambridge: Cambridge University Press.

Troyansky, D., (1987), 'Monumental Politics . . . French Monuments aux Morts', *French Historical Studies*, Vol. 15, No. 1.

Warner, M., (1981), *Joan of Arc – the Image of Female Heroism*, London: Weidenfeld and Nicholson.

Watkins, L. and Worcester, R. (1986), *Private Opinions and Public Polls*, London: Thames and Hudson. See also Harding *et al*, 1986, *Contrasting Values in Western Europe*, MacMillan.

Webber, J., (1993), 'A Memorial for Auschwitz', in Davies and Wollaston, *The Sociology of Sacred Texts*, Sheffield: Sheffield Academic Press.

Wilkinson, A., (1978), *The Church of England and the First World War*, London: Society for the Propagation of Christian Knowledge.

Wilkinson, A., (1986), *Dissent or Conform? War, Peace and the English Churches, 1900–1945* London: Student Christian Movement Press.

Wyschgood, E., (1990), 'Man-Made Mass Death – Shifting Concepts in Community' in *Journal of the American Academy of Religion*, 58–2.

Young, J., (1989), 'The Texture of Memory: Holocaust Memorial and Meaning', in *Holocaust and Genocide Studies*, Vol. 4, No. 1.

Young, M., (1933), *The Drama of the Medieval Church*, Oxford: Oxford University Press.

# The acceptable face of human grieving? The clergy's role in managing emotional expression during funerals

## Jenny Hockey

The needs of bereaved people have become a theoretical and practical focus among the members of groups such as counsellors, clergy, academics, doctors and social workers, many of whom share the view that the unmet needs of bereaved people can bring difficulties in grieving and therefore in readjustment. While death ritual in non-Western societies often provides an important rite of passage, both for the surviving family and the deceased, many contemporary Western funerals appear not to play so central a role within the social and emotional re-orientation of people who are bereaved. This chapter explores material gathered during a study of the approach to Christian funerals common among Sheffield clergy and their congregations. It argues that if clergy seek to help bereaved people to engage in grieving, this goal may be at odds with conventional approaches to the funeral in the West. 'Uncontrolled' emotional expression is seen by clergy as something difficult to accommodate when they are proceeding with a structured liturgy. When the dominant Western beliefs or metaphors of emotion are examined, it becomes apparent that emotion is commonly understood to be a natural and uncontrollable entity which is contained within the body, a model which underpins the views expressed by clergy during interviews. The therapeutic 'release' of emotion is therefore desired as a way of avoiding the dangers of 'pent up' feelings. However, what interview material reveals is a paradox which stems from the dominance of this model of human emotion. As natural forces, contained within the body, emotions are feared to be potentially unmanageable within the context of highly structured Western funerary ritual, in that they are understood to be unamenable to control. These beliefs about the nature of emotion are questioned through comparison with other cultural perspectives, evident in practices to be found within both Western and non-Western societies. It is argued that by approaching emotion through an alternative set of metaphors, ritual which is both structured and yet expressive can be generated.

## The funeral as therapy

. . . the majority of British people are today without adequate guidance as to how to treat death and bereavement and without social help in living through and coming to terms with the grief and mourning which are the inevitable responses in human beings to the death of someone they have loved (Gorer, 1965:110).

Gorer's account is a now familiar contribution to the medical, academic and popular critique of the post-war management of death within both Britain and America, evidenced today in forms of practical support such as bereavement counselling and hospice care. Its focus is identified by Martins (1983) as a cultural ideal of a discrete and emotionally low-key death. Against this background the present study was generated. The initiative for it came from Brian Cranwell, a practising member of the Anglican clergy and the chairperson of Cruse-Bereavement Care in Sheffield (see Hockey, 1992). Its aim was to explore the extent to which Sheffield funerals met the needs of bereaved people. Rather than drawing upon pre-existing assumptions about the meaning of the funeral and any role it might have within the process of grieving, it was decided to develop some initial insight into these areas from the perspective of clergy themselves and also that of recently bereaved people in Sheffield. This was achieved through a small sample of extended in-depth qualitative interviews with six ministers drawn, equally, from the Anglican, Roman Catholic and Free Churches. Access to clergy was through the snowball method, each minister then facilitating contact with two bereaved people for whom they had conducted a funeral. In this way a considerable body of ethnographic material was generated. It revealed important issues which were then explored through a questionnaire circulated among Anglican, Roman Catholic and Methodist clergy within Sheffield. Questionnaires were returned by 65 Anglican, 4 Roman Catholic and 16 Methodist clergy. Material drawn from interviews with clergy provides the main focus for the current discussion. While there was some evidence of inter-denominational differences in the way clergy approached funerals, the focus of this chapter is the broad range of beliefs and practices which were common to them all.

In his foreword to the report of the full study, Cranwell suggests that:

> At present, almost all the funerals in the Sheffield area are conducted as 'religious' ceremonies, mostly Christian. But as people become more aware of alternatives such as humanist funerals, or the option for non-believers of having no religious service, ministers in the future will be called upon less for the robes we wear and our enhancement of a rite of passage than for the pastoral and spiritual value we bring to bereaved people (Hockey, 1992:vi–viii).

Cranwell also makes reference to 'bereavement literature (which) tells us that how we behave during the events surrounding death has an effect on those nearest to the deceased' (Hockey, 1992:vi). A potentially therapeutic role is therefore being posited for the funeral, a development which Cranwell perceives as consumer-led in his vision of a future where the 'religious' dimensions of a funeral are less sought after by 'non-believers' and people 'aware of alternatives'.

The study showed that Cranwell's concerns about the needs of bereaved people were shared by clergy, providing evidence of their awareness of contemporary therapeutic discourse. For example, one minister, when describing the purpose of a funeral, said that he would:

> . . . try to use the service and the pastoral links with the family at that time to try and help them and comfort them and sort of listen to them . . . all a part of the healing process of bereavement.

When asked whether they ever talked with bereaved people about how they might express their grief, particularly during the funeral itself, ministers made comments such as:

> You tend to get used to . . . telling people that it's a good thing to cry, that you're not embarrassed.

131

Some visible expression is usually good.

I tell them not to be ashamed of having a cry.

I'd say to them, 'you must be natural . . . do what you want to do, don't feel anybody's looking at you, don't feel that you're putting me off, don't feel constrained . . . if you want to cry, cry.

I'd just encourage them to be natural about their grief.

Like Cranwell, these clergy are articulating views in keeping with contemporary bereavement literature, advocating the benefits of expressing grief, particularly in the form of tears. Stiff upper lips are seen, from the perspective of this body of knowledge, to be harmful in that the 'stages' of grief cannot be navigated if grieving itself is not undertaken freely and openly. One minister said:

I think it's wrong for relations to tell people not to cry. Often you get this and I try and encourage folk . . . if they want to cry, to just let it go. We had it in our own family actually . . . my grandparents . . . my grandfather . . . died rather tragically and grandma was told by other relations she mustn't cry . . . she must keep a stiff upper lip . . . and she died within four months and part of it was all this pent up emotion which she didn't feel she should release. And that is a great danger, actually.

These are the aims which clergy sought to integrate into a funeral service which, from their accounts, was also an event characterised by an hierarchical relationship between themselves and their congregation. Its formal structure remained, even though they were able to draw upon a range of 'scripts' in the form of alternative sets of prayers, hymns, bible readings and a specially written sermon. Indeed a lack of structure could be seen as problematic. For example, one minister expressed reservations about a Pentecostal funeral he had attended. Whilst impressed by its sincerity, he said:

. . . but we didn't know what was coming next and I felt a bit lost. I know some of the relations felt a bit lost, whereas if you've got a printed form of service, even if you don't keep to it rigidly, they know where you're going . . . there can be a sense of security. So that's why I use a set service and everyone can join in particular prayers and things . . .

These comments raise the question as to whether the therapeutic aspirations implicit within Cranwell's discussion are entirely compatible with the traditional form of a Christian funeral. Ministers spoke of using the service flexibly, yet, as the material to follow indicates, it is often a limited form of flexibility. For example, the address can provide scope for mourners to participate in the service, thereby orienting it towards their individual needs. Friends, family or colleagues can introduce their own accounts of the person who has died and what his/her death has meant. It is, however, seen by clergy as important that someone making an address is fully in control of their emotions. Ministers made comments such as:

> You have to be just careful really of that sort of input because sometimes people would like to do it and then really emotionally can't cope when it comes to it and so you have an upsetting thing in the service instead of . . . you know, someone breaks down when they're trying to speak and that doesn't help the relations. So you just have to make sure that they know what they're doing and that they can do it.

Another minister echoed these concerns, to the extent that he was not prepared to be flexible in this way:

> . . . the funeral service doesn't particularly lend itself to that, in that the last thing you want in a funeral service is for a young person to get up or even a member of the family to get up and to do the reading for their own family and find that it's too much for them on the occasion, which could be embarrassing for them and for the congregation and for the family as well.

In the example of the address, it becomes apparent that a therapeutic aim to construct a ritual which accommodates the personal feelings of surviving friends and family can be at odds with the structured, emotionally low-key nature of the traditional funeral service. This contradiction is not limited to the rather high-profile act of giving an address. The behaviour of mourners throughout the whole funeral, while expected to be not only 'natural' but also 'uncontrollable', could nonetheless present

Jenny Hockey

problems. In effect, clergy made distinctions between acceptable and unacceptable forms of emotional response. While feelings could be 'pent up', and therefore a 'great danger' to the wellbeing of the individual, they could also become difficult to manage if expressed too forcibly. One minister described such situations:

> Sorrow . . . can be a distraction that I think in the circumstances has to be overcome . . . On the occasion of a funeral it can be very very difficult to do in the course of a liturgy that's taking place . . . if someone goes into an uncontrollable burst there's very very little that can be done other than perhaps a . . . either try and overcome that outburst by continuing with the service in another way or a period of silence which won't be silent. You meet that situation and it's only when you meet it that you have to decide . . . you can think beforehand what you're going to do but in reality when that situation arises what you had thought might be a solution to the problem may not necessarily be so.

Another minister echoed this point:

> People try and be very composed and hide their feelings in church but equally you'll have people absolutely desolated, shaking uncontrollably, tears streaming down . . . my colleague had a funeral recently of a baby . . . mother was uncontrollable . . . spent most of the funeral walking up and down. All he could do was try and get things over as quickly as possible with as much dignity as possible in very difficult circumstances.

He went on:

> It gets awkward when you don't know how people . . . with the mother who's quite likely to leap into the grave which is a situation one faces. That makes prayer rather difficult.

Similarly, the words of a minister who had encountered 'uncontrolled' emotional responses from mourners and was clear in his refusal to allow them:

> I wouldn't encourage them to cry . . . I'd just encourage them to be natural about their grief and there are limits . . . there has to be limits. I mean, I will not allow people, after a certain

length of time anyway, to cling uncontrollably to the coffin as it's disappearing down the hatch. I mean that is not on. For everybody it's not on.

Not only could visible grief create problems for ministers but, in their view, it could also present difficulties for mourners themselves. One minister said:

> There are a few people who make . . . hardly anyone who makes a display of grief by which I mean a demonstrative expression of grief which would attract a lot of attention . . . and where people are overwhelmed by their grief they tend to cry very quietly as if they don't want to spoil the service. They'd like to overcome it . . . but it's just too much to keep in.

Another minister made the point that:

> What I try to do is to say that emotion is OK and tears are very natural. But people are still very concerned about making fools of themselves and so I wouldn't want to reduce anybody to a state that would embarrass them.

From clergy's accounts it appears that an apparently liberal approach to the 'natural' expression of emotion can give rise to problems both for themselves and for the congregation within the context of a formal, structured ritual form. This is not to say that most clergy have not developed strategies for managing a certain degree of unscripted emotional expression. Moreover, the bereaved people who were interviewed often described feelings of numbness and unreality at this early stage of their bereavement. From clergy's accounts, those mourners who did experience powerful emotion were nonetheless at pains to express it in a moderated way – 'they tend to cry quietly as if they don't want to spoil the service'. There are, therefore, ways and means being found through which a degree of emotional release can be incorporated into a traditional funeral service. However, from clergy's accounts, the threat of problematic disruption still appeared to remain very real.

## Metaphors of emotion

Given the felt contradictions being expressed by clergy, the question emerges as to whether they can be erased, or whether, as would seem to be the case at present, *ad hoc* coping strategies are all that is possible. This chapter argues that an exploration of the dominant models or metaphors through which emotion is conceptualised and experienced within Western societies can provide insights which might lead to the generation of alternative approaches to funerary ritual. The prevailing concern with issues of emotional control, not only its excess but also its absence, can be shown to be linked with culturally specific models of human emotions.

While psychiatrists and counsellors have consistently argued the need for free expression of 'inner' feelings – sadness, anger, grief, guilt – social scientists have begun to query the universal nature often imputed to human emotion (see Lofland, 1985; Heelas, 1986; Sarbin, 1986). Sarbin's discussion is particularly relevant here. He argues that contemporary academic theories of the emotions tend to detach them from their contexts and to describe them as irrational. Furthermore, 'Emotion is generally discussed in the abstract, not unlike vision or digestion' (Sarbin, 1986:84). The physicality of emotional experience lends weight to the view that the emotions are universal biological phenomena. Sarbin refers to the belief that they are 'the animal inheritance of our evolutionary ancestors' (1986:93). Part of the explanation for this view, he argues, lies in one of Western society's dominant metaphors, that is of the body as a container. Emotion is conceived of as a natural entity contained within the human body. Sarbin suggests that self-reports of emotional experience – 'being seized by an emotion', 'being overwhelmed', 'being caught in the grip of an emotion' – are often used to provide evidence for this model.

Having argued that emotions are seen as abstract entities contained within the body, Sarbin then links this notion with Western mechanistic models, of both human life and the environment, which have the transmittal of force as their root metaphor. He posits a model of the emotions and their expression which is in keeping with a Western worldview dominated by scientific rationality. Sarbin reminds us that etymologically the word 'emotion' is connected with outward-directed movement, as in migrations. Thus the term 'emotion' can itself be seen as a metaphor or hypothesis which was employed to try to make sense of apparent transmissions of force within the body. For example, the visceral turmoil we know as anger, the rush of blood to the cheeks we know as embarrassment, and the tightening of the throat we know as fear.

In Sarbin's view a more helpful way of understanding emotional experience is to look at it contextually, that is by using the model of an historical act rather than an abstract biological entity when explaining the occurrence of feelings such as anger, embarrassment or fear. Emotions, when understood as historical acts, become, in Sarbin's view:

> . . . intentional acts, acts designed to transform or transfigure
> the world; and the acts are performed by persons as agents,
> not as mechanical automata (1986:83).

To mourn, to be in grief, is therefore an experience which Sarbin understands in terms of a social role, one which the individual enters into, informed, albeit unconsciously, by the range of culturally specific myths, fairy stories or soap operas available to them. Furthermore, if the 'historical act' model, or metaphor, is used, it then becomes possible to distinguish between different kinds of 'historical acts'. Sarbin refers to both dramaturgical and dramatistic roles, or forms of emotional expression. In the former case, individuals are *consciously* seeking to disguise a mismatch between what they actually feel and what they are meant to feel. In the latter individuals are still following a role but are doing so *unconsciously*, in that they are being guided by one of a whole repertoire of culturally available scripts or stereotypes. These he describes as:

> the story-telling of fables, fairy tales, morality plays, bedtime
> stories, movies, soap operas and so on. The stereotypes are
> part and parcel of the myths and folktales of a society (Sarbin,
> 1986:91).

Though guided by stereotypes of this kind, individuals none the less appear to exhibit spontaneously this or that emotional response.

Thus the Western notion, and experience, of being 'overcome with emotion', in Sarbin's view, refers to bodily changes which ensue once the individual becomes *intentionally* involved with a particular dramatistic role. Once set in motion, bodily changes take their course and may not easily be controlled. It is these bodily changes which are highlighted through the contemporary use of the term 'emotion', with the result that emotions have come to be understood and experienced as entities or forces which erupt within the private self.

By setting the interview material presented in the first section of this chapter within the context of Sarbin's discussion, the culturally-specific metaphoric system which underpins clergy's accounts can be explored. It was noted earlier that therapeutic and traditional approaches to funerals were not always reconcilable for clergy and that this contradiction might be understood in terms of the metaphors through which emotion was understood. Further material from interviews helps draw out the implications of this view and opens up the possibility of alternative ritual forms.

## Containment and control

Clergy described grief as 'natural' and, being 'natural', it was also 'uncontrollable', at times 'too much to keep in'. Mourners can 'go into an uncontrollable burst'. One minister described sorrow as 'an outlet for some poor folk who are obviously more emotional than others'. An hydraulic model of the emotions, which can be linked with Freudian theory, appears to inform statements such as 'if they want to cry then let it go'. Ministers spoke of the 'great danger' of 'all this pent-up emotion which she didn't feel she should release' and they describe telling mourners 'Don't try and hold in your feelings'.

From this reading of material we have evidence of the emotions as, indeed, being conceived of as natural forces, located within the body-as-container. Sarbin highlighted the dominance of the mechanistic transmittal of forces metaphor within Western thought and, in this material, it is both the containment and the breaching of the container which is at issue.

We can go further in unravelling the logic of the models or metaphors which underpins clergy's accounts. The root metaphors of emotion as 'the transmittal of forces' located within the 'body-as-container' can be shown to have a series of entailments. While logically consistent, these entailments are also contradictory in their implications, a state of affairs which, I will go on to argue, can be seen to account for a central concern among both clergy and congregation with issues of containment and control. These entailments are as follows:

1 Professional competence as a member of the clergy requires emotional self-control.
2 The loss of emotional control represents a breaching of the boundaries of the self which can be problematic in a public setting in that control, once lost, cannot easily be retrieved.
3 Individuals who control or contain their emotions are in potential psychological danger.
4 Emotion which is expressed deliberately is unlikely to be genuine, natural or authentic.

These entailments can be traced within the material below.

Talking about themselves, rather than their congregations, clergy none the less adhere to the transmittal–of–force metaphor. They see themselves as, at times, easily penetrable or destructable containers. Many interviews involved the recounting of episodes where clergy had discovered a powerful emotional association of some kind between themselves and a family where death had occured, an association which became evident in tears or a tremulous voice from the pulpit:

> I mean I've cried at a funeral before now . . . maybe only for a few second but I have actually had tears come to my eyes.

> I was so involved with this lad and what he was going through that . . . the service had only just started and I just choked up.

> I broke down.

> I was cast down.

> Often you can come from a funeral very drained and fortunately in this parish you go from one thing to another.

What clergy are describing is the assault of inner forces which, despite their belief in the therapeutic value of emotional expression, can be seen from the material below to represent a threat to their professional competence. According to the logic of the metaphoric system underpinning their approach to emotion, these forces can be managed only through the determined application of external forces. Thus they describe how:

I learned of the need to keep a very, very careful check on myself.

I really took myself in hand afterwards.

You've really got to take a very tight hold on yourself and the situation.

Whatever you feel inside, that has to be held in check.

The external forces available to clergy are referred to as 'professionalism', as in statements such as 'somehow you have to get professionalism to take over'.

Thus, following Sarbin's distinction between emotional expression as either a dramaturgical or a dramatic role, Sheffield clergy can be seen to adopt a dramaturgical role in that, at times, they feel a need to distance themselves emotionally from their private feelings. For example, one minister said:

You also have to be a bit careful as a minister about your own emotions, particularly if you know the people involved . . . and there are lots of things. . . . I mean it doesn't help anybody if the minister is reduced to a sort of blubbering mess . . . you've got to be able to carry on taking the service.

We have a parallel here with Bourdieu's distinction between symbolic and practical mastery, the former being a conscious manipulation of the unconscious experience of others, the latter being a familiarity with appropriate social behaviour through means which cannot be articulated (Bourdieu, 1977). It is through making this separation between professional role and private feelings that symbolic mastery is made possible and again clergy talked about their role in both stimulating and controlling the emotional experience of their congregations. Another minister said:

The more personal you can make it, without becoming self indulgent about it . . . because I think that this is a danger that you can . . . on that sort of occasion you can pluck on people's heart strings quite considerably and you've got to restrain yourself a bit and think what you're doing.

In their dramaturgical role, clergy are consciously adhering to a script which ensures adequate impression management. This strategy is legitimated by a belief that their professional role requires them to work on behalf of the congregation who, in keeping with the logic of the transmittal–of–force metaphor, are cast in the role of easily penetrable containers. The minister speaks on their behalf, but ensures that if the 'containers' are breached it occurs only in a controlled fashion. One minister described part of his job as being 'to say those things that relatives are in no position to say for themselves at that time'. Sometimes he speaks directly to individual members of the congregation at the end of his address, any resulting expressions of grief being contained through his strategy of introducing a prayer immediately afterwards:

> The address is followed by a prayer so that if it upsets them they have a chance to put their head down and recollect themselves.

Thus the bowed head which renders escaping distress invisible enables the repair of the temporarily breached container.

Though ministers do provide moments of carefully controlled emotional expressiveness within an overarching formal ritual structure, they still tread a delicate path. Its problematic nature can be seen to stem from contradictions inherent within the logical entailments of a Western model of emotion. Believing themselves required to oversee the mourners' controlled release of emotional 'forces' within the otherwise rigid structure of the funeral, ministers view control of their own emotions to be legitimate, and indeed desirable. However for them to mask all evidence of their own feelings is also seen as undesirable. Again, following the logic of a transmittal of forces, the absence of an emotional response indicates a lack of feeling on their part. If emotion were present within them it would become apparent, regardless of the intentions of the minister him/herself.

Clergy argue that 'if people see you are empathising and you are being genuine, this again helps . . .'. However, given the view of emotions as 'forces', the boundaries of the minister-as-container must be patrolled, and they add '. . . at the same time being in control, which I always am'. Their position remains nonetheless precarious. Control must be exercised with artistry – 'one can't be detached . . . if it's someone you've known for a long period it would be quite insulting to just be a professional'; 'the great thing the priest has to offer is his humanity, not being a professional, being a counsellor'. In the concept of clerical professionalism itself, we have, therefore, a paradox. Professional detachment is double edged, perhaps unsurprisingly, given a view of emotion which inevitably promotes a concern with issues of control. Believing that 'It doesn't help anybody if the minister is reduced to a sort of blubbering mess . . . you have to carry on with the service', they nonetheless understand their professional role as one which requires empathy, the visible manifestation of genuine emotion. Within the course of one interview a minister expressed the views that (1) 'control, when you're in charge, is a very important thing . . . you need to keep tabs on the situation' and (2) 'the situation of the priest is to go in and be crucified with those people and only then do we do our job properly'. These contradictory opinions concerning both the maintenance and the yielding up of control are, nonetheless, entirely in keeping with the logical entailments of the emotion–as–transmittal–of–force metaphor.

Thus far, discussion has addressed concerns about the containment of emotion. However the fourth entailment of the transmittal–of–forces metaphor listed above was that powerful emotion deliberately expressed was quite probably inauthentic in that it contradicts, logically, the view of emotion as a natural force rather than an intentional act. For example, when we deny the authenticity of emotion in statements such as 'He's only putting it on', our metaphoric language describes something adhering to the surface rather than bursting from within the body-as-container.

When mourners do cry loudly, shake visibly, or fail to remain in their seats, clergy are not only at pains to preserve the formal structure of the ritual they are conducting but also, in some cases, may begin to suspect that the force of these expressions is not 'natural', and instead represents a conscious choice on the part of the mourner. If this is seen to be the case, doubt begins to fall upon the authenticity of what is being expressed. It comes to be seen through the metaphor of theatre. As already noted, one minister spoke favourably of his independent evangelical congregation where 'hardly anyone makes a display of grief which would attract a lot of attention'. Similarly, another questioned the authenticity of the 'grief' expressed by schoolgirls at the funeral of a classmate:

> . . . the Headmistress, wrongly I think, encouraged all the
> school to come to the funeral. And it literally was a case of

mass hysteria. You know, one girl started crying and the girl next to her started crying and by the time I'd finished I was dealing with this hysterical crowd of girls, 500 girls. I mean it really was mass hysteria. It wasn't genuine grief. Just being passed from one to another. 75 per cent of the kids in that church wouldn't even know the girl. And so I really had to sort of say 'That's it. No more of this. This is silly'. And I really had to do that, which is not exactly how you like to do a funeral but it was just getting totally ridiculous. So you have situations like that and you just have to be the big, brave, nasty, horrible vicar who . . . and stop it.

One minister spoke of:

. . . folk who almost use a funeral for an exhibition of emotion . . . people who have screamed and cried and yelled . . . fainted and all the rest of it . . . it's all a part, it expresses them . . . sometimes you get people completely out of control, almost enjoying it.

Making his view of emotion clear, he said:

. . . there is emotion and there is excessive emotion.

Loss of control therefore not only disrupts the formal nature of the funeral but can also become 'excessive' and, as result, can be interpreted by clergy as a form of enjoyable exhibitionism or attention-seeking display. The intentionality perceived to underlie 'excessive emotion' is logically inconsistent with a view of emotion as the transmittal of force. Its authenticity therefore becomes open to question.

Interestingly, clergy's adherence to this view was accompanied by an awareness that in other cultures deliberate expressions of grief were not uncommon. Unlike the dismissal of such behaviour as play-acting or hysteria when evident among their own congregations, they saw these practices as therapeutic. For example, one minister described a funeral he had conducted for a Ghanaian family:

At the graveside there was a great expression of grief and emotion which, in a different congregation, I would have called hysteria, but it seemed right for them. I went back to the party at the house afterwards and it really was a party.

Another minister also reflected on cultural variation, saying:

> . . . continental weeping and wailing which is the thing to do
> over there is very very difficult to deal with . . . people wanting
> the coffin open tends not to be very British . . . we have people
> try and act with quiet dignity . . . they often don't manage it
> and then feel embarrassed because they haven't managed it.

Clergy's stress on the natural expression of emotion, which is
consistent with the transmittal–of–force metaphor, therefore
paradoxically admits of limits – 'there is emotion and there is
excessive emotion'. In their discussion of highly visible emotional
expression among Ghanaian or 'continental' congregations,
clergy appear to acknowledge that what is thought of as 'natural'
emotional expression may well vary cross-culturally.

## Alternative metaphors of emotion

Much of the theoretical discussion offered in this chapter may
feel counter-intuitive to the Western reader who is familiar with
the experience of emotion 'welling up' inside them, who may
have 'broken down' in public if they have not had the chance to
'let go' in private. The Western transmittal–of–force metaphor so
powerfully informs our understanding of emotion that the
accounts of more traditional or non-Western death ritual, which
may well include periods of wailing or even self-mutilation, often
inspire one of two competing yet logically consistent responses.
There is the view that these more traditional societies are allowing a freer expression of powerful, universal emotions – sorrow,
anger, fear – and are therefore indeed more 'therapeutic'.
Conversely there is the view that noisy 'emotional' ritual is some
kind of display which reflects intense social pressure rather than
intense grief. Either the structure of the ritual has been cleverly
built around 'natural' responses to death; or, in being structured,
the emotions displayed are on some level contrived, a show of
strength or solidarity. In both cases it is the transmittal of force
which is understood to be either accommodated or artificially
reproduced.

Following Sarbin's argument that this metaphor of the emotions is highly culturally specific to many Western societies, this
last section examines the 'public' expression of emotion, both in

the death ritual of more traditional societies and in the example of an 'alternative' Western therapy, co-counselling. This material demonstrates the possibility of emotional expression which is in keeping with the meaning of the death for mourners, yet which is amenable to forms of ritual structuring which involve both its deliberate initiation as well as its curtailment. As such it would seem to meet the twin aims of members of the Christian clergy and their congregations. When viewed through the metaphor of the 'historical act in all its complexity' (Sarbin, 1986:83) emotion and structure cease to be inherently antagonistic to one another. Huntington and Metcalf examine Durkheim's account of the wailing and mutilation through which death among the native Australian Warramunga is experienced (Durkheim, 1965 [1912]; cited in Huntington and Metcalf, 1979:28–34). They argue that:

> Intense emotion and tight organisation go hand in hand even in these funerals where the obligations of slashing one's thighs or burning one's abdomen are precisely determined by kinship (mother's brother and mother, respectively). The funeral material makes it clear that emotional 'effervescence' does not replace structure but results from structure (Huntington and Metcalf, 1979:32).

They also offer the warning that:

> . . . we can neither assume the universality of particular modes of feeling nor that similar signs of emotion correspond to the same underlying sentiments in different cultures (Huntington and Metcalf, 1979:24).

Only through detailed ethnographic study of a society does it become possible to discern the meaning of ritual behaviour for those involved. Huntingdon and Metcalf also discuss Radcliffe-Brown's account of ceremonial weeping among the Andaman islanders (Radcliffe-Brown, 1964 [1922]; cited in Huntington and Metcalf, 1979:24–28). Rather than focussing on death ritual alone, in seeking to understand the meaning of weeping of this kind, Radcliffe-Brown instead sets death ritual within the context of other Andamanese life course rituals such as initiation and marriage. Social anthropology has argued consistently that to offer universal explanations for behaviours such as wailing at a funeral is misguided. Furthermore, the imperative to categorise such behaviours as either authentic or 'faked' can be seen as eth-nocentric in that it is a culturally specific distinction which imputes an inappropriate clarity to what can be seen as a contin-uum of behaviours. For example, Western theatre often involves actors and audience in a staged emotional experience in which tears may flow on both sides of the proscenium arch and all par-ties expect to leave the make-believe world of Hamlet or Lear with their emotions 'stirred' in some way. The material which fol-lows exemplifies emotional effervescence 'resulting from structure' and provides clues as to ways in which Christian clergy might reconcile their competing aims.

Thus, in Okely's account of gypsy death (1983), she demon-strates a cultural system within which highly visible crying during a funeral is required in order that the spirit of the deceased will not return to bring ill luck to the living. The nature of kinship links between the living and the dead is made apparent through the degree of emotional intensity displayed by surviving family:

> Dramatic expressions of grief are expected from close cognates and the spouse of the deceased. They wail and sob, and appear to have 'fits'. They tremble and fall to the ground, apparently unconscious, when the coffin is lowered into the ground. As each individual excels him or herself in public grief, the onlookers state the exact cognatic relationship to the deceased. When a chair was brought for an older man trembling from head to foot, the murmur went up, 'He's (the deceased's) brother's son.' When a woman was carried rigid from the graveside people said, 'She's his sister' (Okely, 1983:193).

Wright (personal communication) also described highly struc-tured emotional expression in the course of death ritual, in this case among Iranian women. As the ritual unfolds periods of wailing will ensue and then be 'cut off like a knife' in order that a new, quieter phase of the ritual can take place. Smoking is used as a way of calming women whose emotional expression ceases more slowly.

This material indicates the possibility of emotional behaviour which is on some level scripted, intentional and logical. An alter-native set of metaphors for the emotions is to be found within Western society in the forms of 'growth movement' therapy. One example is co-counselling, a therapy which brings individuals together to express emotions intentionally, guided by the belief that emotional expression brings enlightenment or insight (see Jackins, 1975). Time periods are negotiated between individuals and, once work has begun, bodily and verbal strategies are used by both the individual seeking emotional expression and their helper(s) to stimulate that expression. As the negotiated time period expires, so the expression of emotion is brought to a close through attention–switching strategies which return the individual to a calmer emotional state. As Sarbin notes, the bodily changes brought about as a result of intentional emotional expression may endure, but individuals will usually manage their emotional expression in such a way that these changes subside fairly rapidly and they themselves can then take on the role of helper for their partner.

Therapies such as co-counselling explicitly challenge the trans-mittal–of–forces metaphor. They demonstrate the possibility of emotional experience which is both intentional and controlled, yet seen as neither inauthentic when expressed, nor repressed when the negotiated time period elapses. Its therapeutic aim is to provide individuals with access to emotional experience which they might otherwise avoid in the belief that once embarked upon, that experience would engulf them in a painfully uncontrollable fashion.

In adhering to the dominant transmittal–of–force metaphor, clergy have difficulty in recognising the possibility of a dramatistic model of the emotions. Mourners, particularly those who share this view of their emotions, are inhibited from making a positive choice to express their feelings. They can be contrasted with the members of many traditional cultures whose emotional participation in death ritual is unconsciously guided by cultural precedents such as drama, literature, folktales and previous funerary experience. By drawing on the evidence that tight organisation and powerful emotional expression often go hand in hand, ministers can hope to be spared the unnerving experiences of the kind described in interviews. As the material presented in this chapter reveals, 'outbursts' of emotion are often seen to be incompatible with planned, scripted ritual behaviour. As noted above, in the view of one member of the clergy:

. . . you can think beforehand what you're going to do but in reality when that situation arises what you had thought might be a solution to the problem may not necessarily be so.

## Bibliography

Bourdieu, P., (1977), *Outline of a Theory of Practice*, Cambridge: Cambridge University Press.

Durkheim, E., (1965 [1912]), *The Elementary Forms of the Religious Life*, New York: Free Press, cited in Huntington and Metcalf, 1979.

Gorer, G., (1965), *Death, Grief and Mourning in Contemporary Britain*, London: Cresset Press.

Heelas, P., (1986), Emotion Talk across Cultures, in R. Harre, (ed.), *The Social Construction of Emotions*, Oxford: Basil Blackwell.

Hockey, J., (1992), *Making the Most of a Funeral*, London: Cruse-Bereavement Care.

Huntington, R. and Metcalf, P., (1979), *Celebrations of Death. The anthropology of mortuary ritual*, Cambridge: Cambridge University Press.

Lofland, L.H., (1985), The Social Shaping of Emotion: The case of grief, *Symbolic Interaction*, 8, 2:171–190.

Martins, H., 'Introduction Tristes Durees', *Journal of the Anthropological Society of Oxford*, November, 1983.

Okely, J., (1983), *The Traveller Gypsies*, Cambridge: Cambridge University Press.

Radcliffe-Brown, A.R., (1964 [1922]), *The Andaman Islanders*, New York: Free Press, cited in Huntingdon and Metcalf, 1979.

Sarbin, T.R., (1986), Emotion and Act: roles and rhetoric, in R. Harre, (ed.), *The Social Construction of Emotions*.

# A gendered history of the social management of death in Foleshill, Coventry, during the interwar years

## *Sheila Adams*

Since the end of the nineteenth century (in Europe) there has been 'a brutal revolution in traditional attitudes and feelings, (death has) become shameful and forbidden' (Ariès, 1975:85). Ariès suggests that the change in attitudes was accelerated by the displacement of the site of death between 1930 and 1950. In the United Kingdom during this period the social management of death was largely transferred from the private sphere of the home into the public sphere of the hospital and funeral director. This chapter looks at one particular aspect of this change by focusing on the role of the neighbourhood layer–out within the context of informal care found in the working class community of Foleshill, Coventry, between the two world wars. The research undertaken for this chapter suggests that this working class community could not be defined in terms of kinship relations or shared male work experience, but was characterised by the pattern of informal care organised by the women in response to their shared experience of economic insecurity and poverty, the absence of public welfare and the imperative to maintain their self respect. It seems probable that the caring activity of the neighbourhood layer–out, based on a rationality of care, which was informed by her practical experience of care and personal knowledge of her neighbours, played an important part in the organisation of this informal care. The chapter argues that the increased value and status of male, scientific rationality, associated with professional training and the provision of formal care in the public sphere of the hospital, funeral director and male mortician, was a major factor in the decline of the role of the neighbourhood layer–out. The changes in the social management of death were mediated by the displacement of the site of death and legislation which confirmed the subordinate status of the female midwives and nurses in relation to the predominantly male medical profession.

## Introduction

During the period between the two world wars, the informal organisation of care for the dying and the dead body by the female neighbourhood layer–out in working class communities was replaced by the professional care of the dying by the medical and nursing professions and the professional treatment of the dead body by the male mortician. There are few accounts of the care of the dead body in the United Kingdom between death and confinement in the coffin. Among these, Clark (1982), Richardson (1983) and Roberts (1986) describe some of the customs observed by women in the home during this period and Smale refers to the 'casual and off-hand treatment of the corpse' (1984:455) by the male mortician in the embalming room in the 1980s. One explanation of this scarcity of accounts of the care of the dead body may lie in the significance of the role played by women, in the privacy of the home, in the management of this period between death and confinement in the coffin. Haggis points out that 'the failure to acknowledge women's roles, activities and rituals as significant has resulted in a definite information bias' (1990:71). This chapter is based on a research project[1] carried out in 1991 to address that informational bias, by understanding and analysing the role of the neighbourhood layer–out in the organisation of informal care which seems to have characterised the traditional working-class communities of the 1920s and 1930s.

## The working-class community in Foleshill in the interwar years

The population of Foleshill, a working-class community to the North of Coventry city centre, doubled from 5,514 in 1901 to 10.756 in 1921[2], as single men and young families[3] moved into the area, from other industrialised urban areas, looking for work in the new car and electronic industries. By the 1930s, these new industries were prospering and Coventry had the highest rate of working class home and car ownership in the country (Crump 1986). 'Foleshillites' did not share this prosperity. The vicar of St

Laurence's Church, Foleshill said in 1931 that 'St Laurence Church was a Church in a poor district, . . . a Church of poor people'[4]. The more prosperous members of the working class seem to have moved on to the new housing estates developed in other parts of the city where 'builders were greatly surprised by the willingness of Coventry workers to buy new properties' (Lancaster and Mason, 1986:345).

Abrams defines the traditional neighbourhood as a 'densely woven world of kin, neighbours, friends and co-workers, highly localised and strongly caring within the confines of quite tightly defined relationships, above all the relationships of kinship' (Bulmer, 1986:91). However in Foleshill during the interwar years the majority of the residents were migrants and did not have kin living in close physical proximity. The men did not share their work experience, and the larger firms often provided good leisure and sporting facilities, from which women were excluded (Crump, 1986). Many clubs or pubs catered for one particular religious, ethnic or industrial group (Lancaster, 1986). Male work and leisure activities could be seen as potentially divisive factors in this working-class community[5].

All the informants interviewed for this study referred to a close-knit working class community in which 'neighbours wouldn't see others starve'[6]. It seems that the community was underpinned by the caring activity of married women, excluded from official economic activity and forced to help each other in order to survive (Bulmer, 1986). In 1920 'the yardstick by which female work in Coventry was judged' (Castle, 1986:137) was set by Courtaulds, in Foleshill. The firm employed over 2,000 women and enforced a strict work discipline including a marriage bar and sex segregation in production. This work discipline was reflected in many working-class homes where strict sex segregation was often observed despite the shortage of space[7]. In Foleshill it was understood that the married, working-class woman's place was in the home; but it is possible that many of these women were engaged in unofficial economic activity. Five of the informants' mothers took in washing, one made silk furniture fringes at home and another worked as a general help for a family in a nearby village. All the informants' mothers worked as unqualified nurses, in their neighbour's homes, for which they sometimes received cash or payment in kind.

The working-class wives in Foleshill, with little or no suitable storage space and an inadequate household budget, probably shopped daily. This was a task which 'took a long time as you kept stopping to talk'[6]. These frequent, informal and casual contacts between neighbours at the shops and in the streets constructed a 'network of actual social relations' (Bott, 1971:99) on which the women's personal knowledge of each other and their families was based.

## Formal care

In the United Kingdom the social and medical management of childbirth, childcare, dying and death has, since the end of the nineteenth century, changed 'from a structure of control located in a community of untrained women, to one based on a profession of formally trained men' (Oakley, 1979:18). This transition of control was probably facilitated by the almost total exclusion of women from formal medical practice and training, and by the establishment of hospitals 'characterised by a high degree of formal doctor-control which permitted the definition and enforcement of an occupational hierarchy' (Versluysen, 1981:32). The Midwives Act of 1902 confirmed the subordinate status of female midwives and defined their professional skill 'in relation to the expertise and omniscience of the male professional' (Oakley, 1979:21), and the introduction of the National Health Service in 1948 established the central role of the hospital in the provision of health care (Stacey, 1988).

The Midwives Act, 1902, gave the Local Authorities responsibility for the supervision and maintenance of the register of all midwives intending to practise in their area. In 1907 the rules governing the operation of the Act were altered in the light of experience and 'the absolute prohibition with regard to a midwife laying out the dead is withdrawn, and now under specified circumstances she may, at the discretion of the Supervising Authority, do this'[8]. This suggests that prior to the 1902 Act it was not unusual for midwives to lay out the dead. Throughout the 1920s four '*bona fide*' or untrained, and forty 'certified' midwives were registered in Coventry. They returned approximately three forms, for the laying out of the dead, to the Medical Officer of Health in Coventry annually, at a time when there were, on average, nine maternal deaths and 103 stillbirths every year.

The research undertaken for this chapter suggests that the neighbourhood layer-out in the 1920s and 1930s in Foleshill did not practise as a certified midwife although many assisted the midwife. Some informants were sure that a woman could not, and did not, combine the role of assistant midwife and layer-out.

It seems possible that these women, who assisted at the birth and/or acted as neighbourhood layer-out, were the 'handywomen' whose activities the medical profession sought to control with the passing of the 1902 Midwives Act. After April 1905 a midwife was required to pass an examination in order to register her intention to practise as a midwife. In 1907 Dr Snell, then Medical Officer of Health in Coventry, referred to the Midwives Act 1902 as that 'ill devised Act (which placed) on the Official Register as "Certified Midwives" many thousands of absolutely untrained women'[8]. Dr Snell implied that untrained women should not be allowed to practise as midwives because they had no formal training and did not possess either the scientific knowledge required or the formal education (many could not read or write) to enable them to act in accordance with the dominant scientific rationality of the public sphere. One '*bona fide*' midwife in Coventry was removed from the register in 1906 as she had not sent a written request for medical aid 'which caused some delay and the mother's grave condition became fatal'[8]. Working-class women who had practised as midwives prior to the 1902 Act were gradually excluded from midwifery.

During the first two decades of the twentieth century 'modern nursing took into itself the Victorian class structure' (Stacey, 1988:93). Several informants said that their mothers would have loved to be nurses but were excluded by the cost of training. Candidates between 18 and 20 years of age were required, by voluntary and poor law hospitals, to produce a medical certificate and a reference of 'good, moral character'; to have achieved a certain educational standard; and to work a three month probationary period. Voluntary hospitals asked for a premium of between £5.5.0 and £15, which was returned on completion of training; if a student nurse broke her contract with a poor law infirmary without good reason (marriage, poor health or family troubles) she forfeited £5[9]. Parents were usually asked to purchase the 'first lot of uniform, which was a bit expensive if you weren't accepted'[6]. The entrance requirements and the cost of training excluded many working-class women from the formal training required to become a qualified nurse or certified midwife.

The concepts of care and caring are problematic (Graham, 1991). Feminist writers (Dalley, 1988, Graham, 1983, Lewis and

Meredith, 1988) have pointed out that the concept of caring 'can never simply be reduced to a kind of domestic labour performed on people, since it is always encompassed with emotional bonds' (Finch and Groves, 1983:4). Waerness sees that it is important to ask what kind of knowledge underpins caregiving work as the quality of caregiving work is dependent upon the training and skills of the caregiver; and 'the value of kindness and politeness cannot be calculated' (1984:195). She argues that caregiving work may be seen to be underpinned by two different types of knowledge: (a) the scientific rationality commonly found in the public sphere and associated with men, and (b) the rationality of care commonly found in the private sphere and associated with women. The knowledge of the certified midwife, who was being 'incorporated into a male-dominated control structure' (Oakley, 1979:22), appears to be based on scientific rationality and that of the untrained midwife on the rationality of care.

Different types of knowledge have different values and status. Scientific, rational knowledge which can be measured, recorded and stored facilitating its use and transmission to the next generation has high value and status; but knowledge based on interactive cues, practical experience and personal knowledge of the individual, which is difficult to measure, record, store and transmit is undervalued and has little status (Anspach, 1987). In the list of nurses and midwives in the Coventry City Directories[10], the names and addresses of the certified midwives were always printed in bold type, unlike those of the untrained midwife. In 1903 the fee set by the Central Midwives Board for a certified midwife was 10/-; by 1936, when the Local Authority was required to ensure the adequate provision of a domiciliary midwifery service, the fee had risen to £2.10.0 for a primipara (first baby), and £2.8.0 for subsequent pregnancies. The manner of listing and the fees may be seen to reflect the higher status and value of professional training based on scientific rationality.

The fees probably excluded many working class mothers from using the services of the certified midwife, as evidence suggests that untrained handywomen continued to act as midwives. A report 'The Training of Midwives' issued by the Ministry of Health in 1923 states that it is 'essential to obtain better control of the handywomen' by the registration and supervision of all women undertaking maternity nursing for gain. Doctors were warned, by the General Medical Council, not to engage or work with a 'handywoman' as she had not received 'professional training' and threatened the livelihood of the certified midwife[11]. Part 1 of the Midwives and Maternity Homes Act 1926 sought to 'tighten up the law relating to the practice of midwifery by unqualified persons'[8]. In 1906 twenty midwives registered their intention to practise in Coventry, of whom seven had received some training, but the remaining thirteen had no formal training. By 1929 only three of the fifty three midwives practising in Coventry had not received formal training[8]; in 1930 Dr Snell was able to report that 'There is an adequate supply of skilled midwives available in the City and the employment locally of old-time "handywomen" has been suppressed'[8].

The exclusion of the untrained handywomen by the medical profession and certified midwives was justified on the grounds of the greater value of scientific rational knowledge. It is possible that the legitimate activity of the handywomen was confined to the care of the dead body. Morley (1971) suggests that the care of the dead body came to be seen, by the wealthy, as a distasteful task towards the end of the nineteenth century. One layer-out's territory was 'a posh area where you couldn't expect people to do it for themselves'[6].

Access to the formal care provided by the Public Medical Service, Coventry & Warwickshire hospital, Provident Dispensary, Foleshill Nursing Association and certified midwives seems to have been dependent on the payment of a membership subscription, contribution or fee which excluded many of the working-class families in Foleshill. Access to the care provided by the Poor Law Institutions[12], Grey Ladies and Coventry Charity Organisation Society[13] was free; but assistance was dependent on a means test and the satisfactory character of the applicant. Applicants were subjected to considerable scrutiny and supervision. They experienced the 'hidden injuries of class (and) parried these injuries of inferiority which defined their social position by building a basis for their own self respect' (Williamson, 1982:9). Some informants had vague recollections of seeing a Grey Lady and several knew the location of the offices of the Foleshill Nursing Association; but none recalled their families ever using these services.

Excluded from formal care by poverty and the imperative to maintain their self-respect, the working-class wives and mothers of Foleshill were forced to help each other in order to survive. They constructed a system of informal care based on personal knowledge and relationships which responded to individual, particular need. Abrams suggests that informal care is unorganised (Bulmer, 1986); but the system of informal care developed in Foleshill seems to have been organised, the women knew where to go for help and the role or task each was likely to undertake.

## The neighbourhood layer-out

The network of actual social relations constructed by the working-class wives and mothers of Foleshill was the essential context for their caring activities. The role of the neighbourhood layer-out was possibly central in the organisation and provision of their system of informal care. 'There was always someone special in a particular district who was able to cope with births, marriages and deaths'[6]. One man greeted the layer-out with 'Oh, I know I've not got long to go, now I've seen you arrive'[6]. The children knew that 'when this lady went into a house, a new baby had arrived or someone had died'[6]. A boy of ten realised his mother had died when the layer-out arrived at his house[6].

Caring activity based on the rationality of care provides 'flexible and versatile services' (Waerness, 1984:199), characteristics which seem to have defined the work of the neighbourhood layer-out. The evidence from the semi-structured interviews suggests that her work was flexible and varied in response to the individual needs of the dying person and family. 'She used her commonsense and just knew what to do'[6]. She did not have any formal training, her caring activity was not routinised or planned and she did not act in accordance with the dominant scientific rationality of the public sphere. This flexibility probably accounts for some of the variation found in the accounts of her work. It is not possible to say that she was always contacted in the same way or that her work was carried out in a specific 'correct' order.

The caring activity of the neighbourhood layer-out was underpinned by a rationality of care based on her practical experience and personal knowledge of her neighbours. However, she does seem to have observed either 'familiar' or 'regular' norms of behaviour in accordance with her own socio-economic conditions and those of the bereaved family and the community. Familiar norms were observed when she was aware that death was imminent and when she was probably already caring for or helping to care for the dying person; so that she did not change her apron and laid out the body with whatever materials were available in the house or could be borrowed from neighbours. She may have been paid in cash or kind, or not paid at all; the bereaved family were probably members of her network of actual social relations and lived nearby. Regular norms were observed when her services were 'booked' in advance by relatives, the doctor, midwife or undertaker. She might visit to 'weigh them up'[6] and ask the family to make certain arrangements. On these occasions she changed her apron, did her hair and washed herself, and took with her materials, supplied by the undertaker or midwife, which often included a bottle of whisky. She was more likely to be paid in cash, and the bereaved family were unlikely to be members of her network of actual social relations. One layer-out was 'booked' in advance by a wife, but when she was called to lay out the body, the husband sat up in bed and asked for a glass of water[6]!

In 1935 only 56 per cent of bodies were seen after death by a medical practitioner (Polson, 1953). The Births and Deaths Registration Act of 1874 gave a medical practitioner a statutory duty to issue, without fee, a certificate as to the cause of death; but the body did not have to be examined after death, except when cremation was the chosen means of disposal. It is possible that the neighbourhood layer-out certified death for many working-class families and informed the doctor who then issued the death certificate. Polson (1953) cites the case of insurance fraud carried out 24 times by two women over the death of a child. On the last occasion the doctor called to certify the death and found the 'dead' child playing in the garden! Rose (1986) discusses the role of the National Society for the Prevention of Cruelty to Children (NSPCC), the media, insurance companies and the trade unions in the controversy which surrounded the issue of infanticide for the sake of the burial insurance at the end of the nineteenth century.

There were no legal requirements as to the disposal of the body of stillborn infants. In 1919 Dr Snell reported that 'a midwife in attendance instructed a neighbour to put the body on the copper fire. Few people will consider that this procedure is unobjectionable'[8]. The behaviour of this midwife and neighbour could suggest that the life and body of the stillborn baby had little value; 'popular belief was that stillborn babies were not "proper" babies' (Oakley, 1979:44). One mother never got over the stillbirth of her last child, a boy, in 1936. Her oldest son, who was then fourteen, took the baby in an orange box to the Sexton of

Ansty church as the sun was setting. He waited, holding the baby until the sun was dipping behind the horizon before the Sexton would bury the box under a tree[6]. The body of a baby boy, aged four months, was taken to Mr Greenaway who used to make all the coffins for Foleshill. Mr Greenaway would place a baby's body into a coffin occupied by an adult body; the baby's funeral and burial were 'free'[6]. Sometimes the body of a stillborn baby would be taken to the cemetery and placed in the next coffin to be buried[6]. Roberts (1989) and Wilson and Levy (1938) refer to the practice of filling common graves with the bodies of stillborn infants.

The role of the neighbourhood layer-out was not inherited in Foleshill, for the women were not shown what to do by their mothers but seem to have been women who were known to be 'very efficient'[6], a 'very nice lady'[6] and 'spotlessly clean'[6]. They seem to have been the nurses and 'organisers' of the team of women who moved in to care for the sick. When a neighbour was ill or confined the other women 'moved in, someone took the toddlers, someone made a meal, someone did the washing, someone did the nursing or helped the midwife'[6]. Roberts (1986) refers to a similar pattern of behaviour in the working-class community in Preston between the wars. It seems possible that in Foleshill different roles were allotted to each woman by the other women in the team. The nomination of an older woman who was 'particularly authoritative on such matters as the "correct" way to deal with a birth or death' (Clark, 1982:168) was dependent on the neighbours' perception of her character, personality and reputation. A typical description was that the layer-out 'did anything to do with nursing if they couldn't cope. She'd that air of – if you were worried to death and didn't know what to do and all panicky, she'd walk in the door with that air of calm down, Auntie Lucy is in charge'[6].

'When there was trouble, anyone ill, they used to come for her'[6]. The layer-out was probably the first person contacted by others in the neighbourhood when they needed help. She was the first to learn of pregnancies and illness in a family. She knew her neighbours, knew who had the resources and was available to help. Richardson quotes from one of Audrey Linkman's respondents:

> 'You laid the person out, washed them and put them in a
> clean night shirt or whatever you could find – of your own if

they hadn't got anything. It didn't matter whose house it came from. And if my mother was just – you know, if there had been a rush on births and deaths, and she was out of some-thing, she would borrow on different houses and they came on kind of rotation. You didn't borrow off Old Mother Radcliffe, but you could borrow off Susy Radcliffe, who was younger and could replace quicker, you see. So you'd ask if she'd got anything clean to help such a body out. And that's how the street went on. I couldn't imagine it being done anywhere now. All right you get a lot more help, but there's nobody that was respected more in our street than my mother' (Chamberlain and Richardson, 1983:39).

Many of the rituals associated with laying out may be seen as 'a physical and social necessity, . . . imbued with spiritual over-tones', and to parallel many of the rituals associated with birth (Richardson, 1987:17). As soon after death as possible the limbs were straightened, pennies placed on the eyelids, the chin tied with a bandage, the legs tied together and the arms folded across the chest or stomach. In Staithes 'the first thing they did was go for the board – the lying-out board' (Clark, 1982:128). In Foleshill there does not seem to have been a special 'lying-out board' – sometimes a door was used, sometimes the undertaker brought a board. The origins of the lying-out board may perhaps be traced to the use of the parish coffin which had almost disap-peared by the beginning of the eighteenth century[14]. Litten sug-gests that 'a plank was placed beneath the corpse to facilitate its transfer from the coffin to the grave' (1991:124). The use of pen-nies on the eyes probably parallels the use of pennies in the linen binder on the navel of the new-born baby. Tying the legs or feet together also made moving the body easier, prevented the spirit walking and perhaps parallels the tight wrapping of the new-born infant.

The body was then left for an hour, with the windows open to permit the soul to escape along with any unpleasant odours of the sick room. The body was washed, all orifices plugged includ-ing the vagina in women and the penis tied in men, the hair brushed and combed, a man shaved, finger nails cleaned. Sometimes a relative was present to help lift and move a heavy body. One layer-out liked a relative to be present 'so they wouldn't think she'd taken anything; but sometimes they couldn't look and would go and hide in the wardrobe'[6]. The corpse was made clean, presentable and odourless for its viewing by friends and relatives.

The body was dressed in a clean nightgown or night shirt. Women who died soon after or before marriage were often dressed in their wedding gowns. A bride-to-be was 'laid out most beautifully in her bridal clothes'[6]. Some had 'special things'[6], ie. a gown, lace veil for the face, white stockings and gloves; 'burial gowns were beautiful, a bit like christening gowns, all tucked, lace and ribbons'[6]. The undertaker might supply the shroud. This would be plain white for members of the Church of England, unlike Roman Catholic shrouds which had a religious picture sewn down the front, usually coloured, about 18 inches long and 6 inches wide, and rosettes around the neck[6]. Men were sometimes dressed in their best suit; a clergyman was dressed in his vestments[6]. Clark suggests that in Staithes 'in common with the practice in many other areas and classes of society, the material was usually purchased well in advance' (1982:128); but in Foleshill the body was usually dressed in a clean gown, sometimes borrowed from neighbours as these working-class families did not have the resources for special clothing.

The task seems to have been performed with 'a lot of compassion and care, making them nice for wherever they are going'[6]. One respondent recalled the pride of her mother as they watched the cortege passing down the street, 'it was her work'[6]. After the laying out, the body was placed, in the coffin, in the front room or parlour. In the small two-up, two-down working-class houses of Foleshill with steep, narrow stairs, getting the coffin up and downstairs could pose problems. Sometimes the windows were removed and the coffin with the body lowered from the window, 'a lot of the dignity of death went out of the window'[6]; or reluctant male relatives might be persuaded to help carry the body downstairs[6].

Friends and relatives would call to pay their last respects to the deceased. Richardson suggests that the practices of viewing and touching the body 'addressed themselves mainly to the state of mind of those left behind . . . and were thought to help grief' (1987:26). Some informants remembered going to view a body as school children. One 3-year-old girl was very impressed by the purple pom-poms which lined the edge of a child's coffin and wanted these for her own coffin[6]; but another girl, aged 9, who went to pay her last respects to her friend Queenie 'didn't and doesn't want to see anyone else'[6].

The practice of placing the coffin in the front room was 'not very pleasant in them days, 'cos if you'd got no hall entrance you had to come in that way'[6]. Bodies could become quite objectionable, especially in the summer months, and were sometimes removed from the home to be kept in the carriage master's stables[6]. Many different factors mediate the social management of death including the physical location and circumstances of death (housing, war, infectious diseases) and technological developments. Since World War 2 hospitals, public mortuaries and funeral directors have used refrigeration to preserve and store bodies while the retention of the body in the front room has perhaps become more impractical with the widespread installation of central heating since the 1960s.

The neighbourhood layer-out often prepared the house, tea and sandwiches for the mourners on their return from the funeral. One had 'special crockery' kept in a laundry basket[6]; another had 'old silver plated cutlery' which was loaned for the funeral tea[6]; and some lent the mourners their best clothes so that they had some decent clothes to go to the funeral[6]. This borrowing may be part of the 'significant borrowing service' described by Roberts (1986:191). The debt owed to the neighbourhood layer-out for her care of the body, the preparation of the funeral tea and the loan of crockery could be considerable. The high status given to the neighbourhood layer-out by working-class wives and mothers may be interpreted as the social recognition of this debt and perhaps accounts for the nomination of this woman on the basis of her character, personality and reputation by women who did not have female kin living in close physical proximity.

'The evidence with regard to payment is contradictory' (Chamberlain and Richardson, 1983:40). Some were sure their mothers were paid a few shillings[6], one that her mother charged 1/- for laying out and another 1/- for preparing the funeral tea[6], although payment was not always forthcoming[6]. A retired undertaker remembered that his father 'used to give them a few shilling as it helped him a bit'[6]. One layer out was once given 10/- by an undertaker[6]. Some were paid in kind, ie. a bucket of coal[6], 'a nice little parcel with a supper of fish and chips as no-one was wealthy and they knew she wouldn't take money'[6]. One layer-out was always paid in kind, for her husband was known as a 'boozer' and the neighbours knew he would spend any cash she was given on drink[6]. Several informants were convinced that 'their mothers never took money, not a penny'[6]. Some of the neighbourhood layers-out also participated in 'unofficial' economic activity which did not necessarily correspond with payment for laying out. Laying out can therefore be considered as a form of casual work, a form of reciprocity in the working-class borrowing service or a task of love.

According to Morley, payment was introduced by undertakers and the wealthy in the late nineteenth century as laying-out came to be seen as a distasteful task performed by 'incompetent, drunken, snuff-taking hired nurses, who specialised in both midwifery and laying out' (1971:24). However payment for laying-out may have a longer history, as the Poor Law records of the parish of Whitchurch, near Warwick record the payment of 4/- to two women for laying out Mrs James Kemson in January 1771[15]. In Foleshill the average charge during the 1920s and 1930s seems to have been between one and two shillings. The changes in the level of payment for laying-out may reflect changing attitudes to the corpse. Leaney suggests that the language of those advocating cremation at the end of the nineteenth and early twentieth century sought to 'alter popular perceptions of death' by manipulating the 'feeling of intense loathing for the physical remains of the dead' (1989:129). It is possible that as the dead body came to be associated with putrefaction and physical decay, the task of laying-out came to be seen as distasteful. Therefore, the role of the layer-out had less value and status.

Richardson argues that Morley's description of the layer out is a 'gross libel on these women' (Chamberlain and Richardson, 1983:39) who were often much loved and respected members of their community. One was described as 'an angel on earth who was with me day and night in all my trouble'[6]. In fact, Waerness points out that 'attitudes combining personal attachment and payment in a relation are mainly found among working-class women' (1984:204). Payment in cash or kind between working-class women who were members of the same network of actual social relations functioned as a means of maintaining reciprocity in which social care was exchanged for cash or goods. Roberts (1986) suggests that payment was one way of sharing limited resources between kin.

Yet the idea that payment was a form of reciprocity in the exchange of social care does not account for the care taken by some of these women of their appearance and personal hygiene before going to attend a laying-out or preparing the funeral tea.

Roberts suggests that for working-class people their neighbour-hood meant 'the street or possibly the small group of streets in which they lived' (1986:184). Perhaps the neighbourhood layer-out observing regular norms of behaviour was attending those outside her neighbourhood, her network of actual social rela-tions; she was 'booked' in advance to attend better-off members of the working class or the middle class. Some seem to have had a close working relationship with the undertaker. 'They sort of showed them how to do it, and helped them to set up in busi-ness'[6]. Sometimes the neighbourhood layer-out received 'back handers'[6] from the undertaker for calling in a particular firm after laying out the body. For these women, observing regular norms of behaviour, laying-out was a form of casual paid work; although the same women performed the same task, observing familiar norms of behaviour, for their neighbours. Naylor claims that 'laying out women . . . held key roles in connecting under-takers with their source of revenue' (1989:55). She argues that laying-out women disappeared as the demand for 'professional people' increased and as the women priced themselves out of the market by working for the undertaker who gave them the best price. This suggests that the demand for the authoritative older woman who knew the 'correct' way to deal with death declined.

### The eclipse of the neighbourhood layer-out

Since the introduction of the National Health Service in 1948 the provision of health care has centred on the hospital (Stacey, 1988). This is an institutional setting facilitating the enforcement of an occupational hierarchy subordinate to male medical authority (Versluysen, 1981). Moreover, the course of many ill-nesses, particularly acute infections, has changed with the use of antibiotics. Women have less practical experience of home nurs-ing, less knowledge of nursing care which underpinned the knowledge of how to lay out the dead.

The welfare services 'have not first and foremost replaced informal caring, but instead gradually changed its content, as an increasing number of professional educators, advisors and consul-tants have invaded the private sphere' (Waerness, 1984:187). In the early part of the twentieth century, in response to concerns about high infant mortality rates, inspectors from the NSPCC and health visitors employed by local authorities[16] visited working-class mothers in their homes to teach them how to care for their children. After 1948 home nursing of the sick was increasingly supervised and undertaken by the professionally trained female district nurse. 'Women were employed in their own right, using their specially trained skills to help other women but also to monitor and control them' (Stacey, 1988:114). Homes were invaded by experts who questioned the working-class woman's practical experience of care, the basis of the rationality of care which informed her caring activity. The working-class woman probably came to understand that her knowledge of care was inadequate; professional training based on the scientific rationality of care was required to care for the sick. The rationality of care, which had informed the caring activity of the neighbourhood layer-out, came to be seen as inadequate for the home nursing of the sick and the preparation of the dead body for its confinement in the coffin.

Several informants expressed feelings of revulsion and distaste when describing the customs associated with the social management of death during the interwar years; perhaps 'people were only too glad to have it taken out of their hands'[6]. It was not unusual for there to be a delay of a week or more between death and the funeral while relatives were informed and travelled to the funeral from other parts of the country. During this time the body, which could become quite objectionable despite being packed in dry ice, remained in the best room or front parlour, which in overcrowded working-class homes could not be shut off from the rest of the house. The 'smell of death'[6] pervaded the house. Many working class families probably welcomed the introduction of the Chapels of Rest, attached to the undertaker's premises in the early 1930s. The body could be removed from the house and could remain at the undertakers until the funeral. The final resting place of the body changed from the private sphere of the home, associated with the rationality of care, to the public sphere of the funeral director which was associated with scientific rationality.

'The poorer the individual, the lower in the social scale, the deeper his sense of guilt and shame if he cannot promise a decent interment for his relatives' (Wilson and Levy, 1938:64). Richardson (1987) provides an historical analysis of the working class family's desire for a respectable funeral. The provision of a decent interment probably begins with the correct preparation of the body for its confinement in the coffin. The task of caring for the dead body associated with putrefaction and decay (Leaney, 1980) was allegedly undertaken by 'incompetent, drunken, snuff-taking nurses' (Morley, 1971:24). The female neighbourhood layer-out had little value or status. Working class families may have feared that the dead body prepared by the female layer-out implied that they accorded little respect to the deceased. By contrast, a dead body prepared by the professionally trained male mortician[17] might reflect the higher status of scientific rationality and might signify that the family attributed considerable value to the deceased.

## Conclusion

The focus of this paper has been the centrality of the role of the neighbourhood layer-out within the context of informal care, organised by the working-class wives and mothers of Foleshill, Coventry, in response to economic insecurity, the absence of public welfare and the imperative to maintain their self respect. Many different factors mediated the declining importance of the role of the neighbourhood layer-out in working-class communities and the displacement of the site of dying and death during the years preceding and following the Second World War. The site of death was transferred from the private sphere of the home associated with women and the rationality of care to the public sphere of the hospital, hospice and mortuary associated with male scientific rationality. Changing attitudes towards the value and status of the rationality of care and the higher value given to scientific rationality legitimated and justified the displacement of the site of death for many members of the working class.

## Notes

Part of this paper was presented to the Leicester Symposium on Death and Dying, Leicester University, November 1991.

1 The twelve informants, the daughters of neighbourhood layers-out, were self-selected in the sense that they replied to my inquiry about laying-out in the local paper. These semi-structured interviews were conducted in the informants' homes. Patterns of informal care of the 1920s and 1930s were also discussed with a group of fifteen women at a day centre for the elderly. Two retired funeral directors and one retired medical practitioner were also interviewed.

2 *Foleshill Union and Rural District Council Year Books* 1926–7 and 1928–9, held in Coventry City Library.

3 Carr, F.W., (1978), *Engineering Workers and the Rise of Labour in Coventry 1914–1939*, University of Warwick: Unpublished PhD Thesis. In 1921 the average age of men and women in Coventry was 29 years, and in Foleshill 26 years; the majority were unmarried.

4 *Coventry Standard*, April 4th 1931.

5 Sprout, R., (1984), *Reminiscences of Red Lane*. An unpublished document held in Coventry City Library. Red Lane was a street in Foleshill with two-up, two-down terraced houses on one side with the Ordnance Works on the other. The author recalls refusing an invitation to visit an apprentice he worked with as 'I mean, me from Red Lane mixing with someone from Belvedere Road was out altogether'; and that they 'had to go to the Board of Guardians for food tickets' in the summer when the men working in the car trade were 'laid off'.

6 The quotes are taken from taperecorded semi-structured interviews with informants who for reasons of confidentiality remain anonymous in this paper.

7 Red Lane Residents Association, 1983, *Red Lane Reminiscences*, Coventry Resource and Information Service. After 1911, Nurse Gaskin was responsible for the physical and moral welfare of the women employed by Courtaulds. She 'ran Courtaulds . . . they were really frightened of her'. In one working-class home 'brother Bill slept downstairs after three years of age, and was never allowed upstairs with the girls'.

8 *Coventry Public Health Reports*, 1900–1939, held in Coventry City Library. Dr Snell was appointed as fulltime Medical Officer of Health in 1897 at an annual salary of £500, a post he held until his retirement in 1930.

9 The Labour Party, (1927), *The Labour Party and The Nursing Profession*, a report held in the Fawcett Library, City of London Polytechnic.

10 *Spennell's Directory of the City of Coventry & District* 1919–1920, Birmingham: Percival Jones Ltd. and *Kelly's Directory of the City of Coventry & District* 1929 and 1935–36, Addlestone, Surrey: Coombelands Press Ltd.

11 Ministry of Health, (1923), *The Training of Midwives*, London: H.M.S.O., held at the Fawcett Library, City of London Polytechnic.

12 In 1922 poor relief in Coventry was one third of the average provided by County Boroughs. A couple with two children would receive a maximum of 25/- compared with 44/6 plus fuel and rent for a similar couple in Poplar, London (Carr, 1978).

13 *Coventry Charity Organisation City and Society Reports*, 1907–1928, held in Coventry City Library. The society gave 8 and 7 funeral grants in 1922 and 1923 respectively. These decisions seem to have been challenged, as their Annual Report of 1923 states: 'Funeral Grants, a class of application which is seldom easy to meet, few societies include these in their scope of operation. The only class assisted was occasionally that of Ex-service Men and their dependents'. Perhaps some of the Society's workers saw Ex-servicemen as 'deserving' poor; but the questioning of the decision suggests that the poor can be expected to make provision for a 'decent' funeral. The Society's annual report of 1927 includes descriptions of 'The Casual', 'The Genuine Seeker of Work', 'The Habitual Casual', and 'The Well Dressed and Well-

mannered Casual', and suggests that it would appropriate for the committee not to assist applicants falling into these categories. They were the unemployed ablebodied, the 'undeserving' poor.

14 One respondent, a Yorkshire miner, remembers a laying-out board being kept in the village pub, where it often featured in the Saturday night entertainment of the young men!

15 *Poor Law Records*, 1772–73, Parish of Whitchurch, held in the Warwick Country Record Office.

16 Miss M. Strover was appointed health visitor in Coventry in 1905. Her duties included supervising the work of the midwives and inspecting their bags.

17 Mr A., a retired undertaker, attended an embalming course, taught by American lecturers, in London in the mid-1930s. He was the first qualified embalmer to practise in Coventry just before the Second World War and became a founder member of the British Institute of Embalmers.

# References

Anspach, R.A., (1987), 'Prognostic Conflict in Life and Death Decisions' in *Journal of Health and Social Behaviour*, Vol. 28. September.

Ariès, P., (1975), *Western Attitudes toward Death*, London: The John Hopkins University Press.

Bott, E., (1971), *Family and Social Network*, London: Tavistock.

Bulmer, M., (1986), *Neighbours: The Work of Philip Abrams*. Cambridge: Cambridge University Press.

Castle, J., 'Factory Work for Women' in Lancaster, B. and Mason, T., (eds), *Life and Labour in a Twentieth Century City*, University of Warwick: Cryfield Press.

Chamberlain, M. and Richardson, R., (1983), 'Life and Death', in *Oral History*. 11(1) Spring.

Crowther, M.A., (1981), *The Workhouse System 1834–1929*, Athens, Georgia: University of Georgia Press.

Crump, J., (1986), 'Recreation in Coventry between the Wars' in Lancaster, B. and Mason, T., (eds), *Life and Labour in a Twentieth Century City*, University of Warwick: Cryfield Press.

Dalley, G., (1988), *Ideologies of Caring*, London: MacMillan.

Davidson, C., (1982), *A Woman's Work is never done*, London: Chatto and Windus.

Finch, J. and Groves, D., (eds), (1983), *A Labour of Love: Women, Work and Caring*, London: Routledge and Kegan Paul.

Graham, H., (1983), 'Caring: a labour of love' in Finch, J. and Groves, D., (eds), *A Labour of Love: Women, Work and Caring*, London: Routledge and Kegan Paul.

Graham, H., (1991), .'The Concept of Caring in Feminist Research', in *Sociology*, 26:1.

Haggis, J., (1990), 'The feminist research process', in Stanley, L., (ed), *Feminist Praxis*, London: Routledge.

Lancaster, B., (1986), 'Who's a real Coventry kid?' in Lancaster, B. and Mason, T., (eds), *Life and Labour in a Twentieth Century City*, University of Warwick: Cryfield Press.

Lancaster, B. and Mason, T., (1986), 'Society and Politics in Twentieth Century Coventry', in Lancaster, B. and Mason, T., (eds), *Life and Labour in a Twentieth Century City*, University of Warwick: Cryfield Press.

Leaney, J., (1989), 'Ashes to Ashes: Cremation and Celebration of Death in Nineteenth Century Britain', in Houlbrooke, R., (ed.), *Death, Ritual and Bereavement*, London: Routledge.

Lewis, J., (1984), *Women in England 1870–1950*, Brighton, Sussex: Wheatsheaf Books Ltd.

Lewis, J. and Meredith, B., (1988), *Daughters Who Care: Daughters Caring for their Mothers at Home*, London: Routledge.

Litten, J., (1991), *The English Way of Death*, London: Robert Hale Ltd.

Morley, J., (1971), *Death, Heaven and the Victorians*, London: Studio Vista.

Naylor, M.J.A., (1989), *The Funeral; Death Rituals in a Northern City*, Unpublished PhD Thesis: University of Leeds.

Oakley, A., (1979), 'Wisewomen and Medicine Man: Changes in the Management of Childbirth', in Mitchell, J. and Oakley, A., (eds), *The Rights and Wrongs of Women*, Harmondsworth, Middlesex: Penguin Books.

Polson, C.J., (1953), *The Disposal of the Dead*, London: English Universities Press Ltd.

Richardson, R., (1987), *Death, Dissection and the Destitute*, London: Routledge, Kegan Paul.

Roberts, E., (1986), *A Woman's Place*, Oxford: Basil Blackwell.

Roberts, E., (1989), 'The Lancashire Way of Death' in Houlbrooke, R., (ed.), *Death, Ritual and Bereavement*, London: Routledge.

Rose, L., (1986), *The Massacre of the Innocents*, London: Routledge and Kegan Paul.

de Runz, I., (1986), 'The Knowledge of God is among Old Women', in *Civilisations* 36:1/2.

Smale, R., (1985), *Deathwork: A Sociological Analysis of Funeral Directing*, Unpublished PhD Thesis: University of Surrey.

Smith, F., (1946), *Coventry – Six Hundred Years of Municipal Life*, Corporation of the City of Coventry.

Stacey, M., (1988), *The Sociology of Health and Healing*, London: Unwin Hyman Ltd.

Versluysen, M.C., (1981), 'Midwives, medical men and "poor women labouring of child": lying-in hospitals in eighteenth century London", in Roberts, H., (ed.), *Women, Health and Reproduction*, London: Routledge and Kegan Paul.

Waerness, K., (1984), 'The Rationality of Caring' in *Economic and Industrial Democracy*, 5:185–211.

Whaley, J., (1981), (ed.), *Mirrors of Mortality*, London: Europa Publications.

Williamson, B., (1982), *Class, Culture and Community*, London: Routledge and Kegan Paul.

Wilson, A. and Levy, H., (1938), *Burial Reform and Funeral Costs*, London: Oxford University Press.

# Cremation or burial? Contemporary choice in city and village

## *Peter Jupp*

Cremation was legalised in England in 1884 but the English preference for cremation is a post-1945 phenomenon. In 1939, 3.8 per cent of English funerals involved cremation, by 1945 7.8 per cent. In 1967, cremations exceeded burials for the first time. By 1991, 70 per cent of funerals involved cremation.

The field-work discussed in this chapter was part of a wider study: the first full-length reconstruction of the history of the change from burial to cremation in the English disposal of the dead (Jupp, 1993). The study sought to explain how the funeral rites of passage – so conservative in nature – had changed, and changed so swiftly. It examined the conditions under which England became the first Western society to adopt cremation so extensively.

The investigation is important for sociology for at least two reasons. Firstly, attitudes to the physical body may be interpreted as metaphors of attitudes to wider social arrangements; major changes in the practice of the disposal of the human dead may therefore offer a critical lens to examine aspects of changed attitudes to other social institutions. Secondly, 150 years ago, communal rites surrounding the disposal of the dead were far more complex, involving procedures concerning religion, the community, gender roles and the family. Simpler procedures for the disposal of the dead may offer insights into the changing importance of these social institutions.

The overall thesis of this study suggested that one earlier but critical factor in the change from burial to cremation was the transfer from Church to local government of significant responsibilities in the disposal of the dead (Curl, 1980; Brooks, 1989; Jupp, 1990). Other significant factors affecting social attitudes towards dying, death and funeral practices include: changes in health care and provision; changes in residential patterns and rearrangements of forms of communal solidarity; popular religious belief and official Church doctrine; the rationalisation of the funeral directing industry. For all of these reasons, the examination of changes in recent funeral practice is now receiving increasing scholarly attention.

This chapter is concerned, however, not so much with institutional and external pressures promoting the adoption of cremation as with the decisions made at family level by individual families about specific family funerals. From a wide range of questions in structured interviews, it focusses upon one particular decision, the choice between burial and cremation. It presents a partial analysis of the interview data collected from two small samples of bereaved families in an urban and a rural location in the East Midlands. The overall evidence suggests that with the availability of a choice in disposal and the dilution of religious and communal pressures upon funeral decisions, a family's main priorities in funeral and disposal choice are family identity and practical family convenience. The data also offers a tentative hypothesis of the factors determining disposal choice, from which a larger-scale study might proceed.

## Methodology

The fieldwork began with the expectation that a rural-urban comparison would indicate different stages of the trend towards cremation. Useful comparisons might be drawn between disposal choices made by bereaved families in cities and those in villages; also between communities where cremation facilities had long existed and those where such facilities had only recently become available. Cremation choice is clearly only possible where crematoria are accessible. In the event, village respondents included a proportion of London incomers, long familiar with cremation, with whom in-village comparisons could fruitfully be made. (Contrasts between locals maintaining burial and incomers choosing cremation were illustrated in a North Yorkshire fishing village by Clark, 1982). The Fenland village of Fensham, where I had personal contacts, and the city of Leicester were chosen as offering clear contrasts. In each case, it was my intention to contact next-of-kin to investigate decisions taken about family funerals, when deaths had occurred within 12 to 18 months before the interview.

## The rural sample

Fensham (a pseudonym) has a population of about 4,000. Its economy was predominantly agricultural until the last 20 years when new housing developments have encouraged retired people and some commuters.

Burial was the only practical option for the disposal of the dead of Fensham until a crematorium was built at Peterborough in 1959. Before that date, Fensham families choosing cremation had to travel far, to Cambridge or Kettering (where crematoria were opened in 1939 and 1950 respectively). Fensham funeral directors say that cremation was rare before 1959. The cremation rate for Cambridgeshire was well above the national average in 1960 (see below) but Cambridge was too far from Fensham in an era of limited car ownership. As for burial facilities, the Fensham parish churchyard has recently been declared full but is open for ash-internments. The Parish Council Cemetery was opened 60 years ago and had many spaces left. The proximity of churchyard and cemetery facilitates mourners' visits to graves with ease and safety.

Personal contacts supplied me with the names of all the 37 people in the parish who had died within a given 12-month period in 1988–89. 34 of the 37 bereaved families involved granted me an interview. All the families save one allowed tape-recording. The interview was fairly strictly based upon a formal questionnaire, which was identical with that used in the city. This questionnaire had four sections: biographical details of the interviewee and the deceased; the circumstances of the death; the decisions and arrangements for the funeral; and experiences of deaths and attitudes towards a range of death issues. It thus covered a wide range of decisions and attitudes, into which context burial/cremation choice could be set.

## The urban sample

Leicester was especially suitable as a location because in 1902 the city had built the second municipal crematorium in England. Thus, not only was there a local authority preference for cremation, but four successive generations of Leicester people had the opportunity to make a burial/cremation choice. It therefore provided a good comparison with Fensham in terms of longterm availability of choice.

The construction of an urban interview sample in a community offered more problems than at Fensham. It was clear that, with 8,000 annual deaths in the city, a random sample was needed. The small number of personal interviews possible would clearly be inadequate for a quantitative study, but might prove appropriate for a qualitative study, seeking to suggest categories within which funeral decisions might be systematised.

The local contacts at Fensham were not available in Leicester. Thus the most direct way of contact with bereaved families was by access to the specific death certificates. I had originally sought to select my sample from one city ward, but the city's death registers are not compiled according to ward-boundaries. The registers contain the names of all who die within the city boundary. Within these boundaries there are, on average, 15 deaths each day: these deaths are registered in any one of eight registers and are not on public display, so that individual certificates have to be ordered by name and purchased.

The possession of death certificates was thus crucial for a random sample of bereaved families. Other major sources of information, like newspapers, were far less useful. Newspaper obituaries contain only a *selection* of funerals. Funeral directors, like cemetery and crematoria authorities, are generally reluctant to release details of clients, even if it could be established that a particular business or a particular cemetery/crematorium was representative of popular choice. The most direct way to obtain the least biassed random sample was through the death certificates.

Death certificates contain critical information about the deceased: the name, age, occupation, birth and death dates, cause and location of death etc. Even more important, they contain the name and address of the informant (*usually*, but not always, the next of kin) with whom a contact for an interview could be made.

Establishing contact with potential informants, allowing for refusals, necessitated the identification of a series of 40 death certificates. I chose to seek for deaths over a two-week period and in a selected month (choosing one of the months of highest mortality) to enable widest selection and to minimise distortion of mortality by seasonal variation. My choice of year was to match that for Fensham. The choice of month was to ensure that, for the sake of increasing the responsiveness of families to the request for interviews, the first anniversary of the death had passed and that that anniversary did not coincide with major public holidays (like Christmas) when sad memories might be compounded with the pressure of family events.

The series had first to be constructed, because the only available public document is the Index to the year's death certificates. The Index contains the year's deaths in alphabetical order, each name accompanied by a certificate number. I established initial points for the commencement of possible series from newspaper obituaries, selected one register, calculated a numerical series of 40 names and purchased the relevant certificates. These gave me contact details for 40 deaths which had occurred in the city within a two-week period.

The families were all contacted in writing to request an interview. Out of the 31 families contacted, 24 agreed to be interviewed. Of the 24 completed interviews, 3 were with nursing-home staff, in the absence of surviving relatives.

## Initial results concerning disposal choice

Initial results revealed that the difference between disposal preference in the two populations was not so sharp as had been expected. Of the 34 Fensham funerals, 12 (35 per cent) involved burial and 22 (65 per cent) cremation. Of the 24 Leicester funerals, 5 (21 per cent) involved burial and 19 (79 per cent) cremation. This compares with a UK average for 1990 of 30 per cent burials and 70 per cent cremations. The Fensham figure was higher than expected. On this basis, the national trend towards cremation is well-established in city and in village (see Table 1).

**Table 1** Percentage of cremations in the Fensham and Leicester samples, with those for Cambridgeshire, Leicestershire and in England and Wales, 1960 and 1990

|  | 1960 | 1990 |
| --- | --- | --- |
| Fensham sample | Not known | 35% |
| Cambs. cremations | 64% | 78% |
| Leicester sample | Not known | 79% |
| Leics. cremations | 35% | 61% |
| England and Wales | 36% | 70% |

### An intriguing corrective

While the practice of cremation seems so well-established, a different picture emerges when the practice of interment of ashes is taken into account.

Of the 19 cremations in the 24 *Leicester* funerals, eight were followed by the internment of the ashes. Five were buried in existing graves (along with predeceased family members) and three placed in new graves in existing churchyards. Burial and cremation figures are usually calculated on the basis of *the mode of destruction* (burial or cremation). Thus, from one perspective we may say that five (21 per cent) of the funerals in the sample ended at the grave-side and 21 (79 per cent) at the crematorium. From the perspective of *final location of ashes*, however, buried bodies and interred ashes may be taken together, and distinguished from scattered ashes. Thus 13 (54 per cent) of the Leicester sample of deaths were finally disposed of *underground* (as coffined corpses or as interred ashes) whilst 11 (46 per cent) were deposited *above ground* (as scattered ashes).

Of the 22 cremations in the 34 *Fensham* funerals, 16 were followed by the scattering of ashes: 14 in the crematorium gardens, and two at other sites, chosen for personal associations, the North Sea and the New Forest. The remaining six were deposited in the local Fensham cemetery, five sets of ashes being interred and one scattered. Thus, in terms of the final location of human remains, 17 (50 per cent) of the Fensham dead were scattered above ground and 17 (50 per cent) buried below.

The placing of the dead has a social importance discussed, eg by Bloch (1971). Human societies often adjust to the loss of an individual group member by positing a belief in an after-life to which the dead may be ritually and safely transferred. The various modes of disposal provide a reference both to the survivors and to the other dead. Once buried, for example, the human body has a fixed location: it may be marked; it provides a locus for mourning and remembrance; it provides a focus for family identity. It provides opportunities for the bereaved to adjust to their new social situation (eg. as widow, orphan or heir). Churchyards and cemeteries present a concept of and a context for the human person which is both religious and, especially, communal. The private cemetery, by contrast, often intends to proclaim a social class identity, distinguished from the 'common mass' of the dead (French, 1975).

The introduction of cremation has offered new opportunities for the social use of human remains. Ashes are portable: so they may be brought and kept at home, where their purpose is for the sake of the individual bereaved (Thomas, 1975). They may however be taken and scattered, eg at some spot with special associations for the deceased: here the final disposal has a reference to the deceased as an individual, rather than as a member of a group. The implications of cremation in offering opportunities for secondary funerals are immense and deserve further attention (Davies; and Young and Cullen; both forthcoming).

This chapter will return below to the mode of disposal as symbolising the link between the deceased, the family and their local community. It is sufficient to note here that while as a mode of *funeral* the preference for cremation seems firmly established, on the basis of *final disposal*, the situation revealed by this small survey shows a more even balance (see Table 2).

**Table 2** Urban and rural sample

(a) mode of disposal by mode of funeral

|  | village | city |
|---|---|---|
| Cremation | 65% | 79% |
| Burial | 35% | 21% |

(b) final resting-place of remains

|  | village | City |
|---|---|---|
| Below ground | 50% | 52.5% |
| Above/upon ground | 50% | 47.5% |

This suggests the value of a far wider enquiry as to the final disposition of human remains. Such an enquiry might well reveal, *inter alia*, that the English preference for cremation may be more apparent than real.

## Determinants of disposal choice

Further analyses of burial/cremation choice were revealed by comparison of the survey populations, particularly with reference to five factors: age of deceased, type of death (eg sudden or anticipated), religious adherence, strength of community identity (natives or incomers) and social class. Considerations of space mean that only the last two have been chosen here for special attention.

### Natives and incomers: Fensham

Of the sample of 34, 25 (74 per cent) of the deceased were natives: born and bred in that area of the Fens. Of these 25, ten (40 per cent) were buried and 15 (60 per cent) were cremated. The nine incomers were all retired people and from the south east of England); two (22 per cent) were buried and seven (78 per cent) were cremated. These differences in a survey of this size are not necessarily representative, but they suggest that for natives, the burial tradition is still strong and that for incomers cremation is the norm (Table 3).

**Table 3** Fensham survey: disposal choice of natives and incomers (1988–9)

|  | Natives | Incomers |
| --- | --- | --- |
| Burial | 10 (40%) | 2 (22%) |
| Cremation | 15 (60%) | 7 (78%) |
| Total | 25 (100%) | 9 (100%) |

### Natives and incomers: Leicester

In the urban sample, the overall cremation preference of both natives and incomers is illustrated even more strongly (Table 4).

15 (83 per cent) of the 18 natives chose cremation, compared with four (67 per cent) of the six incomers. An indicative comment came from a farmer's daughter in a village within the city boundary:

**Table 4**

|  | Natives | Incomers |
| --- | --- | --- |
| Burial | 3 (17%) | 2 (33%) |
| Cremation | 15 (83%) | 4 (67%) |
| Total | 18 (100%) | 6 (100%) |

The incomers here don't use the cemetery, mind, they haven't got the roots like we have.

## Social class: Fensham

Respondents were generally reluctant to identify themselves with a specific social class. This paper has therefore allocated social class identity on the basis of occupation. When class was analysed by occupation, the sample revealed clear class differences in the disposal choice. 13 (38 per cent) of the Fensham deceased were middle class and 21 (62 per cent) working class. Funerals of middle-class individuals were more likely to have involved cremation than those of the working class. The middle-class funerals had preferred cremation, by 11 cremations (85 per cent) to two burials (15 per cent). By comparison, the working-class funerals were more equally divided, with ten burials (48 per cent) and 11 cremations (52 per cent) (Table 5).

**Table 5** Fensham sample: disposal choice according to class and geographical origin (funerals expressed as % of total funerals (34 = 100%)

|  | 21 working-class respondents | | | 13 middle-class respondents | | |
|---|---|---|---|---|---|---|
|  | natives | incomers | total | natives | incomers | total |
| Burial | 8 | 2 | 10 (29%) | 2 | 0 | 2 (6%) |
| Cremation | 8 | 3 | 11 (32%) | 7 | 4 | 11 (32%) |
| Total | 16 (47%) | 5 (15%) | 21 (62%) | 9 (26%) | 4 (12%) | 13 (38%) |

## Social class: Leicester

Analysed by occupation, 13 (54 per cent) of the Leicester deceased were working class and 11 (46 per cent) middle class. Both class groups preferred cremation to burial, 10/11 (91 per cent) of the middle-class respondents and 9/13 (69 per cent) of the working class choosing cremation (Table 6).

Of the ten working-class natives, eight (80 per cent) chose cremation. Of the eight middle-class natives, seven (87.5 per cent) chose cremation. Of the six incomers, four were middle-class and chose burial. The remaining two were both working-class and chose burial, both for reasons of religious association. The one was Catholic, the other Jewish. The native working class preferred cremation by a ratio of 4:1, the native middle class by a

**Table 6** Leicester sample: disposal choice according to class and geographical origin (funerals expressed as % of total funerals (24 = 100%)

|  | 13 working-class respondents | | | 11 middle-class respondents | | |
|---|---|---|---|---|---|---|
|  | natives | incomers | total | natives | incomers | total |
| Burial | 2 | 2 | 4 (17%) | 1 | 0 | 1 (4%) |
| Cremation | 8 | 1 | 9 (37.5%) | 7 | 3 | 10 (42%) |
| Total | 10 (42%) | 3 (12.5%) | 13 (54%) | 8 (33%) | 3 (12.5%) | 11 (46%) |

ratio of 7:1. This suggests that the native preference for cremation is well established in Leicester, and encourages the estimate that the Fensham data represents a picture of burial/cremation choice at an earlier stage. It is consistent with the view that the middle classes adopted cremation before the working classes.

We shall return to the importance of local association and class identity. At this stage we move to examine the reasons articulated by the respondents themselves as to their burial/cremation choice. What reasons were offered by the 58 sets of respondents?

**Reasons given for disposal choice**

Two introductory comments should be made. First, three external groups are often supposed to have a say in disposal choice: funeral directors, doctors, clergy or nursing home staff. All 55 sets of family-members interviewed said that the burial/cremation choice had been taken *before* the funeral director or clergyman had been contacted, ie, it was a decision taken within the family.

Secondly, 17 of the 55 families interviewed reported that the deceased had never discussed funeral choice with their families. Fensham respondents had either given 'clear directions' about their disposal choice (20/34 = 59 per cent) or had refused to discuss it (13/34 = 38 per cent). Leicester respondents, however, were less likely to refuse discussion altogether (4/21 = 20 per cent). 6/21 (30 per cent) had 'dropped hints' and 11/21 (50 per cent) given clear instructions.

If this sample should prove representative, a reason for the contrast may lie in differences in community structure and the opportunities for family contact and communal support. Questionnaire responses revealed that in the village, family mem-

bers live nearer and neighbours are more friendly. The consciousness that family and local support are available may provide
individuals with the underlying confidence that, when they should
die, family members will 'know what to do' and that neighbours
will support them. The attendance figures for funeral services and
the volume of messages of condolence received after the death
confirms that their trust was rewarded. In the city, by contrast,
the communal safety-net of support is threadbare. Neighbours,
especially, play only a minimal part in bereavement support,
which comes mainly from relatives and friends. Consequently city
dwellers, it is contended, know that they have to make known
their decisions about funeral choice well in advance.

## Reasons for choice: main themes

Asked to articulate their reasons for disposal choice, both for the
55 deceased and for themselves as survivors, the 55 responding
families gave a total of 41 different reasons, clusters of four of
which outweighed the others. 22 (19 in Fensham, three in
Leicester) sets of respondents spoke of *parental precedent*, 12 (six
in each population) spoke of choosing the same mode as their
*marriage partner*, 15 (all in Fensham) spoke of cremation choice
through *fear of the neglect of graves* and 11 (nine in Leicester,
two in Fensham) spoke of burial choice *to enable visiting and
grieving*. Religious preferences were rare.

## Active choice for burial

Of those deceased who had requested burial, what were the articulated reasons ascribed to them by the respondents?

### 1 Parental precedent

Five Fensham people had specifically chosen burial because their
parents had done so. Four were natives, but they included two
Catholics. (Catholics were not allowed cremation until 1965).
Four were over 80, which suggests their pro-burial attitudes were
formed long before the cremation facilities became available in
1959. Also, as the interviews revealed, the older they were,
the more burials they had attended at an earlier age. None was

occupationally upwardly mobile. In Leicester, only one man was buried expressly because his father had been: the farmer mentioned above. His daughter commented:

> He was buried like his parents. No-one in the family's been cremated. I have a double grave myself. I don't fancy cremation. It's so final.

## 2 The marital model

No one in the village had been buried expressly to be with their spouse, though the survey revealed that three were. In Leicester, there were two (including the Jewish family). Three city and two village couples had purchased a double grave – a form of spouse model.

No partners in Leicester had been buried when their spouse had been cremated, and *vice versa*. In Fensham, there were two. One was the widow of a former councillor who, having led a campaign to equalise burial fees in the cemetery, chose cremation for himself. She, a traditional Christian, had always wanted burial. In the second case, a wife had died suddenly shortly after moving to their retirement home. Although she had always requested cremation, her husband decided to have her buried, explaining that he had done this specifically to enable him to grieve.

> She wanted cremation and that's one thing I didn't do. I am pleased I had her buried. I have got somewhere to go. It's a nice cemetery. It takes time. It's two years and I'm just beginning to pull myself together.

One of those who was buried after the custom of his parents was a man in his fifties, killed suddenly in a car-crash. Funeral directors have commented that burial is often chosen by those widow(er)s or parents who suffer bereavement of those untimely or prematurely dead. Survivors seek a focus to accustom themselves to a death which has 'robbed' them of part of their future. Untimely death has been an increasing rarity in this century (especially since 1939) with improvements in health-care and nutrition (Winter, 1988). Its occurrence gives survivors a shock of grief, for which, unlike those with, for example, elderly parents, they are unprepared. Elaborate funeral ceremonies and marked graves can help these survivors' adjustment to their new and unexpected social role.

## 3 Visiting the graves

Those who choose burial may feel that they can count on their graves being visited by their survivors, especially by their immediate families. The graves of all seven villagers and four of the city-dwellers, who had requested burial, were regularly visited. (Christmas, Mothers' Day and Easter are very popular times). It was also clear that the grave functions for some survivors as a valid place for communication:

> I don't like this cremation. It's all out-of-sight, out-of-mind. I go down to the cemetery and I talk to my Mum.

## 4 Religious reasons

Three Catholics (two in Fensham) and one Jew (in Leicester) were among those requesting burial. Although the three Catholics were aware that cremation was now permitted, they preferred the traditional way. All three Catholics in the sample had an active belief in the after-life of the dead which affected their own behaviour.

> My husband thought that the spirit either went upstairs or downstairs. Cos we believe in Purgatory. I said (to him), you don't go up immediately, not unless you're a saint, and you're no saint. I don't think you are not that good that you go immediately to Heaven. I think you have got to atone for your sins. [Do you think Purgatory affects the way you behave?] Definitely, yes.

Attitudes among the five Anglican church-attenders were more vague. They focussed on the after-life as a reunion with former family members, although this is not a New Testament understanding of the next life (Rowell, 1974). For example:

> Yes, we think there is an after-life. She (the deceased) always thought she would meet her Dad and Mum and, er, she was a good-living woman, she would never harm anything, she'd give anything. She would say there was a better life than this one, we had to live a good life on this.

The vagueness was also discernible with her association of access to the next life with some moral qualification.

> She would say there was a better life than this one, we had to live a good life on this.

but added:

> She always thought there was good and evil in everyone. She always found the goodness in people [Did she believe in Hell?] She never really said a lot about Hell, no . . .

This comment is illustrative of a tendency identified by Martin and Pluck (1977) that Christianity has adopted the secular optimistic tone of the age:

> There is a persistent tendency . . . to select the optimistic and comforting elements in the conventional Christian package and to reject or ignore the uncomfortable . . . God is . . . rather like a non-judgemental social worker . . . (who) would never really punish, so hell, the devil, the everlasting fire do not have any very salient place in the general cosmology (Pluck, 1977:21–22)

The choice of burial need not be associated with the religion of the survivor. The Jew's son had lapsed from the faith and saw no connection between the mode of disposal and the quality of after-life enjoyed by the deceased. While few in the sample explicitly disavowed any such connection, the general impression was that neither the funeral nor the mode of disposal had any effect upon the existence or character of an after-life for the deceased. None of the sample of 55 entertained any notion of the traditional Christian doctrine of the resurrection of the body. Yet none was so frank as the Leicester farmer:

> I don't know what we have funerals for. It's just a family get-together. They haven't a religious significance.

## Active choice for cremation

### 1 Parental model
Six *Fensham* respondents gave the parental precedent as the reason for cremation choice. Yet five subsidiary factors were also

revealed:

(a) All six were incomers, from London. They had no local roots in the village which a grave might have emphasised or retained or which would have been readily accessible to relatives. Their parents had all been cremated.

(b) The ashes of all save one were scattered. This is consistent with their absence of local roots and the distance of family survivors.

(c) Four had either no children, or children living at a distance, ie the maintenance of a grave would either be neglected or impose a burden upon distant relatives.

(d) Five had no Church connections or pressing religious reasons for burial choice. The only practising Christian of the six had interred his wife's ashes in the Churchyard, perhaps to help him grieve her sudden death; his own beliefs in an after-life were non-specific.

(e) There are indicators of upward social mobility with four of the families. This is in line with the suggestion that cremation is sought by the upwardly mobile, partly because in the pursuit of ambition they are likely to be geographically mobile and rely less upon loyalty to locality and kin.

In Leicester, none of the deceased had been cremated for the stated reason that their parents had been cremated. Yet it was implicit in the testimony of one widower:

> Members of both our families have been cremated for so many years that anything else seems quaint.

The significance of this category lies in the operation of a different choice from parents. Six respondents who had asked for cremation had buried their parents. These six provide an opportunity for the analysis of change.

In the Leicester sample, there was no 'London effect' and the directions of class mobility were mixed. Four other factors seemed more important.

(a) None of the six deceased had any active religious adherence. Two had been Nonconformists at an earlier age. Nonconformists had lost their proprietorial interest in maintaining burial grounds long before Anglicans and Catholics (Jupp, 1990).

(b) All save one were retired people, no longer economically active in the community, and dependent upon their otherwise independent offspring. Only two of the funerals were well-attended: both those of local business-owners, working up to the time of their death.

(c) All, save one childless couple, had children living locally.
(d) Five out of the six had their ashes interred.

A Fensham–Leicester comparison suggests two significant factors behind the choice of interment of ashes, in the absence of religious conviction and of significant class-identity. These are, first, the local origins of the deceased and, secondly, the local proximity of surviving children. We saw earlier that the portable nature of ashes offered further choices. In the Leicester cases, interred ashes may thus be characterised as a half-way house between burial and cremation. While the cremation choice evades the charge of being old-fashioned or 'quaint', ash-internment serves three functions: it marks local identity, enables convenient access for family visiting, and affords minimal and inexpensive responsibility for maintenance.

In Fensham, the incomers were already distanced from their families and birth-place. Upwardly-mobile natives seemed to be demonstrating their achievements in breaking free from the limitations of family and birth-place by choosing cremation. The scattering of cremated remains is the ultimate symbol of freedom and independence, both from kin, kind and locality. In Leicester, however, the survivors seem less concerned to break links with family and locality: the internment of cremated ashes enables them to have the best of both worlds. It is further suggested that the Leicester natives who chose ash internment represent an intermediate stage in the movement from burial practice to cremation: a transitional stage where *local but urban* families choose cremation for the first time, demonstrating the abiding strength of local and family links by the combination of both modes of disposal.

## 2 The marital model

The general rule was that marital partners usually chose the same mode of disposal as their partners. A double grave clearly bears images of the marital double bed. Yet partners can clearly share partnership in cremation. Five of the widowed in Fensham and three in Leicester had specifically requested cremation because their partner had previously been cremated. The only common characteristic was that each of the eight couples was retired.

The preference for similar choice in disposal may be illustrated by its opposite. One couple had had an unhappy marriage. The widower made a deliberate gesture of reconciliation by choosing to be buried alongside his predeceased wife. Two further comments may be made. First, since the wider incidence of divorce following 1945, cremation is the one means of solving the etiquette problem of how the claims of rival partners for company in disposal may be solved. Second, divorce and re-marriage also contribute to breaking ties of kinship and locality, two of the major ties symbolised by burial and on-site memorialisation.

*3 Neglect of graves*

Four of the Fensham deceased, but none of those from Leicester, had chosen cremation because they feared graves would be neglected. One of the Fensham widows related this concern directly with the doubt that family members might be unwilling or unable to visit or maintain the grave:

My mother preferred cremation because she imagined that her children would move away . . . My Dad died and he was buried, and Mum bought the piece of ground near him, to be buried, but when it came to it, she didn't want it to be burial, she wanted cremation, because my brother, he still lives down (names village) she imagined, well, he won't always live there, after he done working.

It's difficult to visit and that's really a reason why we've had it [cremation] because you don't know . . . what's going to happen to your families when they're gonna move, do you? Now my husband's parents, they both got buried at Fensham Church . . . we don't visit as much as we should.

This woman had moved from the village after her husband's death. Both longevity and opportunities for relocation on retirement are characteristics of our contemporary society. Both inhibit traditional practices of visiting parental graves. Grave 'tending' is regarded as the responsibility of partners and children. Where survivors or children are distant, cremation offers the tidier choice. One Leicester native expressed her intention for cremation precisely because of the traditional expectation:

> We don't want our children to have to go to the cemetery. Parents should learn to let their children go . . . I don't want my sons tied by having to look after our graves.

### 4 Grave-tending

Ashes, when interred, provide a focus for grief. Five of the families where the deceased had chosen cremation spoke of the comfort given them by visiting the interred ashes. All had buried the ashes in an accessible place as a focus or a lens for a continuing relationship. One survivor spoke of the everyday domestic concerns which she could take to the grave-side:

> I often go up to the grave to speak to my husband. Whenever I needed help with anything, I went up and talked to my husband about it. We had a cat. It got lost, for days. Well, I was desperate. I went up to the grave and talked with my husband about it. I told him. Well, later that night, I went down and found that cat in the kitchen. I often ask my husband, 'I say, you've got to help me.'

## Burial/Cremation choice: provisional conclusions

At this stage, some provisional conclusions may be offered. Taking the 58 respondents altogether, it is observable that incomers are more likely to choose cremation than natives, and middle class than working class. The lingering burial choice tends to be associated with working-class identity, local roots and adherence to a religion traditionally stipulating burial. Cremation choice tends to be associated with middle-class identity, incomer status and, if there is a religious identity, adherence to a religion which accepts cremation.

The overall trend is towards cremation: 11 families of the 58 indicated that while the previous generation of their family had been buried, their own had been cremated. No families professed the reverse. The class analysis suggests that the English middle class had adopted cremation before the working class. Given the greater geographical mobility displayed by the middle class, the preference of incomers for cremation is not surprising.

186      

## Illuminating the transition

Of the two communities, Fensham is revealed as a community still in transition from burial to cremation. It may therefore offer evidence as to the reasons for the transference to cremation, evidence which will be less discernible in Leicester where the cremation precedent was set within families one or two generations ago. Two particular characteristics of the native Fensham respondents may illuminate some aspects of the transition.

## Fensham survivors (1) widows and widowers

The 34 village deaths left behind as relicts: one parent, three brothers/sisters, nine widowers and ten widows. Attention will be paid to the widows and widowers.

Of the nine widowers, three were Fensham natives. All three wives were buried. Their choice of burial illuminates three of the best-known reasons for burial. The first was a practising Catholic. The second was a traditional villager, having been born lived and died at addresses on the same street all her long life. The third, mentioned above, had always requested cremation but her husband had her buried to facilitate his own grieving.

Of the ten widows, six were Fensham natives. Only one of the six husbands was buried: the one who had died suddenly in a traffic accident. The remaining five had had all been retired, and all were cremated. All the widows (unlike the widowers) had made plans for their own funerals: they would follow their husbands' model.

Of the five local widows whose husbands had been cremated, one had moved from the immediate area after the funeral. Neither she nor her children counted themselves any longer as members of the village community.

The remaining four reveal one common factor. Each had experienced a difficult time looking after their ill or dying husbands. The periods of terminal illness had proved physically and mentally exhausting for the survivors. In each of these cases, the hypothesis first advanced by the Fultons (1971) seems to fit. The Fultons suggested that the advanced medical treatment now available for the ill and dying, especially combined with the hospitalization often necessary for such treatment, has effected a shift of focus in a family's attention around the time of death. Three generations ago, with deaths taking place at home and elaborate post-mortem mourning procedures still in place, the (local) funeral was the watershed of the death process. By contrast, contemporary death can often prove a long-drawn-out process, for pain and dying can both be medically controlled. The about-to-be-bereaved, in Sudnow's phrase (1967), become worn out by care and duty in their home nursing and their hospital visits. As a result, the death becomes the climax. For the exhausted family, tensions released and energies depleted, the ensuing funeral can only be an anti-climax. The undertaker is directed to 'keep the funeral simple'. Cremation with scattering and without memorial offers the simplest form of disposal. (See Walter, 1990 and Davies, forthcoming, for other forms of memorial activities.)

## Fensham Survivors (2) Children

Of the 34 deaths, 11 had been of surviving partners, leaving (adult) children as the next-of-kin. Six of the deceased had been buried, and five cremated. A significant fact was revealed when disposal choice was compared with occupation.

The occupations of the six local families where the surviving parent had been buried were as shown in Table 7.

**Table 7**

| Occupation of survivor | Of deceased's father | Of deceased's grandfather |
| --- | --- | --- |
| Farmer | Farmer | Farmer |
| Carpenter | Clerk | Not known |
| Drainage worker | Sugar-factory worker | Railwayman |
| Railway footplate man | Railwayman | Drayman |
| Sugar factory worker | Agricultural worker | Agricultural worker |
| Business proprietor | Business proprietor | Farmer |

Compared with their parents' occupations, whatever their class, these six were *static* in terms of occupational mobility.

The occupations of the five local families where the parent had been cremated were as shown in Table 8. These five surviving children were all occupationally upwardly mobile. The first four owned

**Table 8**

| Occupation of survivor | Of deceased's father | Of deceased's grandfather |
|---|---|---|
| Business proprietor | Shepherd and publican | Not known |
| Business proprietor | Motor engineer | Barber & odd job man |
| Shop owner | Land-worker | Small-holder |
| Business proprietor | Agricultural worker | Policeman and agricultural worker |
| Horticulturalist | Bulb-growing labourer | Bulb-growing labourer |

their own businesses. The fifth was an employee, but he owned his own home, whereas his father had been a council tenant.

The hypothesis is tentatively suggested that change in disposal choice is linked with class mobility as determined by occupation. I suggest that local villagers possess two forms of status: an *ascribed* status as children who have grown up in a village where their parents are known, and an *achieved* status according to their success at work.

The local villagers who have followed their fathers' occupation have had no need to indicate or reassert a separate status from their parents: they have inherited their parents' local standing. Whether middle- or working-class, their occupational and local status is identical with that of their parents and they have been content to let both their parents' corpses and their status rest.

Meanwhile, precisely those villagers who have made such a success of their occupations that they have come to occupy a social position superior to their parents have chosen cremation for their parents' funerals. My hypothesis is that they have chosen cremation – not necessarily consciously – to signal their independence of family and local roots. The children's status having been raised by business success rather than by virtue of family inheritance or influence, the parents' role need not be honoured nor their link retained by the permanent internment of their bodies in the neighbourhood where they raised their children.

## A Hypothesis

The factors illuminating disposal choice can now be tentatively tabulated in such a way as to enable wider testing. This Midlands survey suggests the regularities in funeral and disposal choice shown in Figure 1.

A more extensive survey of disposal choice would be able to test the hypothesis that disposal-choice is associated with these factors. The hypothesis suggests that *there are currently three principal determinants of disposal-choice for the family. These are the effect of the death upon the family, along with the economic position and the class-position of the next-of-kin.* The hypothesis, if proved, would indicate that the relationship between disposal practice and the survivors' situation in contemporary society is the same as that posited by the anthropologist Woodburn when he described the funeral procedures of the hunter-gatherer Hazda people:

> when death involves major social readjustments and the risk of conflict and disorder, death beliefs and practices will be more elaborate and more ritualised than where such adjustments involve no reallocation of authority or of assets but are largely a matter of personal feelings (1982, 206).

This chapter suggests that, precisely because the contemporary incidence of English deaths involves few major social adjustments, our society has moved to adopt the simplest procedures that the law offers. Death typically takes place in retirement and in old age. The generations of survivors are usually independent enough of their parents, both domestically and financially, to take these normal deaths in their stride. Abnormal deaths include those that are mass, sudden, or premature. These deaths are met with funeral rituals deliberately designed to act as a vehicle for abnormal grief and to do justice to the lives cut short (Walter, 1991b; Harbert, 1991).

### The wider social context of disposal choice

The foregoing was based upon an analysis of the social situation of families making choices for the disposal of dead relatives. The hypotheses about the survivors' choice of elaborate or simple disposal practices must be set in a wider social context. Three aspects of this context are important.

Funeral choices will *tend* to be

| MORE ELABORATE and tending towards burial and memorialisation | MORE SIMPLE and tending towards cremation and scattering |
|---|---|

**WHEN IN TERMS OF SOCIAL ENGAGEMENT, THE DECEASED WAS:**

| | |
|---|---|
| long-term rural dwelling | urban/suburban dwelling or rural incomer |
| working class | middle-class or upwardly mobile |
| young/middle-aged | retired/elderly |
| economically active | retired/economically dependent |
| parent of dependent children | childless/parent of adult or independent children |
| parent of children living locally | parent of children living distantly |
| a baby or dependent child | |
| a member of a close family | a member of a dispersed family/an estranged family |

**WHEN IN THE CONTEXT OF THE CHARACTER OF THE DEATH, THE DECEASED HAS DIED:**

| | |
|---|---|
| after prolonged home nursing | after long-term hospital nursing |
| at home | in an institution |
| suddenly/unexpectedly | a death long-predicted |
| a meaningless death ie. death was inconsistent with his/her life | a natural death |
| eg. was a victim of accident death or of violent death (murder) | eg. of old age after slow decline |

**WHEN IN A RELIGIOUS CONTEXT, THE DECEASED OR BEREAVED FAMILY WAS:**

| | |
|---|---|
| actively but traditionally religious | non-practising or atheist |
| one that perceived religious or spiritual risk in death | one that assumed no religious or spiritual risk in death/assumed automatic transfer of the deceased to the next life/believed no life after death. |

**Figure 1**

## 1 The role of local authorities in disposal

By the Burial Acts 1850 and 1852, the responsibility for providing land for the burial of the dead began to pass from the religious authorities (principally the Church of England) to local authorities (Curl, 1980; Brooks, 1989; Jupp, 1990). Saddled with these responsibilities, local authorities eventually resorted to cremation as the more economic discharge of their responsibilities. There are three phases in local government's investment in crematoria.

Once cremation had been declared a legal alternative to burial, after *Regina v Price* in 1884, (White, 1990), it was recognised within ten years as offering economic attractions for the newly reorganised local authorities which found themselves running short of available land. Secondly, by the 1930s many more local authorities were deciding to build crematoria, when their existing cemeteries were nearly full and available land in even shorter supply. Thirdly, the Government's Cremation Commission 1947–1951 (Cmd 8009) gave the final encouragement to local authorities in the post-war years when nearly all burials had to be subsidised by the rates. In 1951 there were 59 crematoria, half of which were privately owned. By 1961 there were 161, five-sixths of which were Council-owned. Thus, briefly, cremation became available as an economic option for families because local authorities provided a widespread service. The English public was offered a choice in disposal because local authorities had an economic incentive to provide cremation, whose fees were often set lower than those for burial.

## 2 Changes in family life

Changes in family life have been effected in two relevant ways: the role of women and the use of leisure.

The two burdens of nursing the terminally sick and of mourning the dead have traditionally fallen upon women. In English society, increased labour opportunities for women, combined with a falling birth-rate and smaller families, have meant that there are far fewer women available to perform traditional grave-tending duties or adopt traditional mourning wear. More widely spread wealth has combined with increased leisure-time opportunities to reduce both cemetery-visiting and mourning customs (both in dress and in social activities). Grave-visiting was formerly one of the weekend leisure-time duties. A Fensham incomer told me of the three buses she and her mother had to catch to visit their father's grave near their old London home.

Mourning customs, which once signalled the economic and emotional consequences of a death, have lost their importance now that the majority of deaths occur to the elderly and rarely have adverse economic consequences for the survivors. This means that the 'distancing' of death, as described by Ariès (1981), need not only be a consequence of a death 'taboo'. (See Walter, 1991a, for a valuable discussion.) It is also a help for the about-to-be-bereaved family. The 'distancing of death' has relieved families of many burdens of death-work. The institutionalisation of death and disposal has been performed by hospitals and nursing homes, by funeral directors and by local authorities. The consequences included some initial reduction in responsibilities for home-based terminal care (the institutional location of death first overtook the home-location of death in 1958) but also and permanently from neighbourhood-monitored grief and memorialisation duties. The increasing need for domestic privacy, especially between the wars, has been charted by Roberts (1989) and Adams (1991) in their analyses of, respectively, the decline of the customs of corpse-visiting and of the communal layer-out. After 1945, increased public hospital provision and the rationalisation of the funeral directing industry (Smale, 1985; Howarth, 1992) both served to appropriate former communal tasks. The post-war provision of housing combined with that of (distant) crematoria has reduced enormously the role of neighbours in funeral practices, especially in urban areas, as the Leicester interviews confirmed.

*3 The collapse of religious categories in disposal*

The increased role of family choice in the disposal of its dead members is also a consequence of the transfer of responsibility for the provision of space for disposal from the Church to secular authorities. Behind these lie radical differences in Protestant and Catholic belief about the situation of the dead. Traditional Catholic beliefs about the after-life of the dead were described by Walker (1964) as 'dynamic' and Protestant beliefs as 'passive'. Catholic devotional practices assume the possibility of relationships between the living and the dead. With the English Reformation, Protestants were forbidden former Catholic practices of devotions for, and relationships with, the dead (Duffy, 1992). Only during the First World War were Anglican intercessions for the dead widely encouraged (Wilkinson, 1978).

For Gittings the effect of the Reformation was that 'the ritual ties connecting the living and the dead were severed' (1984:40) as a result of which 'each generation could be indifferent to the spiritual fate of its predecessor' (Thomas, 1973:721). Thus, for 400 years, the dominant purpose of the English Protestant funeral was the disposal of the corpse and the support and edification of the bereaved. The funeral was to have no effect upon the spiritual future of the deceased. Once burial was no longer controlled by the Church, disposal began to lose its religious framework. Hence the shift to the use of the funeral to display secular status (Rowell, 1977: Gittings, 1984; Litten, 1991) culminating in the excesses of the Victorian funeral (Richardson, 1987).

More significantly, the Church of England, having taught for 400 years that the mode of disposal had no effect upon the spiritual future of the deceased, had no doctrinal basis with which to oppose the introduction of cremation. Protestant teaching on the immortality of the soul was only made more prominent by the collapse of belief in the resurrection of the physical body. Despite the regular Anglican recital of the Creed, none of the Churchgoers in the sample, indeed none of the 55 groups of respondents, believed in the resurrection of the body. That collapse lies behind Davies' assertion that:

> what cremation allows to come to the forefront is the otherwise strongly implicit belief in a human soul which leaves the body and continues into another dimension of existence at death. The traditional burial service focuses on the body and its future resurrection. While the modern cremation service explicitly follows that pattern, its implicit message is that the body has come to its end but that the soul has gone on (1990, 33).

Williams has pointed out (1990, 140–1) that the symbolism of cremation fits with atheist belief as well as with modern Protestant Christianity. The end result is the withdrawal of religious interpretations from non-Catholic disposal choice. The salience of family support and convenience in disposal choice has thus been emphasised by the coincidence of Protestant theology with secular control of disposal arrangements.

## Conclusion

The choice of burial or cremation is thus not an open one. It is not, and never has been, a purely private decision unaffected by social context. Concerning religion, the major Christian denominations have moved to adopt a position whereby the mode of disposal has no consequences for the after-life. Concerning space for the dead, control of disposal by church authorities has given way to that by local secular authorities for whom cremation has been financially attractive. Concerning community monitoring of private grief, the nineteenth century decline in mourning customs was accelerated by the First World War and, since 1945, by new housing patterns and increased social mobility. These latter have in turn reduced the role of neighbours in funerals and intensified family privacy. Traditional pressures upon funeral practice, formerly imposed by the Church, religious belief and neighbours, have been very largely removed. It is not surprising that bereaved families have come to make funeral choices that are convenient or meaningful for themselves alone.

## Note

The research on part of which this paper is based was supervised by Professor Eileen Barker at the London School of Economics. It was funded by an E.S.R.C. Studentship. Mr Roger Arber, Secretary of the Cremation Society of Great Britain has given support throughout. To all of these I wish to record my gratitude.

## References

Adams, S., (1991), *A Gendered History of the Social Management of Death and Dying in Foleshill, Coventry, during the Interwar Years*, University of Warwick, unpublished M.A. thesis.
Ariès, P., (1981), *The Hour of Our Death*, Harmondsworth: Penguin.
Bloch, M., (1971), *Placing the Dead: Tombs, Ancestral Villages and Kinship Organization in Madagascar*, London: Seminar Press.
Bloch, M. and Parry, J., (eds), (1982), *Death and the Regeneration of Life*, Cambridge: Cambridge University Press.
Brooks, C., (1989), *Mortal Remains*, Exeter: Wheaton.
Clark, D., (1982), *Between Pulpit and Pew: Folk Religion in a North Yorkshire Fishing Village*, Cambridge: Cambridge University Press.
Cremation Committee, (1950), *Report of the Interdepartmental Committee Appointed by the Secretary of State for the Home Department*, London. Cmd. 8009.

Peter Jupp

Curl, J.S., (1980), *A Celebration of Death*, London: Constable.

Davies, J.D., (1990), *Cremation Today and Tomorrow*, Nottingham: Grove Books Ltd.

Davies, J.D., (1991), 'Ashes and Identity' in *Federation of British Cremation Authorities and Institute of Burial and Cremation Administration Joint Conference Report.*

Duffy, E., (1992), *The Stripping of the Altars: Traditional Religion in England c1400–c1580*, New Haven, CT: Yale University Press.

French, S., (1975), 'The Cemetery as Cultural Institution' in Stannard, D.E., (ed.), *Death in America*, Philadelphia: University of Pennsylvania Press.

Fulton, R. and Fulton, J., (1971), 'A psychological aspect of terminal care: anticipatory grief', *Omega*, II: 91–100.

Gittings, C., (1984), *Death, Burial and the Individual in Early Modern England*, London: Croom Helm.

Harbert, B., (1991), 'Whose Funeral Is It?' *Priests and People*, November 1991, Vol. 5, No. 11.

Howarth, G., (1992), *The Funeral Industry in the East End of London: an ethnographical study*, University of London: unpublished PhD thesis.

Jupp, P.C., (1990), 'From Dust to Ashes: The Replacement of Burial by Cremation in England 1840–1967', *The Congregational Lecture*, the Congregational Memorial Hall Trust (1978) Ltd.

Jupp, P.C., (1993), *The Development of Cremation in England, 1820–1990: a sociological analysis*, University of London, unpublished PhD thesis.

Litten, J., (1991), *The English Way of Death: The Common Funeral since 1450*, London: Robert Hale.

Martin, B., and Pluck, R., (1976), *Young People's Beliefs*, Westminster: General Synod Board of Education.

Prior, L., (1989), *The Social Organization of Death: Medical Discourse and Social Practices in Belfast*, London: Macmillan.

Richardson, R., (1989), 'Why was Death so Big in Victorian Britain?' in Houlbrooke, R. (ed.), *Death, Ritual and Bereavement*, London: Routledge.

Roberts, E., (1989), 'The Lancashire Way of Death' in Houlbrooke, R., (ed.), *Death, Ritual and Bereavement*, London: Routledge.

Rowell, G., (1974), *Hell and the Victorians*, Oxford: Oxford University Press.

Rowell, G., (1977), *The Liturgy of Christian Burial*, London: SPCK.

Smale, B., (1985), *Deathwork: A Sociological Analysis of Funeral Directing*, University of Surrey: unpublished PhD thesis.

Sudnow, D., (1967), *Passing On: The Social Organization of Dying*, Englewood Cliffs, NJ: Prentice Hall.

Thomas, H., (1975), 'Changing Social Attitudes to Cremation', *Cremation Society Conference: Report of Proceedings*, Maidstone: Cremation Society of Great Britain.

Thomas, K., (1973), *Religion and the Decline of Magic*, Harmondsworth: Penguin.

Walker, D.P., (1964), *The Decline of Hell. Seventeenth Century Discussions of Eternal Torment*, London: Routledge & Kegan Paul.

Walter, T. (J.A.), (1990), *Funerals and How to Improve Them*, Sevenoaks: Hodder & Stoughton.

Walter, J.A., (1991a), 'Modern Death: Taboo or Not Taboo?' in *Sociology*, Vol 24, No 2, May 1991, pp. 293–310.

Walter, J.A., (1991b), 'The Mourning after Hillsborough' in *The Sociological Review*, Vol. 39, No. 3, August 1991, pp. 599–625.

White, S., (1990), 'A Burning Issue' in *New Law Journal*, August 10, 1990.

Wilkinson, A., (1978), *The Church of England in the First World War*, London: SPCK.

Williams, R., (1990), *A Protestant Legacy*, Oxford: Clarendon Press.

Winter, J.M., (1988), 'Public Health and the Extension of Life Expectancy in England and Wales, 1901–60' in Keynes, M., Coleman, D.A., and Dimsdale, N.H., *The Political Economy of Health and Welfare*, London: Macmillan.

Woodburn, J., (1982), 'Social Dimensions of Death in four African Hunting and Gathering Societies' in Bloch, M. and Parry, J. (eds), *Death and the Regeneration of Life*, Cambridge: Cambridge University Press.

# Volunteers in the British hospice movement

## David Field and Ian Johnson

Sociologists have long been interested in how organisations function and there is a large body of research literature in this area, especially with reference to business, commercial or industrial organisations. However, as Butler and Wilson (1990) note there has been little work on organisations in the voluntary sector in Britain and, with the exception of their own work, there is 'an almost complete gap in our research knowledge' of the organisational structures of charities (1990:23). Hospice organisations are interesting because they differ in a number of ways from the formal bureaucratic organisations more typically studied by sociologists. One of the main differences between hospice organisations in Britain and other formal organisations is their great reliance on unpaid voluntary labour. Volunteers perform a variety of tasks including counselling and 'befriending', transporting patients, laundry work and staffing reception points. It should be noted that hospice organisations are not all the same. They vary both in terms of their size and in the nature of their financial support, although the 'independent hospice' is still the most typical form. Some organisations are well established, with a range of services, whereas others are small-scale and relatively informal organisations focusing upon just one type of service, eg. day care. This chapter is concerned more with the former than with the latter.

The chapter starts by briefly locating the British hospice movement in its social context and considering the main distinguishing factors of hospice organisations. Within this context, the chapter considers the role of volunteers in the British hospice movement, focusing upon potential problems for both volunteers and hospice organisations. For volunteers, there are potential problems in their preparation and training, in their contact with patients, in their relationships with other workers, and in their membership of the hospice organisation. For the organisations, potential problems exist in the recruitment and training of volunteers, the management of voluntary work, supporting volunteers, the effect of staff turnover upon volunteers, the maintenance of the commitment of volunteers to the organisation and, prospectively, the effect of policy changes in the provision of palliative care. Finally we consider the longer-term issues for the hospice movement posed by the pressures for social change arising from the success of the movement and from changes in the wider social environment within which hospices function. We illustrate our argument mainly with data drawn from our survey of volunteers in the Leicestershire hospice organisation (Field and Johnson, 1993), but we should stress that although our analysis is based upon the limited research into the role of volunteers within the British hospice movement (Almond, 1990; Hoad, 1991) and our own knowledge of hospices, the problems we identify are analytically derived and should not be taken as indications of specific problems in particular hospice organisations. Further, what we identify as a potential problem may be regarded by hospice managers and volunteers as not particularly serious but something which they encounter and deal with as an inevitable part of their everyday activities. We suggest, however, that the potential problems we identify may have significant effects upon both the satisfaction of volunteers and the functioning of hospice organisations.

## Forms of social organisation within the hospice movement

The hospice movement in Britain, as with many other charitable organisations (Butler and Wilson, 1990), has a religious basis although many hospices are 'non-denominational' or 'secular'. The beginning of the modern hospice movement in Britain is conventionally dated from the opening of St Christopher's hospice in 1967. In the early part of its growth and development, the movement was mainly characterised by the provision of in-patient hospice care but, particularly from the late 1970s and in the 1980s, the movement has diversified to provide not only in-patient care but also day care, home care and a variety of other services (Griffin, 1991, Seale, 1989). Hospice services are now an important element within terminal care provision in Britain, with 175 in-patient hospices, 186 day care centres, 360 home care

*David Field and Ian Johnson*

teams and 160 support nurses or support teams in hospitals in 1992 (St Christopher's 1992). Various combinations of these services may be found within individual hospice organisations. From the start, the modern hospice movement depended upon voluntary contributions from local communities to provide both initial capital and other set up costs and continuing running costs. Although there is a great variety in the pattern of funding between different hospice organisations, typically around half of their running costs each year are raised by charitable contributions from their local community. The local community is also the source of the unpaid voluntary workers upon which hospice organisations depend so heavily. In the context of this discussion of the role of volunteers within hospice organisations, four features are particularly relevant. Hospice organisations are infused and sustained by a guiding ideology, they are based on non-hierarchical forms of social organisation and interpersonal relationships, they depend upon unpaid labour, and they are vulnerable to social change.

## The role of ideology

Hospice organisations are explicitly based upon a clearly expressed and coherently articulated set of ideas (an ideology) which is 'embodied' or expressed in the organisational structuring of relationships within the organisation. Ideologies may perform a number of functions in formal organisations. They may articulate the organisation's goals clearly and provide motivation for its members, as in charities, political parties or religious organisations. Corporate ideology, as Mintzberg (1991) argues, may represent a significant force of cohesion and source of co-operation among colleagues within formal organisations. In the area of health care, Strauss and his colleagues (1964) have shown that ideologies can influence staff behaviour and patient care in their analysis of the effect of differing 'psychiatric ideologies' of treatment. Similarly, Towell's study of a group of psychiatric student nurses shows the impact of treatment philosophies on the way in which the students came to perceive their role and how they should interact with patients (1975). All of these functions of ideologies can be discerned in hospice organisations, but perhaps the most significant aspect of hospice ideology is its embodiment in the very form that hospice organisations take.

The ideology of the modern hospice movement involves three core ideas: the commitment to holistic care which pays attention not only to the physical aspects of terminal disease but also to the emotional, social and spiritual needs of patients; the delivery of such care by non-hierarchical multidisciplinary teams in which contributions are based upon the particular knowledge and skills of team members rather than upon their status or formal qualifications; and a definition of care which includes the patient and family as the unit of care rather than adopting the conventional medical focus upon the patient conceived independently of the social environment. The hospice ideology has been promulgated in a wide range of written and verbal forms, with the ideas of Cicely Saunders being particularly prominent (Saunders, 1978, 1981; Du Bois, 1980; Lamerton, 1973).

Apart from hospice organisations, other types of organisations which are characterised by the 'embodiment' of their ideology within their organisational form are utopian communities. In both hospice organisations and Utopian communities, the type of person who is recruited to them and the forms of social relationships which make up the organisation of social activities within them are important for the maintenance and realisation of the core ideas which inform them. For example, both the personal beliefs of their members and the type of 'family' relationships found in religious and 'hippy' Utopian communities are central to the functioning of these communities. In addition, some religious Utopian communities have an established regulation of daily life incorporating religious ceremony and practices as central features. As Kanter so cogently argues, these forms of social organisation are vital to the 'continuance commitment' of members of Utopian communities and are central to their success or failure (Kanter, 1972). Like utopian communities, hospice organisations could be regarded as 'anti-institutions' (Punch, 1974) and as with Utopian communities, hospice organisations recruit particular types of person to them. These are typically people who have a commitment to providing a good quality of life to terminally ill people within a 'family' atmosphere, often as a result of their own particular experiences of death. Hospices are also likely to attract people with a strong religious belief or faith (Hoad, 1991).

## Non-hierarchical organisation

The central feature of hospice organisations which embodies these ideas is the commitment to non-authoritarian and non-hierarchical patterns of relationship. Admittedly, this is the ideal rather than the actuality, and some in-patient hospice institutions have a clearly identifiable hierarchy of authority. As with any form of social organisation, some hierarchical ordering is inevitable and necessary, yet most hospice organisations, like families and some Utopian communities, are not explicitly organised in terms of hierarchical and rule governed patterns. They are, in the terminology of organisational analysis, 'flat' organisations (Kanter, 1990). The early hospice organisations tended to be relatively small single function agencies, typically concerned with in-patient terminal care. As the hospice movement has developed, hospice organisations have tended to become multi-functional, and to increase in size (although there are a number of small scale, uni-functional organisations). These developments are at least in part explicable as responsive to the pressures from institutional donors (eg. cancer charities) and internal organisational developments (James and Field, 1992; Brook, 1984, cited in Butler and Wilson, 1990).

As the study of formal organisations in the Western world has revealed, there are a number of possibly negative consequences for hospice organisations flowing from these developments. The greater size of organisations in advanced industrial societies is associated with a greater degree of formalisation and bureaucratization in the functioning of the organisations, with the emergence of rules and more clearly specified task descriptions and hierarchical patterns of relationship between staff members. As the organisations become more differentiated, more complex patterns of inter-connection are likely to emerge which may lead to greater formalisation of the relationships. Equally important, perhaps, is that the differentiation of functions may lead to the development of different interest groups within hospice organisations with the potential for conflict and tension between different interests within the organisation. The tendency for the hierarchical and formal bureaucratic features of social organisation to become more prominent and central to a hospice organisation is one of the threats to the ethos of hospice care (James and Field, 1992).

## The role of unpaid labour

Hospice organisations depend to a greater or lesser extent upon unpaid, voluntary, labour. While the core goal of providing good quality terminal care is obviously the province of trained and paid professionals such as nurses and doctors, hospice volunteers also contribute to such work. They also provide the main source of transportation of patients to and from hospice institutions, usually without claiming the expenses incurred in doing so. Finally, they also provide a substantial amount of the organisationally essential clerical and ancillary labour within hospice organisations (Almond, 1990; Hoard, 1991; Field and Johnson, 1993). Without such free labour, hospices could not perform the full range of their activities. In this respect hospice organisations share some characteristics of families – a metaphor which some members of the movement use in an attempt to describe its style of care (Johnson *et al.*, 1990). As in families, much of this unpaid labour is provided by adult females, and much of it can be classed as 'emotional labour' (Graham, 1983; James, 1989). As in families, hospice organisations depend upon the fusion of physical labour and emotional caring in much of the work of their volunteers. In this respect volunteers can be important agents in the maintenance not only of the physical but also of the psychosocial and spiritual bases of hospice care – although their contributions to the latter may not always be fully appreciated by either the volunteers themselves or by paid hospice staff. As with emotional labour in general, much of the work of volunteers may remain invisible, or be taken for granted as just part of the 'natural' coping repertoire of the volunteers.

## Pressures of social change

As with other health and social welfare institutions in modern Britain, hospice organisations in the 1990s are subject to pressures for organisational change. These pressures stem partly from external sources and partly from internal factors. Externally, hospices are vulnerable to the general pressures and changes within the health care system at large, particularly the processes of evaluation and audit and the increased pressures to identify unit cost and to demonstrate the effectiveness and efficiency of care. Also, hospice organisations are competing for funds with other voluntary organisations during a period of recession in what has become an increasingly competitive 'market' (Charities Aid Foundation, 1991). This has led them to become more professional and bureaucratic in their fund-raising activities. In addition to these external pressures are the internal dynamics of the organisations. Many hospice organisations have expanded as a consequence of their success, treating more patients, widening the range of their activities, and recruiting more staff. This may mean they become more formal and bureaucratic in order to cope with the additional activities and pressures. Such pressures upon hospice organisations are examined more fully elsewhere (James and Field, 1992). Here we are only concerned with possible consequences in the area of voluntary work.


## Becoming a volunteer

The Volunteer Centre, UK, reports that 31 per cent of the nation's adult population are engaged in regular voluntary work for a formal organisation. A quarter of these work in the area of health and social welfare (Lynn and Smith, 1992). People who volunteer are more likely to be from the higher social groups (A/B), and proportionally more white than other ethnic groupings are likely to volunteer, although the evidence for this is rather scanty. Hospice volunteers are similar to the national picture. They are mainly drawn from affluent, non-working females from social groups A and B, and are most likely to be in middle age or older. Hospice volunteers are also more likely to be more religious than the general population. For example Hoad (1990) reports that 40 per cent of his sample of hospice volunteers were 'actively religious'. In comparison, only 13 per cent of the 76 per cent of the British population who are members of a religion attend religious services or meetings on a weekly basis (British Social Attitudes, 1992). People become hospice volunteers for a variety of reasons. In a study of volunteers in the Leicestershire Hospice organisation (LOROS) (Field and Johnson, 1993) the main reasons given for becoming a volunteer were to help others (62 per cent), as a result of personal bereavement (34 per cent), or more generally in response to the experience of someone's death. Just under a fifth of volunteers had known someone who had died at the hospice and another fifth knew someone who had died whom they wished had died at the hospice and said that these experiences of death had motivated them to become a hospice volunteer. In all 83 per cent of the volunteers in the Leicestershire organisation had experienced the death of someone else.

The reasons for becoming a volunteer and continuing as a volunteer are often different. For example, in LOROS, although the motivation to help others was both an initial reason for becoming a volunteer and one of the rewards of their work identified by volunteers, there were also a range of other rewards which, although not initially reasons for becoming a volunteer, were important for their continuing commitment. Among these rewards were the enjoyment which volunteers received from their work, feelings of reward and satisfaction, the atmosphere at the hospice or day centre, their contact with other volunteers and staff, their contact with patients, and a variety of personal gains which volunteers felt they got from their work. Almond (1990) in her study of volunteers in the Bath hospice describes the volunteers' reasons for continuing as the product of a reciprocal exchange between the volunteer's 'gift of time' and the emotional rewards resulting from the appreciation, gratitude and friendship they received during their voluntary work. Similar findings about volunteer motivation and involvement are reported from a questionnaire study of hospice volunteers in the USA (Siebold *et al.*, 1987). What seems clear is that although the initial, possibly intensely felt, reasons which motivated people to become hospice volunteers may persist, these very quickly become overlaid and supplemented by the direct experiences of volunteers in their work situation. Once the initial intensity of commitment has waned, the routines of everyday work and the satisfactions derived from it may become much more important in maintaining the volunteers commitment and involvement in hospice care than the feelings which initiated their entry to voluntary work. However, for some volunteers as their initial fervour cools down, tensions may develop between their sense of duty to the organisation, wishing to stop their voluntary work, and feeling guilty about letting the organisation down. This is especially likely if their initial motivation to volunteer was based on the experience of the death of someone close to them, because they may feel that they would also be letting that person down or devaluing their memory.

## Potential problems for volunteers

There are a range of potential problems for volunteers working in hospice organisations. Some of these are characteristic of those found in any organisation which had volunteers working within it whereas others are specifically attributable to the nature of hospice organisations, especially the focus of their work upon the care of dying patients and their bereaved relatives. Four main problem areas may be analytically identified: the preparation and training of volunteers; the nature of their contact with patients, their relationships with paid staff and other volunteers; and the extent to which they feel part of the hospice organisation.

## Preparation and training

Much voluntary work is of a nature which either does not need explicit preparation or training for the volunteer to be able to perform it, or draws upon skills and abilities which volunteers already have. In these circumstances the initial orienting session between the volunteer co-ordinator and the volunteer may be sufficient preparation for the volunteer's participation in the hospice organisation. In such an orienting meeting it is likely that the practical tasks and activities which the volunteer is to perform will be identified, together with rules regarding such things as confidentiality, relationships with paid staff and patients, and orienting ideas about the philosophy of the hospice organisation. However, some tasks may require explicit technical training (eg. staffing a telephone exchange) while other tasks involving work with patients or relatives (eg. 'befriending' or counselling) may require other, more intensive, types of preparation. In these situations further training and preparation is obviously required. Given the continuous 'trickle' of recruitment of volunteers to hospice organisations it may be difficult for them to organise such training immediately. Thus it is possible for some volunteers to be inadequately prepared and trained for their work, for a short time at least. Admittedly this is unlikely to be the case in such tasks as counselling, where the perceived training requirements may be such that volunteers are not allowed to commence working for the organisation until they have attended an appropriate course.

## Contact with patients

This may be stressful and upsetting for volunteers but is also an aspect of their work which they are likely to value and find rewarding. The main danger for volunteers is that they may experience distress as a result of becoming 'too involved' with patients or relatives. In these circumstances it is important that the hospice organisation has in place mechanisms to identify such over-involvement, and is able to provide adequate support, including counselling if necessary, to deal with it. Hospice organisations have a reputation for being alert and sensitive to potential emotional problems arising among their staff, and providing appropriate help and support. The question is whether such support also extends to their volunteers, most of whom will be contributing only a relatively small number of hours of work to the organisation and who, therefore, may be comparatively invisible and thus more likely to be excluded inadvertently from such support mechanisms.

## Relationships with paid staff and other volunteers

Apart from the normal tension between people in organisations, volunteers may experience additional problems because of their unpaid 'supernumerary' status. Hoad (1991), in his discussion of boundaries and conflicts between paid staff and volunteers, suggests that there can be tension between them over both the work done by volunteers and over the information which volunteers may want about patients. Paid staff may sometimes be suspicious about the ability of the unpaid volunteers to perform the tasks assigned to them. This may be particularly true in areas such as counselling and patient care, where the professional expertise of the staff may be challenged, or where staff relationships with the patients and their relatives may be seen by staff to be threatened by volunteers' activities and the relationships they develop. There may also be tension between paid staff and volunteers over the amount and nature of information which volunteers are given. Paid staff may be concerned about questions of confidentiality and the ethics of passing on sensitive information to volunteers. Some paid staff may even attempt to control the information given to volunteers in order 'to keep them in their place' and to control their activities. On the other hand, volunteers working with patients and relatives may feel that greater amounts of information are necessary for them to perform their tasks effectively, and may be frustrated by the lack of information which they receive. In the LOROS study a number of volunteers complained that because they had not been given adequate information about the physical problems of patients, they had inadvertently caused the patient pain – by, for example, inappropriately gripping a tender arm when helping a patient into a car or out of a chair. Volunteers also expressed the view that they would like to know when a patient has died. As volunteers are not present at all times (typically being at the organisation only once a week or once a fortnight) it is easy for them to be unaware that someone has died. Many volunteers are diffident about asking or 'bothering' paid staff to find out where the patient is. Finally, in rare cases, there may be problems related to status differences between volunteers and paid staff. Paid staff are more likely to be recruited from social groups lower in the social status hierarchy than the affluent female volunteers frequently found in hospice organisations, and some of them may feel threatened by such 'upper class', lady volunteers. Stylistic differences in speech and ways of expressing themselves may lead the paid worker to (mis)perceive the 'lady volunteer' as someone who is 'dabbling' in their voluntary work for trivial and superficial reasons.

There appear to be fewer problems associated with relationships with other volunteers, but newly recruited volunteers may experience some initial difficulties in their relationships with well-established 'older' volunteers. This is most likely to occur if there is the development of a status hierarchy within the volunteer base of an organisation (usually depending upon the length of service and perceived value of the contributions of volunteers).

## Membership of the organisation

Feeling part of the organisation may be a problem for volunteers. In the LOROS study most volunteers contributed one session a week, many contributed once every two weeks, and it was rare for volunteers to work more than two sessions in a week. Some expressed the view that they were 'only a cog' in the hospice organisation and that their contributions were small and easily replaced. Some voluntary jobs were rather isolating; for example, people who worked at the reception desk at the hospice at weekends or evenings had relatively little contact with hospice staff, other volunteers, or even with patients and relatives. Under such circumstances volunteers may feel a lack of intimacy or any sense of belonging to the organisation and it is in these circumstances that the tension between duty and guilt, mentioned earlier, may become particularly relevant. When volunteers do not feel part of the organisation it may be difficult for them to maintain commitment to and involvement in it.

## Potential problems for hospice organisations

Six potential problems can be identified for hospice organisations as a result of their use of voluntary labour: the recruitment and screening of volunteers; managing the rota of volunteers to provide suitable coverage; supporting volunteers in their activities; the effects of staff turnover on volunteers; the maintenance of the involvement and commitment of volunteers to their voluntary work; and the possible effects upon the use of voluntary labour of changes in the evaluation and funding of palliative care in the 1990s.

## The recruitment and screening of volunteers

These are central activities for any organisation which depends heavily upon such workers. The fundamental potential problem is to attract new volunteers. To give an indication of the scale of such activity, we note that in 1991 Leicestershire had a population of 865,133 with 272,133 of these living in the City of Leicester where the hospice and day centre are located (County Monitor, 1992). From this pool of potential volunteers LOROS had recruited (and retained) nearly 600 volunteers in 1991, partly through the publicity of LOROS events in the local media, which stimulated interest in becoming a volunteer, but primarily by word of mouth. As with other types of volunteering, many hospice volunteers become active simply because someone asks them to do so (Thomas and Finch, 1990) and unless people are continually being asked, potential volunteers will be lost. Yet overactive recruitment may have negative consequences. For example, the use of 'mail shots' to private homes may be seen as an invasion of privacy.

When someone has decided to volunteer, it is necessary for hospice organisations to engage in some sort of screening to make sure that the volunteers are suitable for the work that they are going to be asked to perform and also, if patient contact is involved, that they will be able to handle such contact. These are familiar problems for recruiting organisations. However, not only do hospices have to screen volunteers in terms of their trustworthiness, empathy, and personality, it is also important to ensure that they are not recruiting people who would be adversely affected by their voluntary work. Most hospices operate a system whereby people who are recently bereaved are ineligible to act as volunteers, because of the possibility that they may not have 'worked through' their own grief and so may be unable to help others, or be unable to cope with the emotions which might be aroused by working with people who are dying.

## Managing the rotas of volunteers

This task is often complicated and most hospice organisations now employ one or more paid volunteer co-ordinators specifically to cope with their use of voluntary workers. At LOROS the paid co-ordinators have to cope with slightly over 600 volunteers, most of whom donate up to four hours of time per week. These volunteers are engaged in a range of activities across the organisation in the charity shops and the two centres for patient care. The largest number of volunteers work at the hospice, where they are involved in a range of activities such as staffing the reception desk and telephones, servicing the snack bar, arranging flowers, giving hairdressing to patients, and driving patients to and from the hospice and day centre. At the day centre a slightly smaller number of volunteers are involved than at the hospice, but here the problem of organising the transportation schedules for each daily intake of patients is a complex and sometimes difficult task. In both settings the Volunteer co-ordinators have to cope with volunteers who drop out at short notice.

Organisationally it is important that rotas are managed effectively and for the volunteers themselves it is important that their contributions are organised in an effective and predictable manner and in such a way as to convey to them that their contributions are valued. Arbitrary organisation of rotas and a continual chopping and changing of duty periods may have adverse effects upon a volunteer's commitment. Similarly, an excessive number of requests to 'fill in' gaps in the rotas may have a similar effect. Nationally, the Volunteer Centre UK (1992) reports that a major dissatisfaction of volunteers is poor organisation of their work, with around two-thirds of volunteers feeling that their work could be better organised, and one-third being dissatisfied with the tasks which they were given to do. A small number of volunteers in the Volunteer Centre survey said that they gave up their voluntary work because of its poor organisation. Given the expenses incurred and the difficulties involved in managing a large group of volunteers it has been suggested that some hospice organisations in fact have *too many* rather than *too few* volunteers (Clark, personal communication 1992).

## Support for volunteers

The practical and emotional support of volunteers in their work is important to their satisfaction in their work and for their retention by hospice organisations. At a very basic level, volunteers should feel that they are appreciated by the organisation and by the paid staff working within it. Support of a technical nature may also be important, and may often consist of no more than adequate training and preparation by hospice organisations, for example, advice to drivers on what action to take should a patient become ill when they are being driven to or from the organisation, or training with the switchboard equipment so that the volunteer feels competent and expert enough answering the phones and transferring calls throughout the organisation. Finally, as noted in the previous section, recognising the need for emotional support and providing this in a prompt and satisfactory manner, should it become necessary, is important.

## Staff turnover

This may affect volunteers in a number of ways. Many volunteers, in addition to their general commitment to the organisation, make personal commitments to particular staff members with whom they work and to their ways of doing things. Thus when such staff members leave this may result in problems for the commitment of the volunteers. In particular, where staff changes are associated with more general organisational changes which alter previous working practices, for example the introduction of a new system of rotas or new patterns of patient care, volunteers may personalise these changes and develop antipathy towards both the new staff member, who is seen as responsible, and towards the new methods. This may result in the loss of volunteers from the organisation. Even where volunteers do not leave the organisation they may put less energy and effort into their voluntary work and be less likely to 'put themselves out' to help the hospice organisation when, for example, duty rotas collapse or extra help is required.

## Maintaining commitment and involvement

The preceding discussion suggests that the maintenance of the commitment of its volunteers to the organisation is an important task for any hospice organisation. Satisfaction with their work provides the main basis for such commitment and, within this, the day-to-day rewards of appreciation and support from paid staff play a crucial role. For example, in Almond's study (1990) 18 per cent of the volunteers said that negative staff attitudes would be something which would make them stop being a volunteer. In the Volunteer Centre's national survey (1992) almost a quarter of the volunteers surveyed felt that their efforts were not always appreciated, although this does not seem to be the case in hospice organisations. In the LOROS survey, lack of appreciation did not appear to be a problem, with just under a third of the volunteers saying they received a great deal of support and encouragement from staff and another half of the volunteers saying that the support and encouragement that they received from staff was adequate. The integration of paid staff and volunteers around a set of share core objectives and values is also important to the continuing commitment of volunteers, yet the extent and nature of their work may marginalise volunteers. Despite their centrality as a group to hospice organisations, each volunteer is aware of only a fragment of the total life of the organisation, and most contribute only a relatively small amount of time to it. While individual commitment may be high, most volunteers see or experience only a small segment of the life of the organisation and very few have a clear idea of the full range of activities which go on in their hospice organisation. Yet while each volunteer makes only a relatively minor contribution, these small individual contributions are collectively vital to the functioning of hospice organisations.

## Changes in the provision and evaluation of palliative care

Most hospice organisations are funded in part by voluntary contributions and in part through NHS health authorities. In 1992/3 £31.7 million has been allocated by the British Government to enable health authorities to contribute to the running costs of hospice organisations. With the introduction of new purchaser-provider arrangements following on from the reform of the National Health Service (Working for Patients, 1989), the monitoring and evaluation of hospice services in their use of this funding is likely. Indeed, the National Council for Hospice and Specialist Palliative Care Services has developed and circulated guidelines on contracting with the NHS to all independent hospices (1992). Similarly, guidelines on audit have been developed for the council (Higginson, 1992). In this climate of scrutiny and evaluation it may well be that the activities of hospice volunteers will have to be examined and justified. Are volunteers delivering efficient and cost-effective care? Is their training adequate for the work they perform? In this exercise it may be that, as Clark suggests (1992), some organisations may find that the costs of using volunteers are greater than they realised or that they are 'overvolunteered'. As with the use of volunteers in Community Care, it may be that services provided by volunteers are not necessarily cheaper than those provided by paid staff (Leat, 1992). Regardless of the outcome, volunteers are unlikely to welcome such audit and scrutiny of their work as it may be seen by them as questioning their worth to the organisation. Further, if the pressures of audit and evaluation lead to the transformation of voluntary work into something very similar to ordinary paid work, the attractiveness and rewards of voluntary work for volunteers may be reduced.

*David Field and Ian Johnson*

## Concluding comments

If they are to survive with their ideals intact, hospice organisations must be aware that the social changes which they are facing are both a challenge and a threat. The very success of hospices in meeting the challenge of delivering good quality terminal care to an ever increasing number (and slightly wider range) of patients (Griffin, 1991, St Christophers, 1992) has led to their expansion but with resulting stresses and strains also. In particular their successes may have led to a loss of connection with the core ideas which underpinned the modern hospice movement. Without remaining faithful to these ideas, there is a strong chance that a hospice organisation might lose its sense of identity and uniqueness. If hospices become 'just another health care institution' they may experience difficulty in recruiting the voluntary unpaid labour which is necessary if they are to maintain their full range of services and activities. In this context, hospice organisations must remain sensitive to the cohesive power of ideology and the potentially damaging emergence of hierarchy within them.

The hospice ideology is relatively powerful in structuring hospice organisations, and serves as an important buffer against the endemic pressures towards bureaucratic or professional forms of organisation. As their organisation matures, it may be hard for members of a hospice organisation to maintain the pioneering spirit and enthusiasm of the early days of the organisation and their commitment to the core ideals of the hospice movement (James and Field, 1992). Yet, should the hospice ideology weaken and become less powerful, this may well be important in allowing business, organisational, managerial, or professional imperatives or requirements to gain ascendency within hospice organisations, transforming them into something more like hospitals, residential homes or community care teams. They must also remain true to their ideas because volunteers are attracted to work in hospice organisations in large part because of their commitment to the hospice ideology. When the ideas which hospice organisations embody are seen to change, then so too may the motivation and commitment of their volunteers. It may also be that the general reputation of the hospice organisation declines within its local community, thereby making it harder to recruit new volunteers.

This brings us to a second feature of hospice organisations identified at the start, their non-hierarchical nature. As we have suggested this is an element within hospice organisations which is particularly under threat and is rarely fully achieved. While it may be inappropriate for volunteers to be involved and consulted frequently in decisions which are made within a hospice organisation, nevertheless it is important for the motivation and involvement of volunteers that they are appropriately involved, informed and consulted by the organisation. As hospice organisations become larger and employ more unpaid voluntary workers, there is a danger that such expansion may lead to the emergence of strong patterns of hierarchy and the marginalisation of voluntary workers within them. These trends would be likely not only to alienate voluntary workers but also to undermine the ideas upon which the hospice movement is based. However, it is by no means inevitable that hospice organisations will become transformed into hierarchical and bureaucratically organised institutions. One does not need to be as pessimistic as Punch in his claim that 'there is a crucial sense in which the attempt to establish "communitas" by casting off the corrupting fetters of orthodox institutions is doomed from the start' (1974:323). There are alternative ways of responding to the differentiation of function and increasing size within hospice organisations, as illustrated by the way in which some Chinese, family-based, business organisations have expanded. Within these organisations, expansion has proceeded by developing relatively autonomous units based on functional differentiation of tasks which are linked to each other through a system of personal and familial relationships at higher levels (Whitley, 1992). This type of response to expansion and change can be seen at least in an incipient form within LOROS, where the inpatient hospice, the day centre and the charity shops function as relatively autonomous institutions, each with their own complement of paid staff and separate cadres of volunteers.

Hospice organisations are social systems characterised and sustained by a particular ethos of commitment and reward within which unpaid voluntary workers play a significant role. Given their central role, it is important that the 'reciprocal exchange' of the volunteers 'gift of time' for appreciation, gratitude and friendship (Almond, 1990) is maintained, not merely for the satisfaction of volunteers but also for the functioning of hospice organisations themselves. Given the diversity of the movement, it is likely that some hospice organisations will be more successful in maintaining their 'anti-institutional' ethos of 'holistic care' than others.

David Field and Ian Johnson

## Acknowledgments

David Clark provided the initial impetus to widen our study of volunteers in a hospice organisation, provided an informed and sympathetic forum to try out our initial conceptual fumblings in a seminar at the Trent Palliative Care Centre, and contributed useful steering comments throughout the development of this paper. Subsequently David Ashton helped us with the literature on organisational analysis, although he is not responsible for the use we have made of it. Samantha Buchanan typed the various drafts through which this paper progressed. We thank them all for their contributions.

## References

Almond, L., (1990), *Who 'Cares'? – Community Care in Action: A Study of one Hospice's Volunteers*, University of Bath: MSc in Social Policy Analysis.

*British Social Attitudes Cumulative Source Book*, (1992), London: Gower.

Brook, M.Z., (1984), *Centralisation and Autonomy: A Study in Organisational Behaviour*, London: Holt, Rinehart & Winston.

Butler, R.J. and Wilson D.C., (1990), *Managing Voluntary and Non-Profit Organisations: Strategy and Structure*, London: Routledge.

Charities Aid Foundation, (1991), *Charity Trends*, 13th Edition.

Clark, D., (1992), Personal communication.

County Monitor, (1992), *1991 Census Leicestershire*, London: Office of Population Censuses and Surveys, CEN91 CM 26.

Du Bois, P., (1980), *The Hospice Way of Death*, New York: Human Sciences Press.

Field, D. and Johnson, I., (1993), 'Satisfaction and Change: A Survey of Volunteers in a Hospice Organisation,' *Social Science and Medicine* (in press).

Graham, H., (1983), 'Caring: A Labour of Love' in J. Finch and D. Groves, (eds), *A Labour of Love: Women, Work and Caring*, London: Routledge and Kegan Paul, pp. 13–30.

Griffin, J., (1991), *Dying with Dignity*, London: Office of Health Economics.

Higginson, I., (1992), 'Quality, Standards, Organisational and Clinical Audit for Hospice and Palliative Care Services,' London: National Council for Hospice and Palliative Care Services, Occasional Paper 2.

Hoad, P., (1991), 'Volunteers in the independent hospice movement,' *Sociology of Health and Illness*, 13, 231–248.

James, N., (1989), 'Emotional Labour: skill and work in the social regulation of feelings', *The Sociological Review*, 37: pp. 15–42.

James, N. and Field, D., (1992), 'The routinisation of hospice: Charisma and bureaucratization,' *Social Science & Medicine*, 34: 1363–1375.

Johnson, I., Rogers, C., Biswas, B. and Ahmedzai, S., (1990), 'What do hospices do? A survey of hospices in the United Kingdom and Republic of Ireland,' *British Medical Journal*, 300:791–793.

Kanter, R.M., (1990), *When Giants Learn to Dance*, London: Unwin Hyman.

Kanter, R.M., (1972), *Commitment and Community: Communes and Utopias in Sociological Perspective*, Cambridge, Mass: Harvard University Press.

Lamerton, R., (1973), *Care of the Dying*, London: Priory Press.

Leat, D., (1992), 'Innovations and special schemes,' in Twigg, J., (ed.), *Carers; Research and Practice*, London: HMSO, pp. 95–125.

Lynn, P. and Smith, J.D., (1992), *The 1991 National Survey of Voluntary Activity in the UK*, Berkhamstead: Volunteer Centre, UK.

Mintzberg, H., (1991), 'The effective organisation: Forces and forms', *Management Review*, 32: pp. 54–67.

National Council for Hospice and Palliative Care Services, 'Guidelines for Voluntary Hospices Contracting with the National Health Service', London: Occasional Paper 1.

Punch, M., (1974), 'The institutionalisation of anti-institutional ideas', *British Journal of Sociology*, 25: pp. 312–325.

Saunders, C.M., (1978), 'The philosophy of terminal care' in Saunders, C., (ed.), *The Management of Terminal Disease*, London: Edward Arnold.

Saunders, C.M., Summers, D.H. and Teller, N., (eds), (1981), *Hospice: The Living Idea*, London: Edward Arnold.

Seale, C., (1989), 'What happens in hospices?' *Social Science and Medicine*, 28(6), 551–9.

Seibold, D.R., Rossi, S.M., Berteotti, C.R. *et al.*, (1987), 'Volunteer Involvement in a Hospice Care Program,' *The American Journal of Hospice Care*, March/April: pp. 43–55.

St Christopher's Hospice Information Service, (1992), *Directory of Hospice Services*, Sydenham, London: St Christopher's.

Strauss, A.L., Schatzman, L., Bucher, R., Ehrlich, D. and Sabshin, M., *Psychiatric Ideologies and Institutions*, New York: Free Press.

Thomas, A. and Finch, H., (1990), *On Volunteering: A Qualitative Research Study of Images, Motivations and Experiences*, The Volunteer Centre UK, Berkhampstead: Voluntary Action Research.

Towell, D., (1975), *Understanding Psychiatric Nursing: a Sociological Analysis of Modern Psychiatric Practice*, London: Royal College of Nursing.

Volunteer Centre UK, (1992), *National Survey of Volunteers*, Berkhamstead: Volunteer Centre.

Whitley, R., (1992), *Business Systems in South East Asia: Firms, Markets and Societies*, London: Sage.

*Working for Patients*, (1989), London: HMSO.

# Part 3

# Investigating deathwork: a personal account

*Glennys Howarth*

## Ethnography: the case of the undertaker

This chapter is based on reflections of conducting ethnography with undertakers. The research, designed to provide a sociological analysis of the work of the modern funeral director, was prompted by an awareness of funeral rituals as unsatisfactory or inadequate. Funerals organised along traditional lines often appeared to contain ceremonies that were inappropriate and did not address the 'real' needs of the bereaved. By contrast, a relative lack of ritual at the funeral could leave a harrowing void. It was this inadequacy or deficiency of significant liturgy that led me to question the place of ritual in this crucial 'rite of passage'.

The study, carried out in the East End of London, focussed on the deathwork practices of funeral directors. Exerting a powerful control over the after-death system, they are a key to understanding many of the *post-mortem* rituals of our society. In virtue of their directing role they liaise with the bereaved and with all other agencies to co-ordinate the funeral. Knowledge of the occupational role of the funeral director – key player in the drama and guardian of the body – is crucial to developing an understanding of contemporary funeral customs. To understand the motives (Burke, 1945) which inform deathwork practice, I felt it necessary to adopt an ethnographic approach.

Ethnography has been defined as the 'science of cultural description' (Wolcott, 1975:112). It interprets group dynamics from an 'emic' or 'insider's perspective' by gaining fluency with the beliefs, values and sets of knowledge characteristic of that community (Fetterman, 1989). The intention is that it may 'aid us in gaining access to the conceptual world in which our subjects live' (Geertz, 1973:24).

© The Editorial Board of The Sociological Review 1993. Published by Blackwell Publishers, 108 Cowley Road, Oxford OX4 1JF, UK and 238 Main Street, Cambridge, MA 02142, USA.

That undertakers are generally treated with suspicion established a study of their culture as one ideally suited to the ethnographic method. The Dickensian image of the undertaker, feeding on the insecurities and anxieties of the vulnerable bereaved, is one which is taking the industry a long time to shake off. For example, in a recent radio 'phone-in programme, a contributor stated that he believed:

> When my body's gone it's dead and finished and people are welcome to do what they like with it. The last person I want to get hold of it is an undertaker. It is obscene the way that modern undertakers rip off old people.

Popular commentaries (Waugh, 1948; Mitford, 1963) and contemporary funeral reform groups such as The Natural Death Movement, continue to depict the funeral director as profit conscious at the expense of the bereaved; heartless, yet superficially sympathetic during interaction with stricken relatives; and, conscious of their stigmatised status, highly defensive of the industry.

This negative image of funeral directors, however, lends itself to ethnography. There are a number of reasons why this should be. First, a positivist approach which utilised quantitative research techniques might impel the researcher to strive towards the application of 'theory-neutral' methods of enquiry in an attempt to reduce the effects of bias on the testing process, the overall aim being to verify hypotheses. If the research problem originates from within mainstream culture, with its unfavourable view of funeral directors, the framework within which the study will be conducted is already vitiated by social prejudice. Rather than rejecting popular beliefs, a fieldwork approach values this 'ready-made picture' (Schutz, 1964) of culture. Ethnography, particularly, befits an examination of communities alien to the investigator. Being a cultural outsider, with little working knowledge of the undertaker's marginalised way of life, facilitates the observation of patterns and routines and problematises taken-forgranted behaviour. It is this insight into the ordinary, day-to-day experience of deathworkers which generates valid hypotheses.

Second, the stigmatisation of the funeral industry will influence members' responses to any investigation. Overtures involving formal questionnaires and interviews could be perceived as a desire to undermine further their already precarious social position. In response they may choose to ignore the inquiry. Alternatively, if they agree to participate they may, in their replies, sketch a picture of their work and business ethics which is intended to augment the image of their maligned industry. There are of course many potential rejoinders. A keen awareness of the disdainful stereotype of the undertaker, coupled with an understanding of the taboo nature of the trade, must force the researcher to recognise the industry as highly sensitive and requiring a correspondingly delicate approach.

A third, related factor deserving of consideration concerns the insular nature of the after-death industry. Deathwork is shrouded in mystery and although popular reluctance to confront death must partially account for this, it is beneficial to undertakers that it remains so. Job status, trade secrets and occupational boundaries depend on the construction and maintenance of knowledge barriers which separate the lay person from the 'professional'. Existing on the fringes of 'respectable' society, undertakers devote substantial time and energy to the task of presenting an agreeable face to the world. Manipulating the impressions others receive is part of the life experience of all group members. Breaking down the deathworker's facade in a non-threatening manner to gain access to the 'raw' culture of the funeral director can best be achieved, as with any other sensitive group, through ethnography. The emphasis on understanding culture from an insider perspective acts as an antidote to the undertaker's self presentation. Once trust is forged, the funeral director's strategies for promoting better public relations should be revealed and defences, normally fortified in the presence of clientele, lowered in the fieldworker's company.

The major difficulty with the ethnographic method is that in developing relationships with group members the researcher may, in a sense, 'go native' and be seduced by group values and belief systems. If this does occur the danger is twofold. First, the fieldworker only recognises activity through the cultural perspectives of the community under study. Second, and perhaps more problematic, is that, like the new initiate of a religious cult, s/he is usually unaware of the conversion so that when the data is analysed, the prejudices of wider society have simply been replaced by the prejudices of the group.

## A view from the inside – but how to get in?

Equipped with the theory of ethnographic techniques I set about the fieldwork. I began optimistically by writing to the National Association of Funeral Directors (NAFD) in the hope that contact with the professional association would act as a springboard into the parlour of one of their members. This correspondence elicited only a polite refusal to assist, couched in terms of their lack of any useful information. I interpreted their response as reluctance to sanction the collection of information by an outsider in an investigation which might disclose unflattering characteristics and ultimately damage the profession. I subsequently discovered, however, that during the period of research the NAFD had no means of discovering more than the most basic, volunteered information regarding its members and their working practices and therefore, my supposition that the National Association had frequent and knowledgable contact with its members was mistaken.

The next avenue of attack was to write directly to a number of funeral directors. Letters were sent to a total of six companies. The study was described as a concern with societal attitudes to death and the role undertakers play in preserving funeral customs. The approach was highly tentative and this reflected my assumption that the undertaker would be a reluctant participant who would therefore have to be coaxed and cajoled into assisting the project.

In all six cases I received no reply. Some months elapsed and I began to despair of ever finding a 'gatekeeper' (Hammersley and Atkinson, 1983) to the world of deathwork. Library searches became the mainstay of the project and I spent many hours thumbing through texts on death and seeking obscure pamphlets and ancient tracts on funerals and mortuary customs. The fieldwork became limited to intermittent discussions with others who professed similar interests to my own. On more than one occasion this turned out to be a preoccupation with an afterlife. I often wondered if they were having greater success than I at negotiating access to their research subjects!

Persistence finally paid off and a breakthrough occurred. During an habitual scan of the '*in-memoriam*' pages of the local newspaper, I came across an advertisement listing the range of facilities available at a local cemetery. Enquiries regarding death

© The Editorial Board of The Sociological Review 1993

services were to be addressed to the Superintendent. At this juncture I had no notion of his role in the deathwork system or of the way he could assist me. Nevertheless, I put pen to paper and two weeks later received my first positive reply, inviting me to make an appointment.

## Getting started at the cemetery

Mr Krantz (the names used here are pseudonyms to protect the identity of my respondents), the Superintendent who answered my letter, managed a cemetery in East London. The extensive grounds, consecrated in 1874, have met the burial requirements of successive generations of East-Enders through times of war and peace. Mr. Krantz, who was eventually to become my 'gate-keeper', was a charming, sincere, middle-aged man who demonstrated a great love for his work. His enthusiasm was addictive and one could not fail to warm to him as he spoke passionately of his clients and the cemetery, his funeral and customer anecdotes peppered with humour. In this and subsequent visits to the cemetery he patiently discussed his work, his relations with others in the field and his perceptions and understanding of funeral directors and the bereaved.

## Informant expectations and the researcher

At our initial meeting the Superintendent confessed that he had been unsure of what to expect from me. At that stage I too was uncertain of the direction the study would take. Moreover, true to the ethnographic paradigm, I did not wish to limit the enquiry by formulating strict boundaries. When negotiating access, however, the researcher's problems may be compounded if s/he is unable to provide the informant with a set of hypotheses delineating parameters, aims and survey methods. Presenting the subjects of the study with a clearly defined outline of the objectives and methods of the research is easier for them to grasp and less threatening than the promise of 'participant observation' – which is roughly translated as a desire to spend time observing the group and generally 'poking around'.

Nevertheless, I convinced my contact at the cemetery that my interests were scientific and not sensationalist. Once he had come to accept the sincere nature of the enquiry he gave me introductions to two firms of undertakers whom he thought would react favourably to my research. I interviewed the funeral directors of both companies. Each was happy to answer my questions and discuss in detail their front-stage activities. Each gave accounts of their deathwork which were motivated by the desire to present an impression of their industry as professional and sensitive to the needs of the bereaved. Responses to enquiries on bodywork and lay-out of premises, however, met with a decided lack of enthusiasm. Although interviewing funeral directors is a relatively simple and painless venture, negotiating access to life behind the scenes is substantially more difficult. Attempting to engage with the back-stage and daily routines of these companies meant embarking on a lengthy and careful process of negotiation. Furthermore, it necessitated the choice of only one undertaker to form the basis for the field research. Working with two undertakers, either in tandem or sequentially, would have been almost impossible because of the competition and distrust between firms. A friendly *camaraderie* exists on an informal basis and meeting at cemeteries or loaning vehicles from one another is often a means of information-gathering among undertakers. Access to one another's backstage premises, working practices and company records, however, is clearly a different matter. It did not take long for me to realise that going between two companies would have denied me access to both.

### Early days in the field

Fieldwork, begun in September 1987 and completed in August 1988, was divided into three distinct stages. During the first four months of the project I was involved in delicate negotiations and was somewhat apprehensively finding my way around an unfamiliar culture. Visits to the undertaker were either once or twice weekly, by strict invitation and for the purposes of attending and observing funerals. I would arrive at the premises at an agreed time, travel with the company for the funeral and return to the office after the ceremony. The fact that many of these visits were timed for the afternoon meant that Jon Stone, the funeral director, would invite me to accompany him to the adjacent public house at the end of the days' work.

At this stage I was only allowed to attend the rituals with the express permission of the bereaved. Couching my presence in terms of research for a book on funerals, the undertaker made the request direct to the arranger if he thought it appropriate. That the bereaved were first vetted by the undertaker, and further limited by their personal choice, must have meant that the funerals I attended were unrepresentative. The effect this had on funeral observations at this early stage of the project is difficult to assess. Nevertheless, as it was the ritual performance of the deathworker that particularly interested me, these visits yielded much of importance.

Funeral observations were painstakingly recorded in field notes and written up as soon as possible after the event. Copious field notes were taken detailing funerals and discussions held with, and between, ministers, mourners, funeral and cemetery staff. Growing awareness that the opportunity to write might be preceded by a few hours of informal talk in the pub led me to dictate into a tape recorder in the brief snatches of solitude between the return to the office and the visit to the pub.

## Motivated accounts

It was during this period that many tape-recorded interviews were conducted with the funeral director and members of his staff. In answering my questions I sometimes sensed an element of pleasure that they were being asked to 'tell it like it is'. As a group who are stereotypically assigned to the margins of society many saw the research as an opportunity to explain their work and to dispel some of the popular myths surrounding it.

It would have been relatively simple, therefore, to draw conclusions about undertakers which totally dismissed the pejorative popular conception. I was continually aware, however, of the need to remain alert to the fact that every actor, in whatever walk of life, is preoccupied with the process of self-presentation (Goffman, 1959). Performances are enacted for the purpose of persuading clients and observers. The importance of critically interpreting behaviour and assessing the credibility of informant accounts by checking and cross-checking information – of 'penetrating fronts' (Douglas, 1971) – must be uppermost in the mind of the ethnographer.

For example, tape-recorded interviews with the funeral director (following a precedent set in the early days of our acquaintance) always took place in the front office. Sitting behind the desk, the director played the role (to which he was most accustomed in that setting and which I was later to recognise during arrangements interviews) of 'the giver of knowledge' to the uninitiated. I, like the bereaved, was the receiver. He appeared to view these interviews as a formal mechanism for transferring information about working practices. They were his way of 'setting the record straight' and interpreting the day's events. Comparing his version with my own and that of others, and noting disharmonies, served to illuminate underlying motivation and highlight instances of conflict and tension between the participants. For example, he asserted that there was little conflict between his occupational role and that of the priest. His statement initially masked issues of control over the funeral ceremony. Subsequent contact with church ministers who had no business ties with the company led to an awareness of tension between undertakers and the church and to a more subtle observation of the way in which they negotiated control during the funeral ritual. One minister in particular maintained that undertakers generally attempted to belittle his role in the funeral ceremony. He felt humiliated by the funeral directors' use of surreptitious mechanisms to pay the fee for his services. A strategy employed by one company was to take him behind a tombstone before handing over the money. Following the discussion with this minister I made detailed observations of the exchange of cash between the funeral director and the clergy he employed to conduct the service. On one occasion my field notes reported:

> Having drawn up outside the chapel Jon alone got out of the hearse and went to check that all was ready. The minister was standing at the door awaiting the entourage. As Jon approached he held out his hand in formal greeting. Knowing what was about to happen I was able to observe the furtive exchange of cash as he shook the minister's hand.

Assessing the credibility of field data is an intricate task, as there are many possible explanations to account for the behaviour of an individual at a given time and place. For example, during the early stages of the research the funeral director led me on a guided tour of the premises which included the back regions or rear stage. On this, albeit fleeting, visit I was permitted to view the dilapidated outhouses that comprised the undertakers workshop and mortuary – the sight of which would probably have horrified the bereaved. I was surprised that during the visit he related information and allowed me to view buildings and practices which could have been reported in a manner highly detrimental to the industry. How can this be accounted for?

First, like most research subjects, he was undoubtedly flattered by the interest shown. By providing glimpses of backstage mysteries he exploited my desire to learn more about deathwork and so retained my attention. Second, he may not have considered me a threat to the profession, perhaps trusting me not to utilise unpalatable features of mortuary practice. Third, he may have hoped to shock me or test my endurance in some way. Fourth, it is possible that he was filtering my observations and allowing me to note certain 'detrimental' characteristics. Convinced that he was revealing 'all there was to know' I should then have refrained from probing further. Each, or some combination, of these interpretations may provide the key to his behaviour. That is assuming that the subject *is* motivated by some deception and, moreover, that he is bound to display consistency and purpose in the interaction.

Cross-checking, by comparing the accounts of other informants, should result in the collection of clues which aid the process of analysis. It was during the early days in the field that interviews with other members of the company's staff were conducted by request (or instruction) of the funeral director. The value of the data collected in this way was rather doubtful as, unsure of the reasons for my presence and, initially, seeing me as closely allied with the manager, employees were unlikely to divulge information they may have deemed detrimental to their livelihood. Furthermore, arriving at the premises when expected, being supervised by either the funeral director or his 'right-hand' man, and viewing only front stage ritual activities meant that my observations were limited.

That staff felt apprehensive and yet obliged to allow me to interview them did, however, provide an insight into the autocratic nature of the funeral business. Every employee took instructions from and reported directly to the director. There was no chain of command, no pyramid structure of hierarchy – all power accrued and radiated from the funeral director. The company's rationalisation for this structure was that it ensured the smooth running of the funeral ceremony. My own observations revealed that in frontstage activities it constituted a ritualised mechanism for guarding against 'spoilt performances' (Goffman, 1959).

## Intensive fieldwork

It was not until after Christmas that fulltime participant observation became possible. The undertaker agreed that I could spend several weeks on the premises and would be free to observe and participate in a range of back stage activities. These including laying-out, embalming, coffin assembly, dressing the corpse and presentation. Attendance at funerals, sitting-in on arrangements interviews and accompanying staff on removals continued on a permission-only basis. As fieldwork became more intense and my role changed from being exclusively an observer to enjoying greater participation in the undertakers' work, I was able to overcome the remaining obstacles to access. Initially my activities were supervised by the director. It was only a matter of days, however, before more pressing business took him from my side. Once this precedent had been set I was left on a regular basis to make my own way.

## Ethical considerations

Continuing to restrict access in situations that involved the bereaved was presented to me as the need to avoid further distress to clients. Jon Stone considered that in face-to-face encounters the presence of an observer would have bewildered and perhaps offended his customers. For example, having an uninitiated observer trailing workers in the process of collecting bodies would, he believed, have done little to enhance business aspirations.

Because the research was carried out overtly and variously interpreted by respondents as an interest in 'attitudes to death', or, 'the work of funeral directors', there was never a problem about making notes during interviews with deathworkers or when observing their non-ceremonial practice. When attending funerals or arrangement interviews, however, that is, when face-to-face with the bereaved on a non-interview basis, I refrained from note-taking as I did not wish my purpose to be misconstrued and perhaps viewed as voyeuristic and intrusive.

Although death is an everyday event for the undertaker, bereavement is possibly the most traumatic crisis that an individual may ever experience. Consequently, in any non-formal contact with the bereaved I felt it important to make my presence as unobtrusive as possible. In front-stage situations I camouflaged my appearance by dressing in a fashion appropriate to the funeral company. When Jon Stone first invited me to observe a funeral he advised on the manner of dress: 'black skirt, white blouse, black cardigan and coat'. I drove to and from funerals in the front seat of the mourning car alongside the driver and devoted overt observations and comments to the role of the funeral workers. During arrangements interviews I was aware of playing the role of trainee funeral director as I felt this would encourage the bereaved to recognise that my interests lay with the work of the undertaker.

## Field diaries and fieldwork relationships

Field diaries are always advocated in ethnography. In the study of death and dying they are especially valuable. Even before the fieldwork began I kept a research diary and this was vigorously maintained throughout my time with the company. As a source of analysis it was an invaluable companion to field notes. Returning to these texts some time after the completion of fieldwork and asking retrospective questions of the data inevitably revealed gaps but mostly aided the process of analysis and disengagement. Reading through diary entries in conjunction with field data enabled me to identify changes in both the direction of the study and in my own approach to the research. Prior to meeting with undertakers and in the early days in the field I had experienced strong feelings of apprehension. As I became acquainted with deathworkers, diary entries founded on *a priori* stereotypes diminished and questions and *foci* altered as the collection and analysis of data propelled me in new directions. For example, an interest in learning details of the deceased evolved into descriptions of 'the box' and snatches of conversation between funeral workers. A diary entry for the second funeral I attended began: 'Funeral of Mrs X. 82 years, white, British, lived locally, died in hospital, mahogany veneered chipboard coffin.' Less than a month later an excerpt from my diary revealed that: 'It wasn't until we arrived at the crematorium that I realised I

had no idea as to who was in the box'. Charting my own development and initiation into the world of funeral directing, in part
highlighted by shifts in the taken-for-granted nature of aspects of
deathwork, produced insights into the stages of becoming an
undertaker and of the neutralising and accounting tactics they
employed. Two of the most commonly-used techniques aimed at
negating the distressing aspects of deathwork were 'dehumanis-
ing' and 'distancing'. Both relied on the workers ability to desist
from viewing the corpse as a person and treating it as a com-
modity. To assist in this task they created physical space between
themselves and their charges – restricting bodywork to the back
regions of the premises. A further tactic was the use of argot.
The body, referred to with the bereaved as 'Mr', 'Mrs', 'Mum' or
'Dad', in private or backstage became 'the bod', 'the thing' or
'the case'. Coffins were likewise renamed and become simply
'boxes' thus losing their association with death and the corpse.

The research diary also acted as a mechanism for maintaining
sanity. I frequently had reservations about my involvement in
deathwork: the initial horror of witnessing bodywork, a tangible
sense of tempting fate and a concern about the course of my
relationship with the undertaker – a constant need to respond to
his image of me as a 'carefree and affable young woman' clashed
with my self-perception as a serious researcher. Recording inner
feelings in the diary played a significant role in keeping me in the
field.

When access had been negotiated no questions were asked or
information offered by either the funeral director or myself about
personal relationships. The fact that I am female, however,
doubtless had an important influence on the shape and direction
of the study. I am often tempted to believe that it was primarily
this factor which opened the doors and lifted the lids to the
undertaking industry. In many ways gender proved to be an asset
which on occasions I consciously exploited: studying the undertaking trade, a predominantly male industry, I was certainly
encouraged to do so. It was by virtue of my gender, however,
that I became closer to the company receptionist and through her
to the undertaker's staff. Exchanging confidences formed the
basis of a bond between us and her goodwill undoubtedly
strengthened my relationships with other employees. I subsequently found it easier to talk with the staff and soon became
privy to the nods, winks, unspoken language and jargon which
formed a large part of their work situation. At other times being

a female researcher was extremely problematic and one can feel tremendously vulnerable as a woman working in such an alien environment[1].

## Leaving the field

The final phase of fieldwork stretched from June to August 1988. By the end of May I had collected and analysed considerable data and there was little more of value to be gained from remaining with the company. My attendance at the shop became infrequent and I concentrated on following up contacts with deathworkers and other organisations either linked to the undertaker or gained through independent approaches. In this way I was able to cross-check and test out much of the data and analysis formulated during the case study.

When fieldwork finally came to end, in the last week of August, the data lay untouched from that time until May of the following year. I then painstakingly ploughed my way through research diaries, field notes, transcripts, cemetery and company records, trade journals and photographic evidence. Data from all sources was repeatedly considered and cross-referenced. Transcripts were broken down by themes and annotated in note books in the order they occurred to avoid losing their context. Recurrent themes were extracted and indexed. The process was repeated for field notes and other written documentation. This aggregation of information greatly assisted the generation and testing of ideas and analysis. Reference to existing theories, such as Burke's work on dramaturgy (1945), Goffman's consideration of the self (1959), Lefebvre's insights into the utilisation of space (1991), Turner on the body (1984), and Johnson's contribution to the sociology of the professions (1972), enhanced analyses established in the field. Back in the university, discussions of the data with colleagues helped me to relocate the novelty of deathwork and further distance myself from the undertaker's account of his working practice.

## Generating theory

Martin Hammersley reminds us that what we 'discover' in the field, 'is never a simple reflection of what exists' (1991:23). In this

study of deathwork it was my interest in the performance of ritual and the fact that my activities had been closely supervised
and restricted to the front stage that coloured my observations in
the first four months. Using Glaser and Strauss' grounded theory
approach (1967), conceptual categories were generated from the
data at hand and substantiated and expanded through further
observation. If back-stage access had not been gained the study
would have been severely limited and the analysis would have
taken on a very different guise.

It was prolonged admission to the back stage that led me to
examine bodywork and the division of labour within these hinter
regions. Observation and discussions of the variety of roles and
tasks each worker performed provided an insight into the way in
which *they perceived* events and behaviours. It was here that I
came to realise that deathworkers were distinguished from one
another according to their level of skill and their proximity to the
polluting aspects of bodywork. Occupying the lowest positions in
the status hierarchy, the funeral assistant, who was responsible
for collecting dead bodies, suffered the 'sharp end' of death pollution. Apart from tasks such as washing and dressing, his work
could be reduced to a 'hump and dump' role requiring little skill.
By contrast, the embalmer was tasked, not with handling the
body or its waste but with *cleansing* the corpse and expelling
impurities. He neutralised the harmful effects of decay and
through reconstruction and cosmetic work refashioned or
'humanised' the body (Howarth, 1992). It is the pseudo-scientific
nature of work such as embalming that forms the basis for the
industry's claim to professional respectability – a status fundamental to the ideology of the modern funeral director.

Theorising in participant observation is not always achieved
through 'standard methodological recipes'. As Whyte insists,
'(p)robably most of our learning in (the) field is not on a conscious level. We often have flashes of insight that come to us
when we are not consciously thinking about a research problem
at all' (1981:213). There were many instances throughout this
study when 'flashes' of inspiration or intuition led to theorising.
Interpreting deathwork through the dramaturgical metaphor and
locating funeral directing within the sociology of the professions
are two examples. Reading through pages of field notes describing and commenting on numerous funeral preparations, I was
struck by the repetition of words and phrases such as 'make-up';
'presentation'; 'padding'; 'dressing'; 'positioning'; and 'the use of

scripts'. The metaphorical relevance of the theatrical analogy became clearer as I delved more deeply into working practice.

The use of flowcharts is sometimes recommended in analysis. In the funeral company I found these provided valuable clues into the social organisation of deathwork and used them at every opportunity to follow the course of the bereaved, the undertaker and the body. Once familiar with the whole of the premises, I mapped their dimensions and intricacies in detail. Distinguishing between back and front regions and locating those who dwelt in each, enabled me to work with concepts of spatial boundaries and junction points. Overlaying the map work of the undertaker's shop with a flow chart of the movement of the body through the premises, noting its treatment at each stage, provided the groundwork for an analysis of the 'humanisation' of the body.

## Conclusion

When conducting ethnography, researchers are no less a part of the world they enter than the people found therein (Hammersley and Atkinson, 1983). My interactions with deathworkers and the context in which we observed each other and exchanged ideas have been influential in moulding what I observed, the way in which I observed it, and what I believe it signified. In terms of the ethnographic model I began this study with the aim of understanding the motives of the group. Throughout the research I strove to suspend pre-fieldwork prejudices and, at the other extreme, to avoid being captivated by the funeral director's subjective and motivated account of his world. As noted earlier, there is always a danger in ethnography of 'going native'. Perhaps one of the most useful ways of combatting this possibility is to maintain scepticism in the field. This inevitably will affect relationships and interaction with members of the group under study. It need not detract from developing an understanding of 'insider' values. Indeed, healthy circumspection should augment a critical analysis of data.

After I had invested considerable time in the field, a degree of trust and acceptance did develop between myself and group members. Simply becoming a familiar face in the undertaker's premises and co-existing in times of crisis and routine, transformed the nature of my presence from 'stranger' (Schutz, 1964) to 'taken-for-granted'. I soon realised, however, that although undertakers have much in common there are inevitably sub-culture within the community. My field notes and recollections of the research experience demonstrate that in attempting to become a member of the group I played a variety of roles. In these I was either more or less accepted at different periods of time among different people. For example, my relationship with the funeral director began as one in which he was continually aware of my status as researcher. Over time, as daily routines became more familiar to me, my role changed as I could no longer sustain the aura of uninitiated curiosity. My presence, although flattering to the undertaker, became commonplace. I was then able to move freely among his staff and around the premises. Towards the end of the fieldwork when my visits became less frequent our interaction was more hasty, formal and less convivial. In the space of a year I had thus passed through the ranks of 'stranger' to, 'contributor to group culture', finally to return to the status of 'outsider'.

## Notes

1 A thorough discussion of the experience of female researchers is explored by Easterday, *et al.* (1977), Warren & Rasmussen (1977) and Warren (1988).

## References

Boston, S. and Trezise, R., (1987), *Merely Mortal: Coping with Dying, Death and Bereavement*, London: Methuen, in association with Channel Four Television Company.

Burke, K., (1945), *A Grammar of Motives*, Englewood Cliffs, NJ: Prentice Hall.

Douglas, J.D., (1971), *Understanding Everyday Life*, London: Routledge and Kegan Paul.

Easterday, L. *et al.*, (1977), 'The Making of a Female Researcher', *Urban Life*, Vol 6, No 3, October.

Fetterman, D.M., (1989), *Ethnography, Step by Step*, London: Sage.

Geertz, C., (1973), 'Ritual and Social Change: A Javanese Example', *American Anthropologist*, 59, pp. 32–54.

Glaser, B. and Strauss, A., (1967), *The Discovery of Grounded Theory*, New York: Aldine.

Goffman, E., (1959), *The Presentation of Self in Everyday Life*, New York: Doubleday.

Hammersley, M., (1991), *Reading Ethnographic Research*, London: Longman.

Hammersley, M. & Atkinson, P., (1983), *Ethnography: Principles in Practice*, London: Tavistock.

Howarth, G., (1992), *The Funeral Industry in the East End of London: an ethnographic study*, University of London: unpublished PhD thesis.

Johnson, T.J., (1972), *Professions and Power*, London: Macmillan.

Lefebvre, J., (1991), *The Production of Space*, translated by Donald Nicholson-Smith, Oxford: Basil Blackwell.

Mitford, J., (1963), *The American Way of Death*, London: Hutchinson.

Rock, P., (1979), *The Making of Symbolic Interactionism*, London: Macmillan.

Schutz, A., (1964), 'The Stranger', in A. Schutz (ed.), *Collected Papers, Vol II*, The Hague: Martinus Nijhoff.

Turner, B.S. (1984), *The Body and Society: Explorations in Social Theory*, Oxford: Basil Blackwell.

Warren, C.A.B., (1988), *Gender Issues in Field Research*, London: Sage.

Warren, C.A.B. and Rasmussen, P., (1977), 'Sex and Gender in Field Research', *Urban Life*, Vol 6, No 3, October.

Waugh, E., (1948), *The Loved One*, Boston: Little, Brown & Co.

Whyte, W.F., (1981), quoted in Rock, P., (1979), *op cit.*

Wolcott, H., (1975), 'Criteria for an Ethnographic Approach to Research in Schools', *Human Organization*, Vol 34, No. 2, Summer.

# Awareness contexts and the construction of dying in the cancer treatment setting: 'micro' and 'macro' levels in narrative analysis

## Kirsten Costain Schou

'Dying' as a socially constructed process in chronic illness makes its initial, definitive appearance for the dying individual in the treatment situation. For both the sociologist and the patient, awareness of dying is a central concern, for there can be no dying in the social sense without awareness (to whatever extent) of dying. The redefinition of illness in terms of incurability or terminality is an ambiguous *medical* process in many cases, and this ambiguity poses definitional problems for the dying person and for the sociologist researching dying, just as surely as it does for the clinician. Definition of dying occurs in micro-interactional contexts, between professionals and patients, but these interactions are shaped partly by discourses and goals belonging to (and shaping) macro-institutional and organisational contexts. It is argued here that narrative analysis of patients' accounts of diagnosis and prognostic discussions with clinicians can and should explore the construction of dying on both micro and macro levels. Methodological emphasis on the presence of both levels in narratives of 'private' experience allows for consideration both of the personal experience of individuals and of the larger discourses which belong to the organisation of medical work and to biomedicine generally. Intersecting of 'micro' and 'macro' influences and perspectives can be viewed in terms of 'local worlds' (Kleinman, 1992; Gregory and Longman, 1992) and their intersection with 'social worlds' *via* their sub-worlds (Strauss, 1978). Reference is made in this chapter to the narratives of a man with terminal lung cancer, to illustrate some of the 'voices' belonging to both local and social worlds, and operating in accounts of personal experience.

## 'Dying' as a definitional problem

'Dying' poses enormous definitional problems for both patients and clinicians, and therefore for sociologists who wish to study it as a social process. Determining when treatment for cancer should become 'palliative' rather than 'radical', deciding/revising definitions of prognostic likelihood, determining when an individual becomes expressly 'terminal' as opposed to 'incurably ill' or as having advanced disease – these are some of the definitional tasks of treatment management that have enormous practical and existential implications for the patient. Given the ambiguity that continues to surround awareness of even the *diagnosis* of cancer in many cases, it is hardly surprising that *prognosis* remains an ambiguous issue, frequently neutralised or actively avoided by treatment professionals in discussions with patients. It should be noted that, within the general context of ambiguity, there is much variation in 'openness' from centre to centre, unit to unit and clinician to clinician. *Types* of institutions are likely to differ in policies – both formal and informal – of openness with cancer patients: for example, open awareness is a foundational aspect of the philosophy of hospice in Britain. Openness with cancer patients in busy general hospitals, however, is more likely to be heavily compromised, and specialised cancer treatment institutions tend to fall, roughly speaking, somewhere in between regarding 'truth-telling' about diagnosis and prognosis. Also, the biomedical ambiguity surrounding the aetiology and course of many cancers, as well as the heterogeneity of response of different individuals and groups to the 'same' disease and treatment, produce great technical difficulty for the clinician in making prognostic assessments.

Prognostic ambiguity in cancer is indicative of the continuing elusiveness of chronic illness in the biomedical framework generally (Corbin and Strauss, 1988; Conrad, 1990). Medicine as a whole has become increasingly technological over the past 30 years, a development that has not wrought much change in the lowering of incidence or raising of cure rates of chronic illnesses like cancer. Rather, as a result in part of improved diagnostic and treatment techniques, more people than ever are diagnosed and living longer with chronic, life-threatening illnesses from which the majority will eventually die (Gerhardt, 1990). These developments arise from the increasing explicitness of medical investigations into the physical body, afforded by technology. The medical professional is historically (and increasingly publicly) seen as the manager/guardian of that technology (Freidson, 1970) and thus manager of awareness of its aims and products.

Through technological advancement, the body has become a much more 'public' object for medical analysis, and the 'awareness' rituals of death and dying (Glaser and Strauss, 1966) – 'the patterns of ceremony, speech and silence' of dying have been removed from the domestic sphere and relocated in the medical (Armstrong, 1987:652). This relocation of death from the private to the public sphere has not done away with contradiction and ambiguity in awareness issues. Williams (1989) has noted that while British public opinion has consistently approved euthanasia, there is still much equivocation over awareness. Whether or not to restrict awareness in medical practice has traditionally hinged upon the degree of certainty regarding diagnosis and prognosis (McIntosh, 1974), certainty that continues to be virtually unattainable in cancer treatment. But infallibility is central to the medical model, a model which serves as a 'central "structured metaphor" through which death is still encountered in Great Britain today' (Hockey, 1990:63). The image of medical knowledge as infallible is maintained in Britain in part through the relocation of dying from the home to the hospital, a place in which there is a discrepancy between high technology and 'confused moral or religious codes which offer few guidelines concerning the management of such knowledge and skill' (Hockey, 1990:78). It is in the charting of the medical 'awareness contexts' in which death and dying are initially defined that the sociology of death and dying finds some of its most central topics and methodological challenges.

The term 'awareness context' (Glaser and Strauss, 1966) refers to the structures and processes involved in the production and management of awareness (of diagnosis, prognosis, implications of information, etc.), and connotes the emergent and pervasive nature of this phenomenon, suggesting interaction between both 'micro' and 'macro' contextual features in its production. The term 'deathwork' might arguably be interchanged with 'awareness work': the degree to which one is able to undertake 'deathwork' as a dying person, and the extent to which the actions of agents in the medical and community settings can be seen as relating to 'deathwork' is dependent upon the 'awareness context' of death and dying for the dying individual and those close to

her. Following the interactionist distinction between biophysical
and social events (Freidson, 1970; Miller, 1978), there can be no
dying (in the social sense) and no deathwork without awareness
of dying (and no awareness without interpretation), however partial or limited this may be.

## The importance of a micro < – > macro contextual relation in data

The interpretation of (interdependent) 'micro' and 'macro' phenomena, ie of interaction between actors/agents in specific contexts and of organizational structure and ideology, is the means
by which an awareness context is constructed. I shall argue here
from a symbolic, interactionist perspective, that it is the awareness context that makes death and dying available for, or
obscures it from, sociological analysis. Also, in pursuing death
and dying as highly contextual social processes, rigid distinctions
between 'micro' and 'macro' processes and influences are unhelp-
ful. In order to be 'real', definitions of social reality must deal
with both micro and macro levels. A focus on both meanings
and structural factors is necessary to avoid one-dimensional sociological explanations of complex phenomena (Bury, 1991). What
is needed for the development of contextual understanding are
concepts and explanations that both afford and are constructed
by dialectical movement between levels. Both levels can be
'heard' in narrative accounts of experience, in the form of the
various 'voices' employed by the speaker and the various functions a single account may serve. As the researcher's contextual
understanding deepens through analysis of verbal accounts and
observation in interactional settings, the micro – > macro polarity is replaced by an appreciation of the dialectical, micro < – >
macro causal relations which form the substance of contextual
analysis.

One perspective in which the seeming polarity of micro and
macro is reconceptualised in terms of processes of social change
is Strauss' interactionist 'social world perspective' (Strauss, 1978).
Strauss describes social worlds in terms of Mead's emphasis on
'the endless formation of universes of discourse – with which
groups are coterminous' (p. 120). Social worlds (like medicine or
politics) have at least one primary activity with related clusters of
activities, sites where these occur, technology supplying modes

for carrying them out, and organizations devoted to furthering aspects of these activities. All of these features can be converted analytically into *subprocesses*. One focus of analysis is the 'segmenting' of social worlds in the intersecting of specifiable sub-worlds (intersecting occurs between *segments*, defined by 'micro' sub-processes – it does not occur between 'macro' global worlds). 'Power processes' are central to any study of social worlds, and include 'the allocating, assigning, and depriving of resources' by those who control membership and activities within these worlds. Social world analysis involves the examination of macro universes of discourse and the micro sub-worlds of interaction which they inform and which also inform them.

Another complementary perspective to Strauss is Kleinman's (1992) approach to development in health and illness as 'shared emergence and patterned change within local worlds in which experience flows between, within, and around us' (p. 129). Just as power processes and the control of resources are central to the study of social worlds, local worlds are arenas in which claims to resources must be defended. 'Local worlds' are intrinsically moral worlds, 'particular local patterns of recreating *what is most at stake* for us' (my italics). Local worlds are 'moral landscapes' in which actors must justify their need of resources which are limited (Gregory and Longman, 1992). Narrative retellings of experience describe the local worlds of individual speakers and reveal intersection with the local worlds of others. Thus local and social world issues are not rigidly separable, but intersect in the analysis of processes that form and constrain them both.

Kleinman distinguishes between the micro-context contained in the words of participants in research and the 'larger-scale forces' of the macro-context, and emphasises the need for a dialectical movement in analysis between micro- and macro levels. However, the voices of both macro and micro influences (and therefore both social and local worlds) are interwoven in actors' narratives of experience (Gregory and Longman, 1992). In analysing narrative, the researcher must attend to the various 'voices' contained within it: the (re-)construction of identity, the (re-) framing of experience, the definitions of constraint, the presence of discursive 'interpretive repertoires' (Potter and Wetherell, 1987), and the 'defense of moral adequacy' (Silverman, 1985), to name some potential elements in the construction of accounts of personal experience. In this way, the relationships between local moral worlds, intersecting subworlds and social worlds can be established.

I would like to illustrate with reference to one patient's narrative how the micro-level interactions involved in 'breaking bad news' about inoperability relates to the more macro-level discourses and structures surrounding the issue of prognosis and 'truth-telling' generally in the treatment of cancer patients, and which both construct and are constructed by the organisation of medical work in this area. An embedded concern here is the process of *definition* by which this patient begins to be a 'dying' person when a potential, radical treatment calendar (surgical removal of the mass and radiotherapy) is replaced by a palliative radiotherapy calendar. The awareness context (arising as a product of major discourses which allow or disallow specific activities, the organisational context of work characteristic of the social world of the institution, and the specific interactions of specific individuals within it) in which this change in trajectory is managed obscures the full definitional significance of the change: a terminal prognosis.

## Managing awareness at the start of palliation for a terminal cancer: the interdependence of 'micro' and 'macro' contextual features in interview narrative.

The work from which the ideas presented here were developed was a longitudinal study of the diagnostic and treatment experiences of 33 cancer patients receiving radiotherapy at a large regional treatment centre in the North of England. Several semi-structured interviews with each patient over a period of several months were transcribed and analysed using a Grounded Theory approach (Glaser and Strauss, 1967). In addition, several hours each week of data collection was spent observing consultations in a weekly prescription clinic at the treatment centre.

The treatment centre is a regional radiotherapy centre serving a wide catchment area, also providing chemotherapy and inpatient care for cancer patients undergoing treatment. Several thousand patients each year are treated on an outpatient basis, with a smaller number treated as inpatients. Most of the patients in this study were receiving radiotherapy as outpatients. Patients are referred to the centre from district or general hospitals, or *via* specialist clinics held in several regional hospitals by the centre's own consultants. The centre is a very 'visible' institution in the immediate community and in the catchment area generally, through its long history, first as a convalescent home for the poor and then as a cancer treatment centre, after the Second World War. Its name has become synonymous with the word 'cancer' and is associated in the minds of community members as a place for those with 'no hope' of recovery, and with pain, suffering and death, particularly for those whose relatives were treated there 20 or 30 years ago. Modern treatment techniques have greatly improved the experience of radiotherapy however, and the centre has been steadily developing its modern service (both technologically and in terms of relations with patients and their families). It is now a 'centre of excellence' with an international profile, and an important teaching facility. This change in image has not penetrated images of the centre held by the community at large, and the name of the centre still serves as a diagnosis of cancer for prospective patients. Many patients in my sample felt the name of the centre should be changed so that it could be distanced from its past image.

The atmosphere of the centre is exceptionally 'upbeat', and patients new to it found their negative preconceptions completely changed after their first visit to Prescription clinic to be set up for treatment. The centre was experienced as a supportive environment, affording patients much contact with other patients in the waiting rooms (a main source of information and support). Much of the organisation of staff and their work is geared to the maintenance of a unified, cheerful and informative service: patients are continually asked if they have any questions, and radiography and nursing staff are responsible for monitoring 'how patients are doing' as they move through the treatment calendar. Each patient attends a weekly Review clinic under a particular consultant but patients have the most contact with radiography and nursing staff, who are responsible for making referrals to the consultant if problems with treatment effects arise. Consultant staff and their registrars are almost entirely male, while the radiography and nursing staff are predominantly female, reflecting continuing patterns in medical institutions generally.

The centre is in transition, shifting away from the image of the 'workhouse' and its historical reputation as a place of last resort for dying people condemned to pain and suffering, toward that of a modern, state-of-the-art cancer treatment centre offering efficient and friendly service. Changes in practice within it also reflect a broader transition in medicine generally, from the patriarchal, rigidly hierarchical organisation with 'closed awareness' as the rule, to a more open, informative service ethic, in which lower status staff work alongside high-status medical professionals. With regard to hierarchy it can be said that the organisation of this specialist cancer treatment centre falls somewhere between the large, general acute-care institutions, from which most patients are referred, and the hospice. As in hospices, the emphasis in the centre is placed more on team-work than on hierarchy – although the hierarchy remains – with lower-status staff in possession of a strong 'voice' in decision-making and all aspects of the work of the centre. The transition taking place within medicine has not occurred in its entirety, nor is the current ideal of 'open awareness' as yet achieved but, at this point in the discursive shift away from old norms of practice, the goals and techniques of *both* paternalistic medicine and of a newer, more 'open' orientation apply.

The centre offers treatment for a wide range of cancers, largely those of the head and neck, lung and breast. Thus patients in any of its waiting rooms will differ greatly from one another in symptomatology, depending on diagnosis and treatment site(s), and in the extensiveness of the disease (the waiting rooms always display a broad dimensional range of what 'cancer' can be and mean, and of who 'cancer patients' are. Study respondents spoke at length of the positive effect this contact had on their own struggle to define their experience, even though it often meant seeing people who were dying, or who had more advanced disease than they). The actual treatment work of the centre consists, in general, in debilitating the disease in the newly diagnosed, minimising progression in those with recurrences or advanced disease, preventing local recurrence, making surgery possible by shrinking tumour growth, and alleviating or minimising symptoms caused by disease progression. For some patients, behind this work will lie the possibility of disease eradication, more likely as a result of a successful *combination* of treatment modes rather than on the strength of a particular mode, and this possibility will shape their treatment calendars for as long as it remains a justifiable goal for treatment. If at all possible, a radical, cure-directed treatment trajectory is envisaged for each patient. This may, however, only *amount* to palliation in actual outcome, with professionals speaking of success in terms of survival time rather than disease eradication (and here I use the term 'palliation' in the broadest sense, referring to the treatment of 'symptoms' and effects, as distinct from that which ultimately affects underlying disease processes). Sometimes intensive, radical treatment is needed to forestall disease progression and extend life, although ultimately death from the disease is the probable outcome. The most frequently used treatment plan among newly diagnosed patients is a radical one with palliative expectation, and this may be 'palliative' in any of the senses given above.

Although the patients were newly diagnosed, 25 per cent were receiving palliative rather than radical treatment for advanced disease. Most of this latter group became formally diagnosed as terminally ill as the study progressed, and half of these patients had died at the completion of the study. Awareness of prognosis was profoundly ambiguous, but the theme of prognosis ran underneath all respondent's discussions about treatment. I had access to the TNM statistic ('tumours nodes metastases') where available, and was told by the consultant presiding over the prescription clinic each week what the prognostic assessment was for each study participant (the fact that I was privy to this information while many patients were not raises important ethical questions for research). The purpose of obtaining prognostic expectations of consultants for each patient was not to test what the patient appeared to be saying about prognosis (finding out 'the truth' and seeing whether they knew it or not), but to identify the different 'trajectory projections' for treatment (Corbin and Strauss, 1988) of treatment managers and their patients. The obscurity of the prognosis issue, on the one hand, and its pervasiveness, on the other, prompts questions about how death and dying might be allowed or dis-allowed in the social world of treatment, and the implications of this for sociological research into death and dying.

## Palliation vs 'Radical' Treatment

The definitional context in which the awareness of terminal illness initially begins for the cancer patient is the treatment situation. There is no facile boundary between the end of mainstream 'treatment' and the beginning of 'dying' in many instances: dying will begin in the larger context of an illness calendar already in existence, involving treatment (often much treatment) and continuing to involve it, often in treatment centres the public mandate of which is 'cure'. Being terminally ill may begin at diagnosis but diagnosis and treatment usually overlap; and awareness of the terminal prognosis will dawn as the significance of the treatment calendar is revealed. In the case of recurrence, this must be defined as such, in the medical setting by medical agents, and then further defined, as lying beyond the focus of radical or curative treatment, before the definitions of 'incurably' and then 'terminally' ill can be applied. Treatment calendars are constructed and managed within large organizational and institutional structures, involving many sub-worlds. Management of the treatment calendar within this varied geography forms the interactional context in which awareness, first of the cancer diagnosis and then of dying, begins.

The medical determination of an individual as being 'incurably' ill will thus invariably take place within an institution ostensibly devoted to 'curing' disease: on a ward or in a specialist outpatient clinic, within a large 'acute-care' general hospital, or within a treatment centre devoted to the disease in question. In either case, the official, public institutional mandate is to eradicate disease or to stop the disease process, while in both cases, much of the actual work performed is aimed at the *management* of chronic illnesses (Corbin and Strauss, 1988). In the case of the cancer treatment centre studied here, this emphasis on the work of the institution as primarily 'curative' is subtle but pervasive. The *actual* work of the institution (as defined by its biomedical *effects*) will be primarily palliative, however, and herein lies the definitional difficulty for the patient.

Having sketched some aspects of the context in which the definitional problem of 'dying' initially emerges, I will briefly describe the method employed before going on to the narrative example.

## The importance of a micro < – > macro relation in analysis and analytic constructions

The interdependence between 'micro' interaction and 'macro' structures is revealed in the nature of the discourses which allow for and sustain both. Awareness of dying consists in the spaces cleared for it in interactions between individuals and in the policies and ideologies of the institutions in which these interactions take place as social worlds; the substance of both is discourse and the modes of activity that discourses make possible.

My Grounded Theory analysis (Glaser and Strauss, 1967; Strauss and Corbin, 1990) consisted in generating conceptual labels with which to describe discrete discursive features of the interviews, gradually moving from the level of data description to the delineation of relationships between excerpts and between conceptual groupings of excerpts. As relationships within and between conceptual groupings were developed, these became categories, each of which was part of an emerging, explanatory theoretical framework. Grounded theory method consists in analytic induction through the process of constant comparison/contrast of data excerpts with other excerpts, of individual excerpts with conceptual groupings of excerpts, and of each part of the developing explanatory framework with every other part. The method encourages the construction of conceptual terms by the researcher that have relevance for both micro and macro perspectives of the social world, and that deal well with both issues of structure and of process.

In glossing some of my key analytic constructions, I wish to underscore the importance of a micro–macro conceptual relation in sociological analysis, as well as provide necessary background for the narrative example to follow. I am concerned in this discussion with how 'dying' begins to emerge in the treatment setting within an ambiguous awareness context, and with the general implications of its definitional emergence (or non-emergence) for sociological research in death and dying.

The substance of my analysis was ideas about the structuring and use of calendars, trajectories, definitional tasks, and awareness contexts in the process of becoming diagnosed with and starting treatment for cancer. First, there are three main contextual features forming the macro-context of diagnosis and early treatment experience in which all the above play a part:

1 The nested nature of diagnosis, treatment calendar establishment and prognosis. Patients were mainly diagnosed in one of three large general hospitals before being referred to the treatment centre for radiotherapy (some for both radiotherapy and chemotherapy). However, the process of diagnosis includes the establishment of treatability with various modes and schedules of treatment, and this may involve further tests in the hospital setting. Treatment calendar establishment is thus a shared task of surgical and consultant staff at the referring hospital, *and* of staff at the treatment centre. For some patients, diagnostic

processes form part of 'treatment' (as in the removal of a tumour for diagnostic tests). Establishing treatability and implementing a treatment calendar involves assessments of prognosis. The treatment calendar itself can function as a statement of diagnosis for patients ('I'm going to have radiotherapy at [the centre], I must have cancer') or prognosis (inoperability resulting in narrowed treatment options and reduced chance of 'cure'). The degree to which each of these issues (diagnosis, treatability and prognosis) is exposed to the patient corresponds to the degree of 'openness' in the awareness context set up in interaction between patients and professionals, and other patients, family members, friends etc. These interactions are shaped in part by influences from the cultures of the institutions involved (in this case one large teaching hospital, two district hospitals, and the treatment centre, also a teaching institution) and by the broader culture of medicine generally.

2  The structure and role/impact of the various calendars and trajectories involved in diagnosis and the start of treatment: both those that are personal or private, and those related to illness and treatment, and of the agents responsible for them.

3  The definitional tasks and strategies of patients in diagnosis and treatment through which sense is made of experience, and new rhythms in daily living are set up.

A *calendar* is any concrete plan involving the ordering of action over time, and the notion of stages to be negotiated at specific times/places along a trajectory. Calendar construction is an essentially linear mode of structuring and organizing all aspects of living, pervasive in Western culture (although certain groups within Western society have very different conceptions of time as non-linear, as, for example, in North American Indian culture). The individual *illness and treatment calendars* of patients are experienced in a context of individuals' *personal/private and life calendars*, and of those calendars that punctuate both personal and community life and that are tied to the *calendar year* (the latter refers to the actual organisation of time into days, weeks, months and to specific points within that organization, like Bank holidays and Christmas, that serve as markers of a general and communal context. Jewish people in Britain will still experience Christmas as a calendar event even though they do not experience it as a religious occasion or as involving required rituals, like present-giving etc.). Illness and treatment calendars are bound up in the public and non-public agendas of medical institutions, just as they are specific to individual patients, and part of their private calendars.

A *trajectory* is also linear and time-bound, but is used here to mean a *projection*, whereas the calendar is a concrete *plan*, composed of mini-plans in the form of *schedules* (the notion of the illness 'trajectory' and the distinction between a trajectory *plan* and the trajectory *projection* are given in Corbin and Strauss (1988). I have conceptualised this distinction in terms of calendars and trajectories). Trajectories are the templates for calendars. A trajectory formulation in diagnosis and treatment is based on ideas about what could/should/might happen at different points in an experience over time, based on probability and the assessment of contextual features. A calendar, on the other hand, is based on what *will* happen at certain points along a specific trajectory projection. As the trajectory projection changes, so does the calendar.

Treatment trajectories exist in the minds of treatment planners and managers – they are *not* exposed in their entirety to patients directly (except in rare instances) but are instead intuited by patients and indicated partially or hinted at by practitioners to patients. Information about them is implicit in the details of the treatment calendars for which they are the template. Treatment calendars, on the other hand, are made known in varying degrees to patients (otherwise they could not be implemented) and can be discussed by patients and others to an extent by virtue of their 'public' (or semi-public) nature. They are subject to change however, as the agent/treatment manager sees the disease trajectory as changed, and thus adjusts the treatment trajectory accordingly, following it through the implementation of a new treatment calendar. Patients have their own trajectory ideas of course, and these are developed through the tackling of various definitional tasks and strategies.

*Definitional tasks* are both tasks and strategies undertaken and employed to provide meaning and context within the unique experience of diagnosis and treatment for the newly-diagnosed person with cancer. The act of *comparing and contrasting* with other patients' experiences and between one's own observations as a patient is a useful *activity* in that it leads to the development of a more *dimensional* view of the experience, and it may become a conscious *strategy* to this end. It is also a *task*, central to gaining understanding and developing a *context* within which to locate one's own experience as a patient. At the point of diagnosis, most patients lack any sense of a trajectory for their experience, and the calendars they have been using/constructing and living have been temporarily interrupted and postponed through the process of becoming diagnosed. These processes are pervasive and general to the overall task of making sense of experience. There are other, allied tasks pertinent to different stages in the experience. In the context of diagnosis as a definitional problem for example, specific tasks for the patient include establishing an open awareness context (to whatever degree), interpreting significance of diagnostic information in relation to prognosis, and reinterpreting symptoms once the diagnosis and/or prognosis is announced. Definitional tasks for the diagnosing professional(s) include establishing and altering trajectory projections, gauging the awareness context and revealing the diagnosis to the patient.

Finally, *awareness contexts* are a pervasive aspect of diagnosis and treatment contexts. A context wherein questioning and discussion are encouraged and little is witheld from the patient is an *open awareness context*, whereas one in which passivity is required of the patient and information closely guarded and rarely volunteered would be a *closed awareness context*. Much of the definitional activity of patients in this study was aimed at moving from an essentially ambiguous awareness context to a more open one. In the past, the very fact of the nature of the diagnosis was often a closed issue. Currently, while most patients readily realise they have cancer (although professional's use of the word 'cancer' is still surprisingly minimal), the issue of *prognosis* remains off-limits much of the time, and elaborate awareness contexts are constructed to keep it from arising, or to minimise its significance.

There is great difficulty in studying the social process of dying when diagnosis and prognosis remain ambiguous or closed issues in treatment calendars comprised of and enacted through interactions between clinicians and patients. Much 'deathwork' is actually managed at treatment centres officially devoted to curing disease through the management of acute illness or radical treatment calendars for chronic illness. In the case of palliative radiation treatment, the terminally ill patient will be surrounded by other patients for whom there is still the possibility of disease eradication. In such situations, there is a pervasive, public emphasis on 'cure' that forms an intimate part of the 'service ideal' of the treatment centre, even though the actual *work* of the centre is essentially palliative. Especially at the start of the 'incurable' palliative treatment trajectory, the awareness of being terminally ill is managed in such contexts. In these contexts as well there is an observable gap between modern socio-medical theory, which increasingly stresses the importance of 'truth-telling' (Britten, 1991; Armstrong, 1987) and of 'the patient's view' (Armstrong, 1984), and clinical practice, in which there is little space and time for either. The treatment context is an ambiguous one as regards the issue of dying, because of the simultaneous presence within it of two competing discourses (Britten, 1991), one of professional 'openness' in dealings with the patient-as-autonomous-person in which the psychological and social being of the person is recognised, and the older one of paternalism, wherein the goals of biomedicine are primary. For the modern cancer treatment centre studied here, the service ideal consists in the open provision of information within a context in which disease is targeted for 'cure' or eradication. This public 'service ideal' (conveyed to patients in statements by staff about the 'success' of the centre in treating cancer) conflicts with the reality of the problems and work of the service, which include the biomedical ambiguity of cancer, the limitations and fallibility of treatments and medical knowledge, and the limitations on resources.

## Mr H: A narrative example

Mr H was a lung cancer patient who had initially presented at the Casualty department of a large local hospital because of what he thought was an asthma attack. He was initially diagnosed with pneumonia, and had spent a week in hospital before being referred as an inpatient to a 'chest specialist' whose 'assistant' eventually told him he had a 'growth'. Mr H. counted this interaction (described below) as his cancer diagnosis, although he could not recall the word 'cancer' being used by professionals. He was then referred on to another consultant be 'set up' for palliative radiotherapy. His diagnostic process involved much uncertainty regarding operability of the tumour mass in his right lung. This issue was a prognostic issue, because without surgical removal of the mass, palliation with radiotherapy was the only treatment option, given the extensiveness of the disease. Mr H. seemed aware of the significance of the radiation treatment calendar eventually selected, although clear discussions of prognosis apparently had not occurred. The excerpts below are taken from Mr H's account of the diagnostic process during which he began to be defined as someone with a terminal disease.

*Transcription key*: (.) = slight pause; (1) = seconds;
r:r = extended sounds; __ = emphasis;
- - = words spoken closely together;
[ ] = editorial comments.

*Excerpt 1*

PH: They took uh you know they took a piece out of the lungs anyway for test (.) a:and they told me that they were going to do further test (.) and (2) this, he was uh one of Dr C's [hospital consultant's] assistants you know he came along and he said to me he said (.) oh you've got a growth uh in your:r, right lung you know no problems we're going to remove the lung and all this (1) a:and then eh (.) you know he said uh, we'll go into all these other tests though so:o (.) it was waiting for them you know and uh (.) then I had them (.) and he came along on the Friday and he-he says, oh he says uh surgery's out (.) and uh, then Saturday, Dr. C came along (.) well surgery hasn't been ruled out yet but we haven't studied everythink (.) properly yet and (.) see you on Monday he never came on Monday (.) and so, about Monday dinnertime, his assistant turned uh you know the— these two that came round, and so I pulled them up and I said, I said I want to know what's happening you know I said (.) Dr. C said he was coming back today and I said he hasn't been I said and, one's saying one thing and other's saying another thing.

Here the 'diagnosis' (a 'growth' on the lung) and treatment calendar are conveyed to Mr H by junior staff (treatment is apparently minimalised as 'no problem'). The presence of junior or non-senior staff ('assistants', registrars, housemen etc.) as treatment managers in patient's narratives about diagnosis and treatment was pervasive in these interviews. The pronouncement that Mr H is operable is made initially by Dr C's 'assistant', then changed by the same junior to inoperable. Dr C as treatment manager then contradicts this to say that surgery is still a consideration, but fails to reappear to confirm this later on. Instead, the two juniors appear and Mr H challenges them to clarify the situation. Mr H undertakes to 'open' the ambiguous awareness context surrounding the issue of his treatment (and prognosis).

*Excerpt 2*

PH: So:o they [the two juniors] sat down on the bed you know and said (.) well, there isn't anything what we can do for you (.) we've made an appointment for you to see a gentleman called Mr A [Radiotherapy consultant] from ——— [Treatment centre] tomorra afternoon (.) a:and so I said well (.) I said I been here I said for 2 weeks I said now taking up a bed I said what somebody wan—else could probably have had I said it, you could have said this two weeks ago (.) well we didn't know how to approach you I said well, I said in the first place I says when — when you's found it in the lung I said you came straight out with it I said since then you've gone round corners (.) well we don't know really how to you know how to approach different people (.) so I said well I think it's better to know the truth than be messed about.

Junior staff are again in the position of conveying the new treatment calendar to Mr H, the subtext of which is prognosis (the threat that he may be 'untreatable' and thus incurable is given voice in the phrase 'there isn't anything that we can do for you'. Whether or not Mr H is recounting what was actually said cannot be dealt with; rather, in his choice of phrase he gives some indication of what he has *heard*). Details of the actual calendar are given (the new treatment manager and the new institution) by way of indicating the transition from one treatment calendar to another. Mr H raises the issue of wasted resources caused by his taking time and space that 'somebody else' could have had, a direct result of the ambiguous awareness context set up by staff. In response to this, the two juniors are heard to admit to the ambiguity, invoking *individualism* as the reason for the delay in breaking the bad news: each patient is different, and so poses an interactional difficulty for staff, hence the ambiguous awareness context.

*Excerpt 3*

PH: A:and <u>then</u> (1) when I went in to see [the radiotherapy consultant] yesterday it was Mr A hisself who was—a-at <u>first</u> he got called away there was an emergency (.) but <u>he</u> started going round corners with me at the beginning you know (.) and I said to him I says I <u>know</u> what's wrong with me I says I've come here I said to see whether (.) you can do anything for me you know I says I wouldn'you know that's, that's what I'm <u>here</u> for and so we might as well talk about it (.) and then the—the coloured gentleman (.) <u>he</u> came, and took over because Mr A was called away on an emergency like so I only <u>saw</u> Mr A hisself for a couple of minutes and (.) so it was a coloured gentleman who talked to me and (.) he was sort of a bit, evasive but he:e he m-more or less pointed it out to me you know so:o (.).

Mr H is again charged with having to 'open' up the ambiguous awareness context in order to discuss treatment specifics. He describes himself doing this in a direct and responsible manner reminding the consultant that he is there to receive a service he and his staff should provide. Throughout his narrative, Mr H is careful to depict his own active role in the opening of the awareness context in interaction with reluctant professionals. As before, the treatment calendar is discussed eventually by Mr A's registrar, as Mr A as treatment manager must attend to 'an emergency' elsewhere.

*Excerpt 4*

PH: I mean <u>why</u> didn't they tell me this [inoperable tumour mass and palliative — non-curative —- radiotherapy course] right at the beginning they must have known at the beginning but they didn't tell me (.) I mean, what it w—- the what he said to me he said well (.) he said you don't really know how to approach people how they're going to <u>take</u> it and that (.) well I suppose everybody is different I mean I know, you know some people who <u>do</u> they just throw the towel in don't they you know they (.) they seem to lose interest. . .

The 'this' of Mr H's account is still ambiguous: has he understood the prognostic implications of inoperability (and of the reluctance of professionals to deal with him directly)?

Alternatively he may have interpreted the shift away from surgery to radiotherapy alone as confirmation that he has *cancer*, and not just a 'growth' that can be removed, 'no problem'. He will not know that his radiotherapy calendar of five days is a palliative one, and will go on to wonder aloud in subsequent interviews why others are having 5 *weeks* of treatment instead. He will also alternate between talking about having to face up to the inevitability of his death from cancer, and his hope that maybe 'the treatment will work'. He will need, throughout the process of his dying, to both grieve and hope, preferably supported by a treatment environment that allows space for the 'awareness of dying' to develop.

In this last excerpt, individualism is explored by Mr H, who concedes that 'everybody *is* different' and that 'some people' do react to bad news by giving up. Mr H went on to describe how the registrar at the treatment centre had expressed admiration for Mr H's ability to 'take' the news (but what news has he taken?), and how he had joked that Mr H should become a counsellor for other patients:

> He said to me he says I think we ought you ought to come
> and work for us counselling other people [laughs]!

Mr H describes himself as an exemplary individual in a difficult situation, and how this exemplary behaviour was noted by professionals who have fallen short of their duty to provide an open awareness context in relation to the issue of treatment (the subtext of which is prognosis). In so doing Mr H uses 'individualism' to defend his 'local moral world'; Mr H is not 'some people', who would have 'lost interest' or reacted badly. Much interview space in interviews with terminally ill patients is devoted to describing instances of exemplary coping and rationalising instances of failing to 'cope' (the interview situation itself is one in which moral justification of one's actions and thoughts is implicitly demanded). Mr H is aware of the moral imperative in this situation to 'cope well'.

Within these narratives of experience there are interwoven contextual features relating to both the local world of this particular man as a person and a patient and the larger social world of the institutions involved and of medicine itself. The continuing obscurity of Mr H's terminal prognosis is maintained by an ambiguous awareness context. The micro-interactional contexts reconstructed by Mr H in his accounts are shaped in part by macro-level discourses (like 'individualism') with their roots in biomedicine, and by organizational features (the pervasive use of juniors to carry out difficult relational work at particularly sensitive places in the early treatment calendar, for example). The 'awareness context' surrounding the issue of Mr H's cancer and its prognosis is shaped on both micro-interactional and macro-organisational levels. Private and public constraints and aims of both individual actors and social worlds are interdependent at both micro and macro levels; this interdependence is the means by which local and social worlds (through their sub-worlds) intersect.

'Individualism' and 'minimisation' are two modes of discussing treatment by agents implicated in Mr H's accounts. Individualistic accounts of treatment and its effects are often accompanied by minimisation of the impact and even the importance of treatment (extensive radiotherapy schedules were repeatedly referred to as 'a precaution' by agents in the treatment centre and in the three hospitals from which patients interviewed were referred). These complementary modes of speaking about treatment interfere with two complementary definitional tasks for the patient in dealing with treatment and illness, and these are also given voice in Mr H's narratives. The patient, with little initial understanding of the disease and its treatment, must construct a more dimensional view of both. This involves comparing and contrasting with other patients, those with different diagnoses and treatment calendars and at different stages of the disease.

Developing a dimensional context within which to locate *personal* experience enables the patient better to manage the treatment calendar and the personal calendar (and this becomes particularly important in terminal cancer when illness and treatment calendars frequently shift to the foreground and the personal calendar recedes to the background). Dimensionalising and contextualising is facilitated by an open awareness context, in which comparison and contrast with the treatment calendars of others, and the questioning of staff in the treatment situation about treatment can take place.

However, 'individualism' mitigates against open awareness of treatment and related issues, the central one being prognosis. Within an individualist conception of the treatment experience, doubt may not easily be cast on treatment procedures or on the knowledge and judgement of treatment managers (particularly the latter). Doubt in the treatment situation is not publicly admissable *except* in relation to the individual patient, her individual body, and individual disease process. The general culture of medicine stresses the image of the practitioner's skills as beyond doubt, and of his judgement as certain, while emphasising also the paternalistic role of the doctor in protecting the patient from doubt (particularly from doubt about the practitioner and medical knowledge). In so protecting the *patient*, the doctor also safeguards her judgement and knowledge by disallowing the patient's scrutiny of it (scrutiny that might lead to doubt). Within the specific culture of the treatment centre studied here, formal statements were made to new patients about the importance of *not* discussing treatment with any other patients, 'because everyone is different'. Also, the introductory material for radiotherapy patients produced by the centre gave this prohibition repeatedly, stressing that all questions about treatment were to be addressed to clinic staff (radiographers and nursing staff) rather than to other patients (all of the patients interviewed chose to ignore the 'no talking' rule, although they expressed feelings of guilt in doing so).

This attempt by professionals to restrict awareness and control what is being discussed in its waiting rooms and clinics reflects the importance of controlling knowledge of the *work* done by medical professionals in maintaining their position *as* professionals with 'expert' status. This status is preserved by the maintenance of the exclusive claim to medical knowledge and its dissemination by the medical professional. It is important that 'treatment' (the work of the centre) be seen as 'esoteric and unevaluable by laypersons' (Freidson, 1970:45) so as to preserve professional autonomy and the image of infallibility so central to medicine's concept of 'profession'. Individualism is employed to wave away queries about treatment's efficacy (and thus the efficacy of professional's work).

The public face of treatment is conveyed most often by an *ideal trajectory projection*, in which 'cure' is the goal, through minimisation of both the importance of non-primary treatment as a mere 'precaution' (use of this word appeared to be standard for all discussions of radiotherapy and chemotherapy with patients who had had surgery first), and minimal discussion of its potential effects on the ill person (including the effects of the illness and treatment *calendars* on the personal calendar). There was a tendency in both the three hospitals and the treatment centre for the seriousness of treatment in general to be minimised in descriptions of it ('it's no problem, we'll remove the lung').

Rather, any problems with treatment are located discursively in the patient: adverse effects are the body's (particular body's) reaction *to* treatment. Treatment is there to 'fight' the disease and is therefore 'good'. Adverse effects are 'bad' but primarily stem from the body's failure to act more positively. Absence of cure is 'bad' but occurs because the specific disease process is too intractable or because the particular body (and, as is increasingly suggested, mind) has not proved competent enough to make use of the inherent curative powers of treatment to 'fight' the disease (the pervasive emphasis in the psycho-oncologic 'coping' literature on 'fighting spirit' – Greer *et al.*, 1989: Watson *et al.*, 1991 – is an enormously moral aspect of the emphasis on individualism in treatment.)

This emphasis on individualism originates in the biomedical model of disease and treatment which shapes medical practice. In the biomedical model, disease processes are considered identifiable as 'entities' through a reductionist process of isolating linear cause and effect relationships in specific diseased organs. Emphasis is placed on the affected part and the nature of the disease involvement in the body, so that interventions can be targetted at the isolated diseased organs or area. Gaining biomedical knowledge about the patient within this model depends upon the careful observation of the particular disease in the particular body of the particular patient. The clinical profile of a disease is built up as individual cases are observed and documented. Thus the validity of the clinical profile is seen in this model to depend on accurate observation of each *individual* case.

While 'individualism' has its roots in the dominant biomedical model of disease, and in the very real biomedical ambiguity and unpredictability of those processes called 'cancer' (as well as the great biological and psychological diversity of individuals who are ill with cancer), it is nevertheless employed in the diagnostic and treatment settings to dis-allow doubt about treatments which are themselves only partially understood, and which are certainly limited in their powers. In maintaining a discourse of individualism (and accompanying minimisation) in which discussion of these limitations of medical knowledge and practice is prohibited, the deviance of the *patient* is the focus, and an open awareness context (one in which prognosis can be discussed and re-discussed as the illness progresses) is not possible. The macro-contextual features of individualism and the ambiguity that sustains it, which emanate from biomedicine and biological reality, thus have implications for the management of medical work and the treatment organization, for the micro-context of the patient's illness, treatment and private calendars (management of which is contingent on ideas about treatment and prognosis), and for the researcher concerned with how 'dying' becomes available for sociological analysis in the medical (treatment) setting in the first place.

The 'same' contextual feature can operate in different ways depending on different actors' purposes. Individual treatment managers may use the discourse of individualism to excuse themselves from not being more 'open' ('we never know how each person will react'), from not giving more information about the effects of treatment, its limitations and about prognostic likelihood. 'Individualism' thus gives them a rationale for generally maintaining a closed or ambiguous awareness context with patients. Keeping the awareness context closed or ambiguous for individual patients gives agents greater power generally in controlling and guarding resources, and thus has implications for the treatment organisation. If awareness is to be restricted anyway, interactions like explaining to an individual patient the move from the possibility of cure to a palliative treatment plan can be given over to less experienced junior staff, freeing the consultant or surgeon for other, more technical work. This practice may become a feature of the organisation, and of the educational work of the institution as a teaching hospital, in which patients are an educational (and research) resource, and students a labour resource. In this regard, 'individualism' may simply be facilitating the perpetuation of a longstanding organizational feature in the centre – the use of junior or non-senior staff to do difficult interactional work – at a time when discourses are shifting from an emphasis on suppressing prognostic issues to having to provide clear information.

Conversely, patients may use 'individualism' to justify themselves as *deserv*ing of just those resources professionals have to manage and may wish to restrict (namely, the time and personal attention of senior treatment managers). Because patients are unique individuals, they are worthy of 'special' treatment and consideration *as* individuals (as *persons*), and cannot be reduced to the level of the 'case', having this unique personhood discounted in impersonal treatment. Defending one's right to *personal* treatment and consideration by professionals involves establishing that one's individual, private experience is important. It must be remembered that this right is not implicit in the treatment situation, and is constantly threatened by the general public knowledge of the strain on resources in the Health Service. Also, just as professionals may use 'individualism' to explain away or minimise the vagaries of treatment effects or limitations ('everybody reacts differently'), patients may invoke their individuality to explain disturbing treatment effects; they are not reacting 'perversely' but responding differently because of a more positive 'uniqueness' (and not necessarily because they are more ill), a more emotionally (and morally) neutral explanation.

## Conclusion

The treatment calendar (consisting of interactions between individual agents in specific settings) is both revelatory of, and a means of protecting, the secret of dying. The awareness of dying begins in a complex interactional context shaped by dominant discourses arising from the larger social worlds of medicine and of the treatment institution, used in different ways in the fulfillment of local world concerns of the individual interacting agents. The way in which these agents and their work is viewed (by them and by others) affects awareness. Awareness can be shaped by non-senior staff, operating as a treatment management resource, and by the teaching mandates of institutions in which patients are an educational and research resource. Also, because there are changes occuring in medical discourse involving the patient, away from paternalistic 'closed awareness' and toward 'truth-telling' and 'open awareness', the secret of dying is both still a secret and, if not told, a lie (Armstrong, 1987). Both 'regimes of truth' are involved in the awareness contexts of treatment, further complicating the issue of awareness of dying.

Any sociology of dying must address the issue of how the terminal prognosis is constructed and conveyed to the patient (for without it the patient in the *social* sense, and likewise for research purposes, would not otherwise *be* 'dying'), and address the political and power issues involved in constraining awareness of prognosis. Secondly, in addressing the issue of definition in its entirety, the relation of the 'micro' level of interaction and of the patient's private world or local world to the 'macro' level of the encompassing social world of the institution in which this defining process is undertaken, and to medicine generally must be established. The twilight zone of biomedical prognostic uncertainty and the obfuscation of the *issue* of dying in both actions (like failing to confirm test results) and in discourse are key issues for the sociology of death and dying: 'Truth and its accompanying discourse generates the very phenomena – people, ideas, objects – which will become the focus of its analysis' (Armstrong, 1987:655). If 'dying' as a social process is to be studied, its construction, on both micro and macro levels, and that of the awareness contexts within which it is allowed or dis-allowed, must be problematised and made an analytic focus.

# References

Armstrong, D., (1984), 'The patient's view', *Social Science and Medicine*, 18, 9:7437–44.

Armstrong, D., (1987), 'Silence and truth in death and dying', *Social Science and Medicine*, 24, 8:651–7.

Britten, N., (1991), 'Hospital consultant's views of their patients,' *Sociology of Health and Illness*, 13, 1:83–94.

Bury, M., (1991), 'The sociology of chronic illness: a review of research and prospects,' *Sociology of Health and Illness*, 13, 4:451–68.

Corbin, J. and Strauss, A.L., (1988), *Unending Work and Care: Managing Chronic Illness at Home*, San Francisco: Jossey-Bass.

Conrad, P., (1990), 'Qualitative research on chronic illness: a commentary on method and conceptual development,' *Social Science and Medicine*, 30:1257–63.

Freidson, E., (1970), *Profession of Medicine: A Study of the Sociology of Applied Knowledge*, New York: Harper and Row.

Gerhardt, U., (1990), 'Introductory essay: qualitative research on chronic illness: the issue and the story,' *Social Science and Medicine*, 30, 11:1149–59.

Glaser, B.G. and Strauss, A.L., (1967), *The Discovery of Grounded Theory: Strategies for Qualitative Research*, New York: Aldine De Gruyter.

Glaser, B.G. and Strauss, A.L., (1966), *Awareness of Dying*, Chicago: Aldine De Gruyter.

Greer, S., Moorey, S. and Watson, M., (1989), 'Patients' adjustment to cancer: the mental adjustment to cancer (MAC) scale vs clinical ratings,' *Journal of Psychosomatic Research*, 33, 3:373.

Hockey, J., (1990), *Experiences of Death: An Anthropological Account*, Edinburgh: Edinburgh University Press.

Kleinman, A., (1992), 'Local worlds of suffering: an interpersonal focus for ethnographies of illness experience,' *Qualitative Health Research*, 2, 2:127–34.

McIntosh, J., (1974), 'Process of communication, information seeking and control associated with cancer: a selective review of the literature,' *Social Science and Medicine*, 8:167–87.

Miller, R.S., (1978), 'The social construction and reconstruction of physiological events: acquiring the pregnancy identity,' in N.K. Denzin, (ed.), *Studies in Symbolic Interaction: An Annual Compilation of Research*, Vol.1:181–204, Greenwich: JAI Press Inc.

Potter, J. and Wetherell, M., (1987), *Discourse and Social Psychology*, London: Sage.

Silverman, D. (1985), *Qualitative Methodology and Sociology: Describing the Social World*, Vermont: Gower Publishing Co.

Strauss, A., (1978), 'A social world perspective,' in N.K. Denzin, (ed.), *Studies in Symbolic Interaction: An Annual Compilation of Research*, Vol. 1:119–28, Greenwich: JAI Press Inc.

Strauss, A. and Corbin, J., (1990), *Basics of Qualitative Research: Grounded Theory Procedures and Techniques*, Newbury Park: Sage.

Watson, M., Greer, S., Rowden, L. *et al.*, (1991), 'Relationships between emotional control, adjustment to cancer and depression and anxiety in breast cancer patients', *Psychological Medicine*, 21:51–7.

Williams, R., (1989), 'Awareness and control of dying: some paradoxical trends in public opinion,' *Sociology of Health and Illness*, 11, 3:201–212.

# Sociologists never die: British sociology and death

## Tony Walter

British sociology is not well represented in the vast and growing literature on death. One exception is medical sociology's research into the social aspects of dying but other sub-branches of sociology have been strangely quiet about our mortality. This chapter briefly reviews British sociological theory, sociology of religion, community studies, the body, deathwork, gender, ethnicity, gerontology, teaching, and social policy. Some possible explanations are reviewed. Finally, there are indications of a recent renaissance of interest, among some British sociologists, of which this book forms a part. Two future scenarios for the sociology of death are sketched.

I start with two observations. One, this *Sociological Review Monograph* is the first collection of papers devoted entirely to the subject of death and written by a wide range of British sociologists – not just medical sociologists. Two, the editor has had little difficulty in finding papers. What does this mean? Is there a brand-new British sociological interest in death and dying? Or are we only now recognising an interest that has been there for a while but has not been identified as such?

In this chapter I will explore how this monograph fits, or fails to fit, within British sociology. First, I will argue that, though death and dying have been widely discussed in certain circles for some time, British sociology – with the major exception of medical sociology – has been somewhat late on the scene. Second, I will suggest some hypotheses for this lack of sociological interest. Third, I will discuss the prospects.

Leaving aside the period of the Gulf War, every week for the past three or four years has seen articles in the serious dailies and Sundays on hospices, bereavement, undertakers, the cost of funerals and so forth. This interest is but the most recent manifestation of a 30-year-old movement to humanise dying and bereavement (Lofland, 1978; Armstrong, 1987). The movement relies heavily on the development of improved pain control for the dying (especially as pioneered by Cicely Saunders and the hospice movement), along with the researches of psychiatrists (such as Elizabeth Kubler Ross, 1970; and Colin Murray Parkes, 1972); and American social scientists (eg Feifel, 1959; Fulton, 1976; Kastenbaum, 2972; and Glaser and Strauss, 1965). The stream of deathly publications from these and many others has long since become a torrent. Simpson's (1987) English language bibliography on *Dying, Death and Grief* lists 1700 books – not articles – published in 1979–1986. When we consider the social sciences, we find particularly strong representation from anthropologists, historians (especially French historians), psychologists, and North American sociologists.

Books by British sociologists are notably absent from Simpson's bibliography. An update to 1992 would change that somewhat, though several of the recent publications – Rory Williams, 1990; Jenny Hockey, 1990; Douglas Davies, 1990; and Tony Walter, 1990 – on the British way of death have been as much influenced by anthropology as by sociology. The one British sociologist to have made a major impact in the field of death and dying is Geoffrey Gorer (1955, 1965) – although, significantly, he is quoted far more often by American sociologists and by British psychiatrists than by British sociologists. Gorer's pointer to the social nature of our mortal being is something that, until recently and with the exception of medical sociology, British sociology has quite simply ignored.

What about articles? In autumn 1991, I looked at the *British Journal of Sociology* since 1980, and *Sociology* and *The Sociological Review* since 1983. Among the 800 or so articles, there were only eleven (1.4 per cent) whose titles in any way hinted at a concern with death: they covered AIDS, risk theory, industrial injury, the mortuary, press reporting of deaths in Ulster, Durkheim on suicide, and articles by myself on Hillsborough and on the concept of death as taboo. Only five of the titles (two of them being my own) contained the words death, dying, dead, bereavement, or mourning. Doubtless one or two more touch on the subject, though not indicated by their titles or in their abstracts (eg James, 1989). If these mainline journals accurately reflect British sociology, then it would seem that its practitioners spend a lot of time in football stadia and shopping malls discussing hooliganism and post-modernism, but keep their awareness of human mortality separate from their sociological endeavours.

But the picture is certainly not quite that simple and it certainly is in process of changing.

## Sociology in the UK: theory

Berger and Luckman (1967) consider death as *the* anomic condition and root cause of the problem of meaning (Mellor, 1993), a view to which psychiatrist Colin Murray Parkes (1972: 84–5) assents. Human cultures are therefore to be understood as ways of creating reifications that keep at bay the ultimate meaninglessness that derives from human mortality. Berger and Luckmann's concept of 'the social construction of reality' has been enormously influential but, somehow, its roots in an anthropology that centres on human mortality have been largely forgotten, until very recently.

Durkheim, of course, introduced the concept of *anomie*, not least within the context of a particular kind of mortality, namely suicide (1952). But since Durkheim, *anomie* studies zoomed off into every area of relative *anomie* (urban dislocation, delinquency and so forth) and forgot the ultimate *anomie* of death – even in the United States where both *anomie* studies and death studies have been major sociological industries (although not together).

It is only in the last two or three years that British sociological theory has begun to incorporate human mortality. As Mellor discusses in more detail elsewhere in this volume (see also Mellor and Shilling, 1993), Giddens' recent work (1990, 1991) identifies death as something that modern society keeps out of public consciousness; but it is certainly not something that the reflexive late-modern self can ignore. Hence death is, in Mellor's phrase, publicly absent but privately present. But Giddens (1987: ch. 7) also highlights violence as a feature of nation states, and – unlike most other sociology textbook writers – he has not ignored the industrialised war machine that is so central to modern societies (1989: ch. 11). It may be that risk rather than rational problem-solving is the hallmark of late modernity (Beck, 1992).

Bauman (1992a, 1992b) has focussed even more sharply on how society handles death, suggesting a shift from modernity to postmodernity. Postmoderns, he suggests, are like nomads looking at most for the next camp and more aware of where they are and where they have been than of where they might be going – somewhat different from the modern pilgrim who is 'going somewhere'. For the postmodern person, 'nothing seems to be immortal any more. But nothing seems mortal either' (Bauman, 1992a:170). In some circles, both traditional and modern ideas of 'the good death' are becoming fragmented, with each dying person encouraged to find their own spiritual and/or psychological path (Walter, 1993). But if postmodernity transforms the way we approach death, one might also ask whether death challenges postmodernity? Can there really be a postmodern death, characterised by the irony, paradox and playfulness of postmodern life, or does death reveal a more serious need for meaning that undermines postmodernity? This should surely be an important question for theorists of postmodernity, as well as for those concerned to understand the social construction of death and dying.

As Frankenberg (1987:135) has pointed out, communal modes of dealing with death can be used as indicators of particular kinds of society. This is in effect what Durkheim did in his study of suicide, what Ariès (1981) does in his dazzling, if flawed, survey of historical epochs in Europe, and is perhaps what Norbert Elias (1985) might have done had he written about mortality rather earlier than the last years of his long life. Bauman (1989) challenges sociologists to consider what the Holocaust as a patterned form of death has to tell us about modernity. But with this notable exception, British sociologists have preferred mode of production, patriarchy and other such concepts as key societal indicators.

The recent interest in the sociology of time is also putting mortality back on the agenda (Adam, 1990; Young, 1988). An important article here is Frankenberg's (1987) critique of studies of the 'life cycle': human life does not go on for ever in circles, it comes to an abrupt end. He does not find Glaser and Strauss' (1965) concept of 'trajectory' satisfactory either, as it denies the individual any kind of control. Pilgrimage is a more realistic concept that does justice both to our biological end and to our ability to give meaning to our own lives.

There is, therefore, some exciting recent work that is making the fact that we are a species whose members will both die and know it, central to modern sociological theory. Whether this will lead to substantial further work, both empirical and theoretical, remains to be seen. When it comes to substantive areas of

sociology, there is not much to build on, with the major exception of medical sociology, to which we will turn before going on
to look at some other substantive areas where the canvas is still
virtually untouched.

## Medical Sociology

Medical sociology is the one substantive area where there has
been substantial death research. Mortality statistics have long
been a part of epidemiology and are used as a more or less reli-
able indicator of inequalities in health between different class or
ethnic groups (eg Townsend and Davidson, 1982). I will focus
here, however, on mortality not as a sociological resource but as
a sociological topic. How does British society manage the dying,
the corpse and the bereaved?

Of the three, dying has received by far the most attention from
medical sociologists. Since the 1970s, there has been a considerable
growth in interactionist studies within the institutional settings in
which most people draw their last breath, in particular the hospital
and the hospice – much less so the nursing home and the residential home for elderly people (though Hockey, 1990, is unusual in
comparing such a residential home and a hospice). Much of the
research (Field, 1989:3) has replicated American research of the
1960s into two questions concerning cancer patients.

One question concerns the process of how patients and their
relatives do, or do not, become aware, of a terminal diagnosis.
Glaser and Strauss (1965) identified different 'awareness contexts', and their work has encouraged the subsequent shift in the
USA away from the 'conspiracy of silence' and 'mutual pretence'
that characterised relations between medical staff, relatives and
the cancer patient toward more open communication (Novack et
al., 1979)[1]. McIntosh's study in Aberdeen (1977) found considerable reluctance on the patients' as well as the doctors' part for
open disclosure of a terminal diagnosis, feeling this would undermine hope, but more recent evidence from other parts of the UK
indicates a shift (though slower than in the USA) toward more
open communication (Bowling and Cartwright, 1982: ch. 3;
Field, 1989; Seale, 1991b).

The second question concerns the process of dying. Although
Kubler-Ross' (1970) psychological theory of emotional stages
through which the dying patient passes is by far the best known

outside of academia and features strongly in the training of British nurses and doctors (Field, 1984:432; 1986:273), also influential have been the sociological concepts of dying trajectories (Glaser and Strauss, 1968) or timetables (Roth, 1963) by which the process of dying is institutionally managed and routinised. This research clearly reveals a conflict between the infinitely various psychological needs of the dying and the needs of their institutional carers for predictability and routine. It has been a useful corrective to the psychological models that otherwise dominate medical and nursing training. Sociological research has revealed both that doctors are not as open in their communication with the dying as they claim to be and why dying patients are rarely treated as individuals (Field, 1989; McIntosh, 1977). Psychological research has been instrumental in promoting a new model for relating to the dying, but sociological research reveals how difficult it is to operate that model in institutional practice.

Thus British sociology of dying has been useful, not least in teaching student doctors and nurses (eg Field, 1989) and as part of the movement toward more humane dying; but one has to say that the theoretical input has been almost entirely American. Whereas British practitioners of other disciplines (such as Parkes and Saunders (du Boulay, 1984)) have led the international field in research into death and dying, British medical sociological research in this area has been derivative.

That much of this research has been conducted within hospitals is perhaps not surprising, given death's medicalisation, the fact that most people now die in hospitals, the relative ease of conducting research within institutions, and the greater power of the medical establishment (compared with, say, voluntary bereavement organisations) to finance substantial sociological research. In addition, sociology is now an established part of medical training and there are many contacts between sociologists and teaching hospitals. But if at the public level death has been medicalised, at the private level it has been individualised – reflected perhaps in the tendency of self-care groups of bereaved individuals to look for advice not to sociologists but to psychologists (an exception being Jenny Hockey's recent research sponsored by Cruse-Bereavement Care).

The hospice movement is widely recognised as having been pioneered in Britain and an important line of sociological research, over the past decade, has been the evaluation of the hospice model. Developing often as bottom-up initiatives in the community, and fitting within a free-market and plural concept of health care, there is considerable concern by health authorities as to how hospices fit into the overall pattern of provision and whether they add to or drain scarce resources. Hospices themselves are concerned about their future development and growth and about the relative roles of volunteers and paid professionals. Sociologists, historically geared toward planning and monitoring rather than simply allowing markets and charismatic individuals to run their course, have therefore become involved in hospice evaluation. So far, the conclusions seem to be twofold: that pain control innovations have been taught to hospitals by hospices but that, overall, there are major pressures that are causing hospices to operate increasingly like hospitals. In this area, British sociology is making a significant contribution to the continuing development of a British innovation: the hospice (Clark, 1991, 1993a, 1993b; Higginson and McCarthy, 1989; Hoad, 1991; James and Field, 1991; and Seale, 1989, 1991a).

Outside the hospital and the hospice, two major studies from the Institute for Social Studies in Medical Care have interviewed several hundred people retrospectively about the last year of life of a close relative (Cartwright *et al.*, 1973) and about their own loss of an elderly spouse (Bowling and Cartwright, 1982), together with interviews with the person's general practitioner and nursing staff. These studies have been particularly valuable in revealing many of the practical and social problems experienced, balancing up the psychological literature's focus on emotional problems. Recently, the 1973 study has been replicated.

Public concern about AIDS has injected vast sums of money into sociological research and in particular into medical sociology (see, for example, Aggleton and Homans, 1988; Aggleton *et al.*, 1989; Small, 1993)[2]. The 1991 edition of *Medical Sociology in Britain* identifies AIDS as the largest single category within the research projects section, with 32 projects, and it is the largest grant-receiving area by far. In their review of this work, Berridge and Strong (1991:135) comment that 'AIDS has proved part of the answer to British sociological unemployment in the 1980s' and they welcome the belated legitimation of the sociology of sexual behaviour. Otherwise their verdict on the intellectual significance of all this research is less than fulsome:

Sociology may have got the big grants but most of the research has focussed on practical rather than sociological problems.

AIDS has brought a revival of positivist social science; and conceptual development has played a very minor part.

We are witnessing the creation of a policy-oriented AIDS research empire divorced from mainline sociology.

Despite the empirical richness of much of the research of British medical sociologists into death and dying[3], mainline sociology does not seem to have noticed. Of 21 articles to which a leading medical sociologist recently drew my attention as evidence of interest in death and dying by British sociologists, only one (James, 1989) was published in a general sociology journal. All the others were in *Social Science & Medicine*, *Sociology of Health & Illness*, or nursing or medical journals. This reflects British medical sociology's marginalisation from mainline sociology – medical sociologists tend to publish in medical or nursing journals, or maybe their sound empirical grounding does not appeal to the more theoretical interests of some mainline sociology journal editorial boards[4]. The influence of medical and sociological research on dying in the UK has been far more on medical and nursing students than on other sociologists.

Which brings us, briefly, to the teaching of medical sociology. Medical sociology textbooks vary considerably in their coverage of the British way of death. Hart's (1985) text for 'A' level students does not mention the subject, except for a few entries on death rates, an extraordinary omission. Turner's more theoretical text for undergraduates (1987) has but two and a half pages. It is only when we come to certain (but not all) texts for medical students (eg Patrick and Scambler, 1982) that we find substantial treatment of the subject, or a complete textbook devoted to it (Field, 1989). This seems to suggest that it is the requirements of medicine and nursing, rather than the agenda of sociology, that is driving the teaching of death and dying within medical sociology (Field, 1984, 1986).

The dominance of medical sociology, or rather of medicine-driven sociology, in death and dying is shown by the fact that the only academic institution in the UK where there is currently any kind of sociological focus on death and dying that is not institutionally defined as medical sociology is the sociology department at the University of York. One might perhaps add the LSE, with two PhD theses (on funeral directors and cremation respectively) submitted recently (Howarth, 1992; Jupp, 1993) and the award of the T.H. Marshall fellowship to Glennys Howarth to study the work of coroners.

If medical sociologists get most of the credits for a sociological understanding of the British way of death, the proviso must be added that their work does not amount to a sociology of death. Rather, it constitutes a sociology of *dying*. A sociology of death would also have to examine the management of the corpse, modes of disposal, ritual, bereavement, the media treatment of death, etc.[5]. What little work on these subjects has been done by medical sociologists naturally tends to cover those areas where medicine still claims some territory – medical certification of death and the work of coroners (Prior, 1989), and the health of the bereaved (Bowling and Cartwright, 1982). This then is not a criticism of medical sociology, merely a comment on its limits.

Frankenberg (1987:123), however, argues that this focus of sociological interest on certain aspects of dying has a conservative function. A sociology with a time-honoured tradition of demystifying the more oppressive and uncomfortable aspects of life in Britain might be expected to follow Gorer's (1965) lead in demystifying the ways in which elements of our society pretend that death (like poverty, racism or sexism) does not exist. But instead, medical sociologists have helped to demystify death-denying practices within the hospital and developed a 'useful social technology of helping to ensure a smooth passage to the other side' for those who die in hospital. 'In so doing they avoid discussion of the implications of knowledge and acceptance of death on the nature of life.' Helping people to ease out of this life, out of sight in hospital or hospice, is a humane rather than a radical sociology. I would not criticise it for this very real achievement, but it is nevertheless curious for a sociology that prides itself on radical demystification to limit itself in this way – one can but hope that the belated interest shown by major theorists such as Giddens and Bauman discussed above may open the door for a challenging as well as a comforting sociology of death.

I will now turn to see whether other sociologists have taken analysis and critique out of the hospital into the rest of society.

## Sociology of Religion

Peter Berger (1969) powerfully re-stated Weber's observation that religion is in large measure in the business of producing theodicies to keep at bay the meaninglessness of suffering and the terror of death. Malinowski (1962:97) had been of the same opinion:

> Death, which of all human events is the most upsetting and disorganising to man's calculation, is perhaps the main source of religious belief.

One would therefore have expected sociologists of religion to have majored on suffering, death, dying and mourning. They have not. Turner's (1991:229) examination of British sociology of religion texts reveals that, with the exception of Berger, death barely gets a mention.

A major concern of sociologists of religion in the 1970s was secularisation. Given Malinowski, Weber, Berger, *et al.*, one would hypothesise that secularisation, in so far as it has occurred, derives in large measure from the declining immediacy of death. With most people living now to old age and dying out of sight in hospital, death is now less visible (Blauner, 1966) and this could be a significant reason why people no longer turn to religion. Further, a decline in fear of death would lead to a decline in fear of hell, hence the declining hold of religion on everyday behaviour.

Historians of secularisation have indeed addressed this possibility (Chadwick, 1975: 104–6; Gilbert, 1980: 61–3), as has the Italian sociologist Acquaviva (1979:197–8), but British sociologists of secularisation touch on it only in passing. Brian Wilson's classic *Religion in Secular Society* notes religion's traditional concern with death and burial, commenting that scientific explanations have now ousted religious interpretations, leaving death as 'an embarrassing private trauma in which almost any outside solace, except from intimates, has become an intrusion' (1969:93). His later books touch only briefly on the decline of the fear of hellfire (1976:19) and on the observation (1982:157) that death is one of those 'parts which rationality has not yet reached' which may in part account for the continuance of religion. Martin's magisterial *General Theory of Secularisation* (1978) fails to consider the evidence that the extent to which various national churches have retained control of burial has affected the extent and nature of secularisation in each country (Jupp, 1993). Undergraduate level texts on secularisation often do not even have death in the index (eg Glasner, 1977; Lyon, 1985). Why have sociologists of secularisation failed to consider the obvious?

Is it because there was no British sociology of death with which they could have engaged?

Moving on from secularisation, what about the rest of the sociology of religion? Towler's massive survey of religion in Leeds included the subject[6], but remains unpublished. Roger Grainger's (1988) fascinating book *The Unburied* has unfortunately made little impact on the sociology of religion. Among mainline sociologists of religion, one has to go back to Bill Pickering's (1974) short article on rites of passage. The ritual handling of death in England is largely through the established church but the Church of England, in contrast to youthful sects, has received remarkably little sociological research – and that includes its funeral rites.

In 1990, however, this deathless sociology of religion itself died, almost without warning. Davies, Jupp, Walter and Williams, in four totally separate publications, presented theoretically-framed, empirical material on the religious aspects of the modern British way of death. In 1992, for the first time, the annual conference of the Sociology of Religion Group of the British Sociological Association included a section on death, an innovation repeated in 1993. 1993 also saw the publication of a volume on the role of the hero's death in modern as in traditional pilgrimage, though not all the contributors to this are sociologists (Reader and Walter, 1993). In the associated field of religious studies, Shirley Firth (1989, 1993a, 1993b) is currently publishing on death practices among Hindus in Britain.

Why the long silence by those studying the one institution centrally concerned with death? And why the recent revival (to use a metaphor from both death and religion) of interest? I think the answer has to do with secularisation.

The nineteenth century saw a shift from death as the domain of the church to the domain of medicine. The doctor replaced the priest at the bedside, public health replaced religion as the main determinant of what happened thereafter to the corpse (Ariès, 1981; Illich, 1976). If sociologists of medicine, rather than of religion, study death today I suspect this is partly because institutionally death has become a medical, more than a spiritual, affair; and partly because sociologists have been sucked into holding this belief personally. The first is a good reason, the second a poor show – at least for sociologists who aim to stand outside the reigning weltanschaung.

The usefulness of the concept of secularisation has, in the

1980s, come under major attack. With the revival of fundamentalisms and the continuance of folk religion in many modern societies, few sociologists of religion now argue for any simple secularisation thesis. Religion, *contra* the predictions of the positivists of both nineteenth and mid-twentieth centuries, is clearly here to stay. The revival of interest in death, both popular and among sociologists of religion, is, I think, part of this revival of religion. Many people are beginning to argue that death, like religion, can no longer be swept under the carpet as the kind of thing that does not and should not exist in a modern society.

## Community Studies

Anthropological studies of pre-modern communities typically include substantial and important sections on the handling of members' mortality. This has not been true of British community studies, though W.M. Williams' (1958:66–8) study of Gosforth has a couple of pages on coffin-handling and burial. The best known exception is Chapter 7 of David Clark's study of Staithes (1982).

If only a few community studies mention death, some death studies certainly are rooted in a sociological understanding of community. The most notable of these is Rory Williams (1990) who relates the individual attitudes of his interviewees to their Aberdonian culture. By contrast, Marris' (1958) trailblazing *Widows and their Families*, though emanating from the Institute of Community Studies, did little to relate the experiences of his interviewees to their local community and culture. This shortcoming seems less likely to characterise the Institute's current intensive study of fourteen terminal patients (Young, forthcoming).

In addition, there are also studies of communities struck by disaster. British sociological examples of this genre are Miller's (1974) competent yet strangely forgotten study of Aberfan, and more recent studies of the Hillsborough disaster by Coleman *et al.* (1990), Davie (1993) and Walter (1991b).

## The Body

Turner (1984) has criticised sociology's concept of the disembodied mind, and of course disembodied minds do not die. But the promise that the new sociology of the body will include death on its agenda is yet to be fulfilled. Though Turner's textbook on religion (1991) has a chapter on death and sex, I have already mentioned that his so-called 'embodied' text on medical sociology contains only two-and-a-half pages on death and dying, while the recent anthology on the body by Featherstone, Hepworth and Turner (1991) has chapters on food, the body in consumer culture, and mid life, yet precious little on death and nothing on corpses. Armstrong's (1983, 1989) development on Foucauldian theories of the body certainly has led him to a historical sociology of death. Apart from Armstrong, however, it would seem that the new sociology of the body has yet to look seriously at dying or dead bodies.

## Deathwork

The one exception is Prior's (1989) superb study of the social organisation of death in Belfast. In addition, the routine management of dead bodies has generated a number of doctorates which, despite considerable attention paid to the body, owe more to the sociology of occupations than to recent theoretical sociological discourses on the body. Smale's (1985), Naylor's (1989) and Howarth's (1992) doctorates on funeral directing, and Jupp's on the development of cremation (1992), are as yet unpublished. Meanwhile, Sheila Adams (Warwick) is researching the neighbourhood layers-out of the body in inter-war Coventry, and Howarth is about to start research on the work of coroners. Given the fascinating subject matter of these theses, one wonders why the dearth of publications? Is it because a PhD on death has not as yet been likely to make one particularly attractive as a prospective sociology lecturer – there being only one sociology department that teaches a 'death option' – so the good doctors move out of academia and never get around to publishing?

Along with the dearth of deathwork in community studies, this is all very regrettable. Ritual management of the corpse and of the bereaved varies extraordinarily around the UK (regionally, by class, ethnic group, religion, urbanisation, etc) and we have nothing remotely like a socio-geographical map. We know more about the variation of funeral ritual across scores of pre-modern societies than we do about death within the UK.

## Gender

In the early modern period, care and control of the dying and of the corpse were substantially in the hands of women. But from the eighteenth through to the present century, the medicalising of death has involved the increasing power of (male) doctors over the (female) bedside carers of the dying, while the rise of the occupation of funeral directing has led to the demise of the neighbourhood layer-out (see Adams in this volume). In the meantime, women continue to do the bulk of the often dirty and demanding care of the dying, both in their role as informal carers and in the paid role of nurse (James, 1992).

This de-feminisation of the power to define and control the management of death, while leaving women with much of the dirty work, is currently being challenged in the hospice, bereavement care and natural death movements[7], which are seeking to develop alternatives to male, hospital, technological approaches to dying and grief. Women – Cicely Saunders, Elizabeth Kubler-Ross, Mother Teresa, and Margaret Torrie (founder of Cruse-Bereavement Care) – have become charismatic leaders (James and Field, 1992), bringing the subject out from under the carpet and revolutionising the care of the dying and of the bereaved. And, as concern with the spiritual destination of the deceased wanes, so post-death concern focusses on the bereaved, a disproportionate number of whom (as far as those who have lost a spouse are concerned) are women: correspondingly, the authority of (male) clergy to define post-death care is being supplanted by that of (female) bereavement counsellors and befrienders. A re-feminisation of death is under way, led by women. One might even go so far as to say that this is one of the few areas in which in the past two decades women have radically transformed a part of our culture, though the question of whether this transformation is to succeed or be subverted is still an open one (James and Field, 1992).

It is strange that feminist sociology has not shown any manifest interest in these developments. Maybe it has had other priorities; but it is curious that if feminist historians have researched the de-feminising of death, sociologists should not be interested in its re-feminising. Is it that feminist sociological interest in care of the dying and bereaved is subsumed (and possibly lost) within the very real interest in women's roles as unpaid or underpaid and often exploited carers of the other members of their household? Or have feminist sociologists made what Michael Young terms 'the presumption of immortality', the presumption that being mortal is peripheral to being human and therefore that challenging patriarchy in the care of the dying and bereaved is peripheral to the feminist task?[8] This clearly does not apply to the deaths of fetuses and infants, which have attracted feminist sociological research (eg Oakley *et al.*, 1990).

Funeral and mourning rituals in both traditional and modern societies require males and females to behave in significantly different ways. This has been noted in several studies (Bloch, 1982; Danforth, 1982; Frankenberg, 1987:123; Stroebe and Stroebe, 1987:177–85; Taylor, 1983; and Walter, 1990:ch. 5) but nobody has yet attempted a thoroughgoing analysis of death rituals in terms of gender. Most psychological work on dying and grief has been completely gender-blind; it is high time a sociological approach remedied this. Anthropologist Barbara Myerhoff's (1979) participant observation study of an elderly Jewish community in California is an example of what can be done. She found that the women seemed to age better than men: they were more skilled in the expressive roles of self-care, care of others and socialising, roles in which they could continue to take pride; and their experience of a lifetime of limitation meant that the ultimate limitation of terminal illness or death was something they had some skill in approaching, whereas for some men old age was the first time that their fantasies of omnipotence had been challenged. Dumont and Foss (1972:26–7) review evidence that women have a stronger death-wish than men, but do not theorise this from a feminist perspective. Bronfen (1992) has done a sophisticated feminist analysis of death, femininity and the arts, but this is not sociology. The field is wide open.

## Ethnicity

Hospitals are becoming aware of differing religious and ethnic practices to which they should accommodate and which can be particularly sensitive at and around death. This is in large part the audience for which Firth (1989, 1993a, 1993b) is writing, and is another example of where there is valuable research being done but it is driven by the practical needs of doctors and nurses rather than by the sociological imagination.

From the point of view of a sociological understanding of death, a more pertinent question is: what will happen to the modern, white, bureaucratised, technological, secular management of death now that the first generation of immigrants from the 1950s and 1960s is beginning to die? Will they influence the British way of death, as have white women, will they be assimilated into it, or will they maintain their own traditions in relative isolation? Comparative data from the USA and Australia would make this a fascinating study – I for one cannot avoid the strong impression that the American practice of a communal viewing in the funeral parlour is strongly influenced by the Irish wake, and that the fashion for mausolea has been influenced by Italian customs, though I am aware of no sociological or historical study that examines this.

In the course of my own research on funerals (Walter, 1990), I became aware of an extraordinary diversity of customs even within modern societies, and consequently became convinced that a sociological understanding of contemporary death has to incorporate nationality and ethnicity as well as overarching theories about modernity. Within Britain, I concluded that approaches to mourning in the UK can be broadly divided into English versus Celtic, the one placing great importance on emotional privacy, the other on communal ritual; this was revealed in, for example, differential responses to the Hillsborough disaster (Walter, 1991b:607–8). Certainly many people have identified English funerals and bereavement as ghastly because of the English stiff upper lip.

Elias (1985:26–7), by contrast, argues that emotional privacy is a feature not so much of Englishness as of the civilising process:

> The task of finding the right word and the right gesture therefore falls back on the individual. The concern to avoid socially prescribed rituals and phrases increases the demands on the individual's powers of invention and expression. This task, however, is often beyond people at the current stage of civilisation. The way people live together, which is fundamental to this stage, demands and produces a relatively high degree of reserve in expressing strong, spontaneous affects. . . . Thus, unembarrassed discourse with or to dying people, which they especially need, becomes difficult.

Given that attempting to release emotional reserve is a key part of the current attempt to humanise death, dying and grief, this fundamental question requires sociological attention: does emotional reserve derive from modernity or from ethnicity?

## Gerontology

One would expect that, since most people today die in old age, the social scientific study of ageing would be conducted with this as a clear backdrop. It appears not to be. Taking the journal *Ageing and Society* to represent the sociological strand of gerontology in the UK, I surveyed its first 11 volumes, from 1981–1991. Only five articles (3.8 per cent of the total) and 22 book reviews (also 3.8 per cent of the total) directly address death and dying. Of the five articles, four are by North Americans, leaving only one British sociological article (Seale, 1990) for the entire first ten years of this journal. Of the 22 book reviews, only two were of books that are both British and unambiguously sociological, namely Field (1989) and Prior (1989). This picture is confirmed by Crosby's (1991) register of British social research on old age, 1985–1990, which lists 477 research projects, of which no more than four or five concern bereavement, dying and care of the dying.

One wonders whether the lack of a sociology of ageing in the light of its natural end may be partly due to gerontology's being driven by the old as a problem for society, rather than by death as a problem for the elderly, along with its reliance on the social survey rather than more qualitative methods (Hockey, 1990:11–12). Also, lobbies for the elderly continually strive to counter negative images of old age and of old people, advocating as active a retirement as possible. Such lobbies are unlikely to commission research that sees retirement as a prelude to ultimate demise.

Also significant may be Seale's (1990) conclusion that the problems of the elderly dying, such as having no fit relatives to look after them, are as much the general problems of being old as the specific problems of the dying. Since a considerable proportion of those who die are old, however, this surely is of considerable importance for the social scientific study of death and dying, which has focussed disproportionately on middle-aged and not-so-old cancer sufferers, from whom general theories (notably those of Kubler Ross and of Parkes) have been extrapolated. There is a considerable paucity of sociological (or for that matter, psychological) theories of dying and of grief which makes sense of the experience of the elderly (Littlewood, 1992).

Obviously not all studies in the sociology of old age ignore death. Townsend's classic study of old people's homes (1964:50–1, 85–6) has some telling if brief things to say on how the homes manage the death of residents, but we have to wait for Hockey (1990) to find a study of old persons' homes that acknowledges they may in some cases be places for people waiting to die. Meanwhile in North America, two such studies had been conducted back in the 1970s (Gubrium, 1975; Marshall, 1980; see also Hochschild, 1973).

A major exception is Cartwright *et al.* (1973), and subsequent replications (eg Seale, 1990). Because of its methodology of interviewing the survivor retrospectively about the last year of the deceased's life, this year is *defined* in terms of its being the last – expressed in the book's title *Life Before Death*. Along with Hockey (1990), this is a rare study of old age in which death defines life rather than is incidental to it.[9]

Gerontology shades off into the study of ageing, which shades off into the study of the life cycle. Frankenberg's (1987) trenchant critique of the concept of 'life cycle' raises a number of issues about the concept's eclipse of death as the end, and perhaps defining, point of life.

## Other areas

I have covered some of the obvious sociological subfields where one might have expected human mortality to have some profile. But there are many others too. Certainly the sociology (and more often the psychology) of leisure and of the media has been concerned with violence on television, but this is driven by public concern rather than by sociological questions. It can be argued (Walter, 1989) that if medicine has replaced the church as the manager of death, then the mass media have replaced the church as the interpreter of death, not only in fictional movies but also in news handling of death – for example, in the lengthy attempts after a disaster to find a cause and to establish guilt. But the sociology of the media has not, to my knowledge, examined this not insignificant possibility.

Wright (1986) and Nichols (1986) argue that the sociology of work has ignored industrial injury. Cultural studies has been given a boost by AIDS research money (Berridge and Strong 1991:135), but otherwise seems governed, like the sociology of work, by the presumption of immortality. And so the story goes on.

Increasingly, the more interesting work in sociology cannot be neatly classifiable into subfields (eg Marris)[10]. One major research area for the sociology of death would be to document and analyse the current movement to 'humanise' death, dying and bereavement, and the associated rise of a therapeutic or semi-psychiatric frame for relating to the dying and bereaved (Perakyla 1988); that is, to take over where historians such as Ariès (1981) left off[11]. A stimulating start has been made by Lofland (1978), but she covers only dying and is American in her focus; Armstrong (1987) is also a useful corrective to common assumptions here. Further work might draw on the literature on social movements, on postmodernity, and on sociological analyses of counselling in non-death situations (Clark and Morgan, 1993) and the holistic ideology of modern nursing (May 1992).

## Teaching

In 1990–1, Mike Mulkay introduced an option on the sociology of death and dying into the York sociology degree course, but I know of no other such instances. Otherwise, the sociology of death is taught in the UK as a small part of the sociology of medicine, especially as taught to medical and nursing students (Field, 1984, 1986), and as a small component in some sociology of religion courses. The Open University is currently preparing a course 'Death and Dying', but this is part of the Diploma in Health and Social Welfare, so its approach is practical and multi-disciplinary (Dickenson & Johnson 1993).

The lack of teaching opportunity in this field was reflected in the composition of those who attended the 1991 Leicester symposium on 'Social Aspects of Death and Dying' that prompted this current Monograph. Of the 23 participants (only eight of whom were medical sociologists), only three held full-time lectureships in sociology departments, while another two held joint appointments with medical institutions; the others were all researchers. So long as tenured university lecturers show no interest in the sociology of death, it is difficult to see how options on the subject can be generated – however much it is growing as a research field and however fascinating some of the literature. Given the popularity of the York option, however, I suspect things would change quickly if enough of the death researchers moved to sociology degree teaching posts – a big 'if'. But that could just come about in a few years time when a considerable number of sociology lecturers will retire and more posts for younger lecturers become available.

## Social Policy

To what extent has social policy responded to sociological research on death and dying? There is something of a contradiction here.

On the one hand, social scientific work on death and dying has been a prime example of what Giddens (1990) means by reflexivity – the way in which social practices in the modern world are continually evolving in response to popular understandings of social science knowledge. Communication with the dying in Britain has been profoundly influenced by American researchers (Glaser and Strauss, 1965; Kubler-Ross, 1970) who revealed the personal costs for staff, patients and families of 'mutual pretence'. Sociological evaluations of hospices and of AIDS education may also prove influential, in time. Wilson and Levy's (1938) report on funeral costs was influential in the setting up of the death grant. And Parkes' (1972) understanding of the psychology of grief provides the knowledge base for the British bereavement counselling movement. More generally, Gorer's (1955, 1965) idea of death as the taboo of the twentieth century must, like it or not, be one of the sociological ideas that is most quoted outside of the sociological community and outside of academia. And awareness of declining death rates has surely affected modern consciousness (Armstrong, 1986).

There are gaps. Funeral directing and the cremation and cemetery authorities in the UK (unlike in the USA) do not include popular social science to legitimate their practices. And there are as yet only embryonic signs that sociologists will be asked to evaluate bereavement care in the way they have been asked to evaluate hospice care. Meanwhile, the debate about euthanasia makes no reference to sociological studies, because – unlike in the Netherlands (van der Maas *et al.*, 1991) – there appear to be none. Nevertheless, the British way of death is evolving substantially in response to social science (though not necessarily sociological) knowledge.

On the other hand, with the exception of health policy, social policy journals and conferences in Britain make virtually no reference to all this; this presumably reflects death's public absence, even though it is privately very present (Mellor, 1993). Social policy's distancing itself from death, however, has by no means always been the case, far from it.

Take the management of the corpse. This was a major concern of social policy from the 1830s to the 1930s. From the 1832 Anatomy Act (Richardson, 1989), *via* the public health inspired cemetery legislation of the mid-nineteenth century (Brooks, 1989: Part 1), through to funeral insurance and eventually the death grant introduced by the Atlee government (Wilson and Levy, 1938), the development of the British welfare state has hinged substantially on the British obsession with the financial and sanitary management of its corpses. Without the desire of the Victorian working class to insure itself against funeral costs, our welfare state would almost certainly have developed later and in a very different way.

Since the introduction of the death grant, however, corpse management and financing has no longer been a concern of academic social policy (Hennessy, 1980 being an exception). Cemetery and crematoria managers, funeral directors and clergy, discuss corpse management in considerable detail at their conferences. My impression after attending several such conferences is that their discussions lack any theoretical base, presumably in part because they have been abandoned by academic students of social policy. When corpse management occasionally hits the headlines, as when in the late 1980s Westminster City Council sold off three cemeteries for a few pence, the public and press debate is typically uninformed. We have social scientists to comment on the prospects for hospices, but who is competent to comment on the prospects for our crematoria and cemeteries? Davies (1990), Jupp (1990), Walter (1990) and the York University cemetery research group are now beginning to address these issues, but why the academic silence for the previous fifty years?

## Why?

So far, I have attempted to show that there has been a remarkably low level of British sociological interest in death but that this is beginning to change. Starting with medical sociology in the mid 1970s, and then with several non-medical sociological studies in the late 1980s (only now being published), we see the beginnings of a sociological interest in how Britons die and grieve. Why the lack of interest, and why the recent renaissance of interest?

The simplest sociological answer, proffered by Mellor elsewhere in this volume, is that sociology is closely bound up with modernity and therefore 'modernity's systematic sequestration of considerations of mortality will continue to be reflected in sociological theory and practice'. I suggest below that there may be something in this but by itself it is not good enough. Any explanation must account for the large amount of deathwork conducted by historians, psychiatrists, anthropologists and, in the USA, sociologists (Vovelle, 1980:98–9).Some tentative hypotheses follow.

## 1 The medicalisation of death

This means that death now *is* a medical event, properly studied by medical sociology. In Britain this has entailed marginalisation from general sociology and from sociological theory. Perhaps only as other groups in society are challenging the medical model of death are non-medical sociologists coming to see death as not necessarily or entirely a medical phenomenon. This hypothesis has the merit also of explaining why it is medically trained psychiatrists, rather than academic psychologists, who have led the way in researching personal grief. But it does not explain the broader and earlier sociological interest in death in the USA, stemming from the 1950s.

## 2 The humanising of death

The attempt to humanise death – to see it as a natural rather than a medical phenomenon and to pay more attention to the emotional and psychological aspects of dying and grieving – is tending toward a fragmenting of death. Instead of 'modern death', perhaps we now have a million individual 'postmodern deaths', in which individuals die and grieve at their own psychological pace – or at any rate, this seems to be the hope of death's humanisers. This replacement of doctor's orders by the personal agendas of the dying and bereaved seems to express a key feature of postmodernity: the undermining of the essentially modern discourse of medicine, and its replacement by a million and one personal styles.

In so far as those who commission and read social scientific research on death are overwhelmingly part of this humanising movement, this may help explain the disciplinary spread of this research. Research by psychiatrists, or for that matter psychologists, is valued as part of the process of individualising death. Historical and anthropological deathwork becomes part of death's nostalgia industry – harking back to a pre-modern era, before the scientific and medical discourses of modernity 'ruined' dying, when people died 'natural' deaths and when 'society' knew how to arrange rituals for the dying and the bereaved (Lofland, 1978:88–92). For all his scholarship, Ariès (1981) is essentially nostalgic. It may be less clear to the humanisers how sociology can help either to individualise post-modern death or to sentimentalise pre-modern death – though sociological research on communication with the terminally ill has, in fact, been very useful for the humanisers.

As with the previous hypothesis, this does not account for the three-decades-old North American demand for sociological deathwork. Both the medicalisation and the humanising reaction have surely gone further in North America than in Europe.

## 3 Death is uncommon today

It tends to come to those who have retired, who have passed on knowledge and maybe even capital to their children, and who are socially near-redundant. Death therefore disrupts not society but the individual, who is left alone without traditional rituals (Blauner, 1965; Mulkay and Ernst, 1991; Walter, 1991a:305–6). Death has become a problem faced by individuals rather than by society as a whole – hence the interest by psychiatrists rather than sociologists, not to mention the nostalgic work of the historians and anthropologists. This also could explain the preponderance of research on 'premature' deaths which are seen as 'unnatural' and as particularly difficult for both dying and bereaved to come to terms with.

On the other hand, one can argue that even though somewhat retiring these days, the grim reaper still holds the key to understanding any society. And even if he's out of sight, the hullabaloo about proper styles of dying and grieving, the frequent press and magazine articles about how to die and how even to bury and burn, certainly aren't (Walter, 1991b). Sociologists have little excuse for not being aware of this.

*4 Demography*

With death rather rare, most of us do not have a close bereavement until our 30s or even older; middle age could even perhaps be defined as the realisation that our life will not go on for ever. This often sets off an interest in death, and for sociologists an interest in the sociology of death. That British sociologists are skewed heavily toward the middle-aged may be one simple explanation for the renaissance of sociological deathwork in the UK. This hypothesis also has the merit of being able to account for the earlier interest by American sociologists, the first major cohort of whom reached middle age in the late 1950s and early 1960s – precisely the period when their own sociological interest in death mushroomed.

As a little test of this hypothesis, I made a note of the reasons given by those who attended the Leicester symposium on death and dying in November 1991. Since this was the first such meeting for British sociologists, one may assume it attracted a good cross section of researchers (see Table 1).

**Table 1**

| Reason for interest in death and dying | |
| --- | --- |
| Nursing | 4 |
| Other research led into this area | 7 |
| Death of other | 6 |
| Own death coming closer | 1 |
| Having to take/arrange funerals | 4 |
| n = 19 | |

Seven out of 19 (37 per cent) of this small but significant group were therefore brought into this field by awareness of their own or others' deaths. Unfortunately, participants were not asked to give their ages; my impression was that most were aged between their mid 20s and late 40s, with a handful over 50. Ageing, therefore, seems to be the explanation for some, but by no means all, of this by no means entirely middle-aged group. The large number of undergraduates taking the death option on York's sociology degree also indicates a more youthful interest.

## 5 Idealism

Sociologists have tended to ignore the natural environment, and even more so the individual's body and its inevitable demise (Turner, 1984). Whether this accounts for the lack of interest in death hitherto we will have to wait to see, for the renaissance of interest in the body, as I have already mentioned, has yet to fulfil its promise of a sociology of death.

## 6 Progress

Mellor's comment about sociology being wedded to the project of modernity, of controlling our lives through the exercise of rationality, may well be part of the explanation. Understanding class and racial conflict, patriarchy, deviance, mental illness, the city, the sociology of health and illness, can all be construed as part of the Enlightenment programme of human beings creating a better society and regaining control of their destiny. Perhaps it grates rather that we all will die? Acknowledging this certainly involves an acceptance of a fundamental powerlessness, a difficult lesson for bereavement counsellors – let alone sociologists – to learn (Hockey, 1990:181). Patriarchy and capitalism can be fought but the truth is that, at the end, the fight against death cannot be won. If the sting of death can be drawn, it is typically through religion or through stoicism, not through sociological knowledge. In so far as sociology is inherently a discipline that attempts to empower people through knowledge, its researches can certainly help the dying and grieving but, ultimately, this help is limited. The more the sociologist is into radical empowerment, the less likely s/he is to get into the sociology of death, which could help explain the distance kept by feminist and Marxist sociology.

Against this hypothesis are two observations. First, the sociology of death first flourished in the USA where the myths of progress and of personal omnipotence are far more powerful than in the UK. Second, it may be misleading to say that a society wedded to progress cannot cope with death, for progress *depends* on the old dying and being replaced by the energy and ideas of the young: without death, there could be no progress.

Nevertheless, I would put my money on British sociologists' professional ideology of radical social and personal progress through sociological knowledge as the most likely explanation for their embarrassment that we all die. Their arrival at middle age and the associated appearance of the reaper on the distant horizon helps explain any partial revision of this ideology.

Or perhaps it is simply that the mini-explosion of British sociological publications on death over the past four or so years coincided with a similar explosion in the quality mass media, in which case there is nothing to explain: sociologists are normal members of the chattering class, and have been neither ahead of nor behind their peers.

## The future?

If British sociological interest in death is to develop (and the signs are that at long last it will), a basic question is whether we want a specialism called the sociology of death and dying? or should we seek to introduce human mortality into every facet of sociology?

I am not sure. In the USA, we see a thanatological ghetto, with specialist journals such as *Omega* and *Death Studies*, and the resulting dilution of a specifically sociological approach within an interdisciplinary thanatology with its own hideous deathspeak[12]. Aghast at this spectre, I would prefer mortality to be introduced into general sociology (Bauman, 1992: Mellor, 1993), in much the same way that gender has been. If general sociology should be aware that 51 per cent of us are female, surely it should be even more aware that 100 per cent of us die?

But Mulkay and Ernst (1991:180) raise a problem here:

It is clear that, from an early age, we anticipate, in some general sense, our own and others' eventual demise. However, because the attribute of morality is universal, it does not, in itself, lead to variations in social conduct; that is, we do not behave in any special way when we interact with someone who is going to die at some point in the future which is at present quite unknown.

By contrast, a person's gender, ethnicity, class, age, etc. *do* differentiate them from others and hence do affect social interaction.

So is a mortal sociology doomed either to broad theoretical statements as in Berger and Luckmann (1967), Giddens (1991) and Bauman (1992), or to trivial generalities?

To answer this we will need more theoretical publications that are clearly focussed on specific instances of modern death, such as Bauman's work on the Holocaust (1989); and empirical monographs that relate their data to the major concerns of sociology, such as Prior's work on death and rationality in Belfast (1989). At the same time, we should heed Lofland's (1976:8–11) encouragement to be conceptually irreverent: sociological concepts are for understanding the real world, not vice versa, and a sociology that has largely ignored human mortality may well need its concepts and theories radically revising.

Whither then – a sociology of death, or a mortal sociology?

## Acknowledgement

I would like to thank David Field for his comments on a draft of this chapter.

## Notes

1 See Armstrong (1987) for a stimulating critique of the usual account of this shift.
2 For a useful sample of papers arising out of this field, see *Sociology of Health and Illness*, 12(3), Sept 1990.
3 In addition to formal research teams, notably at the Institute for Social Studies in Medical Care, an extraordinary proportion of the limited amount of research on death and dying has been conducted by individuals who, during the period from late 1960s to the early 1980s, belonged to the MRC Medical Sociology Unit and the closely allied Sociology Department at Aberdeen. Remove Nicky James, David Clark, Mike Mulkay, and Tony Walter from the 1991 Leicester symposium upon which this monograph is based, and there would have been no symposium. To this list of one-time Aberdonians, one has to add Rory Williams, Lindsay Prior, Jim McIntosh and Phil Strong. This dominance of the sociology of death and dying by 'the Aberdeen school' is curious, and certainly unintended, when one considers that the MRC unit never had death and dying as a research priority (though it did have ageing as a priority in the late 1970s), that much of this work was initiated by these individuals after they had left Aberdeen or before they arrived, and that some of this earlier (Clark 1982:ch.7) or later (Walter, 1990) work is not medical sociology.
4 Rare attempts to integrate medical sociology and sociological theory include Armstrong (1983), Scambler (1987) and Turner (1987).

5 Kearl's (1989) American textbook suggests the potentially vast scope of the canvas.

6 'Conventional Religion and Common Religion in Leeds', ESRC research project G/0/23/0056, 1981–3.

7 The Natural Death Centre, 20 Heber Road, London NW2 6AA.

8 Many of the death reformers are also practising Christians, yet general discussions about Christian social involvement similarly ignore this area where, for once, they have been influential.

9 Not all the deceased in this study were elderly, but most were.

10 The justification for using substantive sociological sub-fields as the frame for my review is twofold. First, for better or for worse, they have dominated sociology until the 1980s, and still dominate sociology teaching. Second, the vast majority of the sociology of death in this country has been done by medical sociologists, and this becomes apparent immediately one compares medical sociology with the other substantive areas.

11 I hope to address this issue in a forthcoming book.

12 For a review, see Southard (1991:xxiii–xiv).

# References

Acquaviva, S., (1979), *The Decline of the Sacred in Industrial Society*, Oxford: Blackwell.

Adam, B., (1990), *Time and Social Theory*, Cambridge: Polity.

Aggleton, P. and Homans, S. (eds), (1988), *Social Aspects of AIDS*, Lewes: Falmer.

Aggleton, P. *et al.*, (eds), (1989), *AIDS: Social Representations, Social Practices*, Lewes: Falmer.

Ariès, P., (1981), *The Hour of Our Death*, London: Allen Lane.

Armstrong, D., (1983), *Political Anatomy of the Body*, Cambridge: Cambridge University Press.

Armstrong, D., (1986), 'The Invention of Infant Mortality', *Sociology of Health & Illness*, 8:211–32.

Armstrong, D., (1987), 'Silence and Truth in Death and Dying', *Social Science & Medicine*, 24:651–7.

Armstrong, D., (1989), 'Bodies of Knowledge: Foucault and the Problem of Human Anatomy', in G. Scambler (ed.), *Sociological Theory and Medical Sociology*, London: Tavistock.

Bauman, Z., (1989), *Modernity and the Holocaust*, Cambridge: Polity.

Bauman, Z., (1992a), *Mortality, Immortality and Other Life Strategies*, Cambridge: Polity.

Bauman, Z., (1992b), 'Survival as a Social Construct', *Theory, Culture & Society*, 9:1–36.

Beck, U., (1992), *Risk Society: Towards a New Modernity*, London: Sage.

Becker, E., (1973), *The Denial of Death*, New York: Free Press.

Berger, P. and Luckmann, T., (1967), *The Social Construction of Reality*, London: Allen Lane.

Berger, P., (1969), *The Social Reality of Religion*, London: Faber.

Berridge, V. and Strong, P., (1991), 'AIDS and the Relevance of History', *Social History of Medicine*, 4, 1:129–38.

Blauner, R., (1966), 'Death and Social Structure', *Psychiatry*, 29:378–394.

Bloch, M., (1982), 'Death, Women and Power', ch. 8 in M. Bloch & J. Parry, op cit.

Bloch, M. and Parry, J. (eds), (1982), *Death and the Regeneration of Life*, Cambridge: Cambridge University Press.

Bowling, A. and Cartwright, A., (1982), *Life After a Death*, London: Tavistock.

Bronfen, E., (1992), *Over Her Dead Body: death, femininity and the aesthetic*, Manchester: Manchester University Press.

Brooks, C., (1989), *Mortal Remains: the history and present state of the Victorian and Edwardian cemetery*, Exeter: Wheaton.

Cartwright, A. *et al.*, (1973), *Life Before Death*, London: Routledge.

Chadwick, O., (1975), *The Secularisation of the European Mind*, Cambridge: Cambridge University Press.

Clark, D., (1982), *Between Pulpit and Pew: folk religion in a North Yorkshire fishing village*, Cambridge: Cambridge University Press.

Clark, D., (1991), 'Contradictions in the Developments of New Hospices: a case study', *Social Science & Medicine*, 33, 9:995–1004.

Clark, D., (ed.), (1993a), *The Future for Palliative Care*, Buckingham: Open University Press.

Clark, D., (1993b), *Partners in Care? Hospices and Health Authorities*, Aldershot: Avebury.

Coleman, Sheila *et al.*, (1990), *Hillsborough and After: the Liverpool experience*, Ormskirk: Centre for Studies in Crime and Social Justice, Edge Hill College of Higher Education.

Clark, D. and Morgan, D., (1992), 'The Gaze of the Counsellors?' in S. Scott and G. Williams (eds), *Private Risks and Public Dangers*, Aldershot: Gower.

Crosby, G. (ed.), (1991), *Old Age: a register of social research, 1985–1990*, London: Centre for Policy on Ageing.

Danforth, L., (1982), *The Death Rituals of Rural Greece*, Princeton University Press.

Davie, G., (1993), 'You'll Never Walk Alone: the Anfield pilgrimage', in Ian Reader and Tony Walter (eds), *Pilgrimage in Popular Culture*, Basingstoke: Macmillan.

Davies, D., (1990), *Cremation Today and Tomorrow*, Nottingham: Alcuin/Grow Liturgical Study 16.

Dickenson, D. and Johnson, M. (eds), (1993), *Dying, Death and Bereavement*, London: Sage.

du Boulay, J., (1984), *Cicely Saunders*, London: Hodder.

Dumont, R. and Foss, D., (1972), *The American View of Death: Acceptance or Denial?*, Cambridge, Mass: Schenkman.

Durkheim, E., (1952), *Suicide*, London: Routledge & Kegan Paul.

Elias, N., (1985), *The Loneliness of Dying*, Oxford: Blackwell.

Featherstone, M. *et al.* (eds), (1991), *The Body*, London: Sage.

Field, D., (1984), 'Formal Instruction in United Kingdom Medical Schools about Death and Dying', *Medical Education*, 18:429–34.

Field, D., (1986), 'Formal Teaching about Death and Dying in UK Nursing Schools', *Nurse Education Today*, 6:270–6.

Field, D., (1989), *Nursing the Dying*, London: Tavistock/Routledge.

Firth, S., (1989), 'The Good Death: approaches to death, dying and bereavement among British Hindus', in A. Berger *et al.*, *Death and Dying*, Philadelphia: The Charles Press.

Firth, S., (1993a), 'Approaches to Death in Hindu and Sikh Communities in Britain', in Dickenson and Johnson, op. cit.

Firth, S., (1993b), 'Cross-Cultural Perspectives on Bereavement', in Dickenson and Johnson, op. cit.

Frankenberg, R., (1987), 'Life: cycle, trajectory or pilgrimage?', in A. Bryman *et al.* (eds), *Rethinking the Life Cycle*, London: Macmillan, pp. 122–138.

Giddens, A., (1987), *Social Theory and Modern Sociology*, Cambridge: Polity.

Giddens, A., (1989), *Sociology*, Cambridge: Polity.

Giddens, A., (1990), *The Consequences of Modernity*, Cambridge: Polity.

Giddens, A., (1991), *Modernity and Self-Identity*, Cambridge: Polity.

Gilbert, A., (1980), *The Making of Post-Christian Britain*, London: Longman.

Gittings, C., (1984), *Death, Burial and the Individual in Early Modern England*, London: Croom Helm.

Glaser, B. and Strauss, A., (1965), *Awareness of Dying*, Chicago: Aldine.

Glaser, B. and Strauss, A., (1968), *Time for Dying*, Chicago: Aldine.

Glasner, P., (1977), *The Sociology of Secularisation*, London: Routledge.

Gorer, G., (1955), 'The Pornography of Death', *Encounter*, October.

Gorer, G., (1965), *Death, Grief and Mourning in Contemporary Britain*, London: Cresset.

Grainger, R., (1988), *The Unburied*, Worthing: Churchman.

Gubrium, J., *Living and Dying at Murray Manor*, New York: St Martins Press.

Hart, N., (1985), *The Sociology of Health and Medicine*, Ormskirk: Causeway.

Hennessy, P., (1980), *Families, Funerals and Finances*, London: HMSO.

Higginson, I. and McCarthy, M., (1989), 'Evaluation of Palliative Care: steps to quality assurance?', *Palliative Medicine*, 3:267–74.

Hoad, P., (1991), 'Volunteers in the Independent Hospice Movement', *Sociology of Health and Illness*, 13, 2:231–48.

Hochschild, A., (1973), *The Unexpected Community*, Englewood Cliffs: Prentice Hall.

Hockey, J., (1990), *Experiences of Death*, Edinburgh: Edinburgh University Press.

Houlbrooke, R., (ed.), (1989), *Death, Ritual and Bereavement*, London: Routledge.

Howarth, G., (1992), *The Funeral Industry in the East End of London: an ethnographic study*, unpublished PhD thesis, London School of Economics.

Illich, I., (1976), *Limits to Medicine*, London: Marion Boyars.

James, N., (1989), 'Emotional Labour', *Sociological Review*, 37:15–42.

James, N., (1992), 'Care = Organisation + Physical Labour + Emotional Labour', *Sociology of Health & Illness*, 14, 4:488–509.

James, N. and Field, D., (1991), 'The Routinisation of Hospice', *Social Science and Medicine*, 34:1363–75.

Jupp, P., (1990), *From Dust to Ashes: the replacement of burial by cremation in England 1840–1967*, London: The Congregational Memorial Hall Trust.

Jupp, P., (1993), *The Development of Cremation in England 1820–1990: a sociological analysis*, unpublished PhD thesis, London School of Economics.

Kearl, M., (1989), *Endings: a sociology of death and dying*, Oxford University Press.

Kubler-Ross, E., (1970), *On Death and Dying*, London: Tavistock.

Littlewood, J., (1992), *Aspects of Grief: Bereavement in Adult Life*, London: Routledge.

Lofland, L., (ed.), (1976), *Toward a Sociology of Death and Dying*, Beverly Hills: Sage.

Lofland, L., (1978), *The Craft of Dying: The Modern Face of Death*, Beverly Hills: Sage.

Lyon, D., (1985), *The Steeple's Shadow: on the myths and realities of secularization*, London: SPCK.

Marris, P., (1958), *Widows and their Families*, London: Routledge & Kegan Paul.

Marris, P., (1974), *Loss and Change*, London: Routledge & Kegan Paul.

McIntosh, J., (1977), *Communication and Awareness in a Cancer Ward*, London: Croom Helm.

Malinowski, B., (1962), 'The Role of Magic and Religion', pp. 86–99 in W. Lessa and E. Vogt (eds), *Reader in Comparative Religion*, Evanston: Row, Peterson & Co.

Marshall, V., (1980), *Last Chapters*, Brooks/Cole.

Martin, D., (1978), *A General Theory of Secularisation*, Oxford: Blackwell.

May, C., (1992), 'Nursing Work, Nurses' Knowledge, and the Subjectification of the Patient', *Sociology of Health and Illness*, 14, 4:472–87.

Mellor, P., (1993), 'Death in High Modernity', in this volume.

Mellor, P. and Shilling, C., (1993), 'Modernity, Self-Identity and the Sequestration of Death', *Sociology*, forthcoming.

Miller, J., (1974), *Aberfan: a disaster and its aftermath*, London: Constable.

Mulkay, M. and Ernst, J., (1991), 'The Changing Profile of Social Death', *Arch. Europ. Sociol.*, 32:172–196.

Myerhoff, B., (1979), *Number Our Days*, New York: Dutton.

Naylor, M., (1989), *The Funeral; death rituals in a northern city*, Leeds University: unpublished PhD thesis.

Nichols, T., (1986), 'Industrial Injuries in British Manufacturing in the 1980s', *Sociological Review*, 34, 2:290–306.

Novack, D. *et al.*, (1979), 'Changes in Physicians' Attitudes Toward Telling the Cancer Patient', *Journal of the American Medical Association*, 241:897–900.

Oakley, A. *et al.*, (1990), *Miscarriage*, London: Penguin.

Parkes, C., (1972), *Bereavement*, Harmondsworth: Penguin.

Patrick, D. and Scambler, G. (eds), (1982), *Sociology as Applied to Medicine*, London: Bailliere & Tindall.

Perakyla, A., (1988), 'Four Frames of Death in Modern Hospital', pp. 41–5 in A. and S. Gilmore, (eds), *A Safer Death*, London: Plenum.

Pickering, W., (1974), 'The Persistence of Rites of Passage', *British Journal of Sociology*, 25:63–78.

Prior, L., (1989), *The Social Organisation of Death*, London: Macmillan.

Reader, I. and Walter, T. (eds), (1993), *Pilgrimage in Popular Culture*, Basingstoke: Macmillan.

Richardson, R., (1989), *Death, Dissection and the Destitute*, London: Penguin.

Roth, J., (1963), *Timetables*, Indianapolis: Bobbs-Merrill.

Scambler, G. (ed.), (1987), *Sociological Theory and Medical Sociology*, London: Tavistock.

Seale, C., (1989), 'What Happens in Hospices: a review of research evidence', *Social Science and Medicine*, 28:551–9.

Seale, C., (1990), 'Caring for People who Die: the experience of family and friends', *Ageing and Society*, 10, 4:413–428.

Seale, C., (1991a), 'A Comparison of Hospice and Conventional Care', *Social Science and Medicine*, 32:147–152.

Seale, C., (1991b), 'Communication and Awareness about Death: a study of a random sample of dying people', *Social Science and Medicine*, 32:943–952.

Simpson, M., (1987), *Dying, Death & Grief: a critical bibliography*, Berkeley: University of California Press.

Smale, B., (1985), *Deathwork: a sociological analysis of funeral directing*, University of Surrey: unpublished PhD thesis.

Small, N., (1993), *AIDS – The Future Challenge*, Aldershot: Avebury.

Southard, S., (1991), *Death and Dying: a bibliographical survey*, New York: Greenwood Press.

Stroebe, W. and M., (1987), *Bereavement and Health*, Cambridge: Cambridge University Press.

Townsend, P., (1964), *The Last Refuge*, London: Routledge and Kegan Paul.

Townsend, P. and Davidson, N., (1982), *Inequalities in Health*, Harmondsworth: Penguin.

Tuckett, D. (ed.), (1976), *An Introduction to Medical Sociology*, London: Tavistock.

Turner, B., (1984), *The Body and Society*, Oxford: Blackwell.

Turner, B., (1987), *Medical Power and Social Knowledge*, London: Sage.

Turner, B., (1991), *Religion and Social Theory*, London: Sage.

van der Maas *et al.*, (1991), 'Euthanasia and Other Medical Decisions Concerning the End of Life', *Lancet*, 338:669–73.

Vovele, M., (1980), 'Rediscovery of Death Since 1960', pp. 89–99 in R. Fox (ed.), *The Social Meaning of Death, Annals of the American Academy of Political and Social Science*, vol. 447.

Walter, T., (1989), 'Deathwatch', *Third Way*, 12, 5:6.

Walter, T., (1990), *Funerals – and how to improve them*, London: Hodder.

Walter, T., (1991a), 'Modern Death – taboo or not taboo?', *Sociology*, 25, 2:293–310.

Walter, T., (1991b), 'The Mourning After Hillsborough', *Sociological Review*, 39, 599–625.

Walter, T., (1993), 'Death in the New Age', *Religion*, 23, 2: 127–145.

Williams, R., (1990), *A Protestant Legacy: attitudes to death and illness among older Aberdonians*, Oxford: Oxford University Press.

Williams, W., (1958), *The Sociology of an English Village: Gosforth*, London: Routledge.

Wilson, Sir A. and Levy, H., (1938), *Burial Reform and Funeral Costs*, Oxford: Oxford University Press.

Wilson, B., (1969), *Religion in Secular Society*, Harmondsworth: Penguin.

Wilson, B., (1976), *Contemporary Transformations of Religion*, Oxford: Oxford University Press.

Wilson, B., (1982), *Religion in Sociological Perspective*, Oxford: Oxford University Press.

Wright, C., (1983), 'Routine Deaths: fatal accidents in the oil industry', *Sociological Review*, 34, 2:265–89.

Young, M., (1988), *The Metronomic Society*, London: Thames & Hudson.

Young, M., (forthcoming), *The Presumption of Immortality*.

# Notes on contributors

Sheila Adams is working on a thesis on the Role of the Crematorium in the Social Management of Death, at Warwick University.

David Clark has written widely on the sociological aspects of religion, family life, health and illness. He is the author and editor of two recent books which relate to the present volume: *Partners in Care? Hospices and health authorities* (Avebury, 1993) and *The Future of Palliative Care: Issues of Policy and Practice* (ed.) (Open University Press, 1993). He is Co-Director of the Health Research Centre at Sheffield Hallam University and Senior Research Fellow (Sociology) at Trent Palliative Care Centre.

Kirsten Costain Schou studied English Literature at the University of Regina, Saskatchewan, before commencing doctoral studies at the University of Leeds in 1989. Her thesis, entitled *The Quality of Life of Cancer Patients: Aspects of the Social Experience of Treatment* was submitted in 1993. Over the past ten years she has worked in critical care units and hospices in both Canada and Britain.

Jon Davies is Head of the Department of Religious Studies at the University of Newcastle-upon-Tyne. He has written widely in the fields of town planning, housing and urban problems and is currently working on a book on war and religion and another on death in history.

Glennys Howarth is T H Marshall Fellow in the Department of Sociology at the London School of Economics. She has conducted work on independence and autonomy among the old and is currently studying the work of coroners. Her doctoral thesis focused on undertaking and the funeral industry.

© The Editorial Board of The Sociological Review 1993. Published by Blackwell Publishers, 108 Cowley Road, Oxford OX4 1JF, UK and 238 Main Street, Cambridge, MA 02142, USA.

David Field is a Senior Lecturer in Medical Sociology in the Department of Epidemiology and Public Health at the University of Leicester. He has published papers on medical students' attitudes to death, terminal care education and a book *Nursing the Dying* (Routledge, 1989). More recently his research has focused on hospice care.

Janet Finch is Professor of Social Relations in the Department of Applied Social Science at Lancaster University. Much of her recent work has been on kin and family relationships. She is author of *Family Obligations and Social Change* (Polity, 1989) and co-author with Jennifer Mason of *Negotiating Family Responsibilities* (Routledge, 1992).

Jennifer Hockey is a Lecturer at the University of Hull. Trained as a social anthropologist, her primary research area is the management of death and includes work on ageing, residential care, terminal care, bereavement counselling and death ritual. Her publications include *Experiences of Death: An anthropological account* (Edinburgh University Press, 1990) and, together with Alison James, *Growing Up and Growing Old: Ageing and dependency in the life course* (Sage, 1993).

Revd. Peter Jupp completed his doctoral thesis at the London School of Economics. He is currently working for the Institute of Community Studies, directing the National Funerals College project and is an Honorary Research Fellow at the Centre for the Study of Religion and Society, University of Kent.

Ian Johnson has been a GP and community physician in Sheffield and is currently a Consultant in Palliative Medicine at the Leicestershire Hospice.

Jane Littlewood is a Senior Lecturer in Social Policy and Administration at Loughborough University of Technology. She is the author of *Aspects of Grief* (Routledge, 1992) and a co-author of *Applied Research for Better Practice* (Macmillan, 1992). She is currently engaged in research concerning widowhood and maternal experiences of bereavement. She is involved in Charnwood Bereavement Help.

Philip A. Mellor lectures in the Sociology of Religion in the Department of Theology and Religious Studies at the University of Leeds. He has published widely in the areas of religion, social theory and methodology. At the moment he is working with Chris Shilling on a book, *Embodiment and Postmodernity*, which will appear in 1995.

Michael Mulkay is Professor of Sociology at the University of York. He has written on sociological theory and on social aspects of art and humour. He has also published on a wide range of issues in the sociology of science for which he received the J D Bernàl award in 1986. He teaches an undergraduate course on death and dying in order to help himself and his students come to terms with their own mortality.

Neil Small is a Senior Research Fellow at the Social Policy Research Unit, University of York. His current research interests include an examination of the interface between health services and social care. He is the author of *AIDS: The challenge* (Avebury, 1993) and *Politics and Planning in the National Health Service* (Open University Press, 1989).

Lorraine Wallis is a Research Officer on the Inheritance, Property and Family Relationships project in the Department of Applied Social Science at Lancaster University.

Tony Walter is a freelance sociology lecturer and writer, currently working on a book on death in the late twentieth century. Among his earlier books are *Hope on The Dole, Basic Income, Funerals and How to Improve Them* and *Pilgrimage in Popular Culture*.

# Index

Abercrombie, N., 16, 19
Aberfan, 76
Abrams, 151, 156
accidental death, 43–4
Adams, S., 193, 276
Adler, M., 98
Afterlife, belief in, 40, 43, 174, 181–2, 194
AIDS, 87–108, 270
  autobiography and, 94–100
  celebrity and, 100–104
  in the media, 97–101
Alcorn, K., 98
Almond, L., 205
anticipation, of death, 61–4, 65
Archer, M., 23, 28
Ariès, P., 69, 149, 193, 267, 286
Armstrong, D., 276, 282
Aron, P., 99
Ashe, Arthur, 103
Averill, J.R., 71
awareness, of dying, 238, 240–1, 246–7, 251–2, 257, 260, 261, 268

Bauman, Z., 23–4, 25, 26, 28n, 106–7, 266–7, 290
Beckford, J., 15
bereavement, 73, 76, 79–80, 82, 277
Berger, P., 3, 13–14, 15, 16, 19, 266, 272
Berridge, V., 270
Bluebond-Langner, M., 45
body, 232, 234–5
  disposal of, *see* corpse management
  sociology of, 26, 275–6
Bourdieu, P., 140
Bowlby, J., 80

Bronfen, E., 278
burial, 179–82, 187, 192
Burke, K., 233
Butler, R.J., 198

cancer, 238–62
  children dying from, 44–5
  cancer treatment centres, 243–6, 252
Cannandine, D., 70, 78, 114, 125
caring
  formal, 152–6
  informal, 156–63
Cartwright, A., 270, 281
Cavell, E., 120
cemeteries, 174, 283, 284
Charleson, Ian, 99
Charmaz, K., 72
Chatwin, Bruce, 99
Cheal, D., 77, 78, 80
children
  social death and, 42–6
  stillborn, 157–8
Clark, D., 75, 150, 160, 213, 275
clergy
  and funeral directors, 228
  help for bereaved from, 129, 130–5, 138–44
co-counselling, 146–7
Coleman, s., 275
communal grieving, 76, 82, 279
community studies, death and, 275
Corbin, J., 250
corpse management, 164–5, 169–95, 284
Cranwell, B., 130, 131–3
cremation, 169–71, 174–8, 182–6, 187–8, 192, 194